T0301604

TALES FROM ALBARADO

TALES FROM ALBARADO

Ponzi Logics of Accumulation
in Postsocialist Albania

Smoki Musaraj

CORNELL UNIVERSITY PRESS   ITHACA AND LONDON

Publication of this book was made possible, in part, by a grant from the First Book Subvention Program of the Association for Slavic, East European, and Eurasian Studies.

First published 2020 by Cornell University Press

Library of Congress Cataloging-in-Publication Data

Names: Musaraj, Smoki, author.
Title: Tales from Albarado : Ponzi logics of accumulation in postsocialist Albania / Smoki Musaraj.
Description: Ithaca [New York] : Cornell University Press, 2020. | Includes bibliographical references and index.
Identifiers: LCCN 2019050415 (print) | LCCN 2019050416 (ebook) | ISBN 9781501750335 (hardcover) | ISBN 9781501750342 (paperback) | ISBN 9781501750359 (epub) | ISBN 9781501750366 (pdf)
Subjects: LCSH: Ponzi schemes—Albania. | Speculation—Albania. | Post-communism—Economic aspects—Albania. | Albania—Economic conditions—1992–
Classification: LCC HC402 .M87 2020 (print) | LCC HC402 (ebook) | DDC 364.16/3—dc23
LC record available at https://lccn.loc.gov/2019050415
LC ebook record available at https://lccn.loc.gov/2019050416

To
Matthew and Simone

Contents

Illustrations

Acknowledgments

This book has taken many years to complete and bears the sustained labor and support of several communities of scholars, friends, and family. My mentors, Hugh Raffles, Janet Roitman, and Bruce Grant have each spent countless hours of reading and providing critical feedback on the early version of the book. To Hugh I owe many thanks for inspiring a way of thinking ethnographically beyond convention and for reminding me to attend to the pleasures of writing. Janet transformed my way of thinking about money, value, and wealth, in anthropological and philosophical terms. I am thankful for the hard questions and the theoretical challenges that she continues to bring to my attention. In addition to being an encyclopedia of socialist and postsocialist scholarship, Bruce continuously reminded me to question my own common sense and pushed me to provide more thick description of the imponderabilia of everyday life in Albania that I often take for granted. I am thankful to all three of them for the great care that they have continued to provide throughout the past several years. The idea for writing about the pyramid schemes in Albania first emerged in a conversation with Claudio Lomnitz who also provided critical theoretical and methodological insight on the early stages of my research. I am thankful to him for encouraging me to pursue this book. At the New School, my work benefited from the stimulating classes and conversations with Ann Stoler, Gustav Peebles, Ben Lee, Hylton White, and Vyajyanthi Rao.

In Albania, I have benefited from the warm welcome and support by various institutions, old and new friends, and family. I thank in particular Rozeta Koçi who provided research support and friendship and accompanied me during many interviews with former participants in the pyramid firms. I thank Auron Pasha for offering me an internship at the Institute for Development and Research Alternatives (IDRA). I also thank IDRA's staff for the friendship and for helping me identify and contact pyramid schemes' participants. Among others, I thank in particular Florian Babameto, Oni Xhelaj, Emona Ferhati, and Marjeti Dumi.

The Institute of Cultural Anthropology and Study of Art (IAKSA) (then known as the Institute of Ethnology) provided much intellectual support during the time of my research and has continued to be a reference point during subsequent visits to Albania over the years. I thank Gerda Dalipaj, in particular, for the passionate conversations, the walks and runs at *liqeni*, and for inspiring me with her own research and poetry. During the course of my research and over the past several years, Blendi Kajsiu, Armanda Hysa, Eni Papa, Gentiana Kera, Andreas Hemming, Shaban Sinani, and Albert Doja provided feedback and exchanged ideas about my book at various stages. Other friends in Albania, both from the past and made along the way, indulged me on conversations about my research over numerous coffees in the ubiquitous Tirana cafes. Among others, I thank Ada Musaraj, Eldira Gjipali, Alda Skëndaj, Lori Mengri, Jugera Bilali, Mimoza Kaçi, Mirlinda Naçi, and Evis Hoxha for sharing their time and ideas with me.

My time at the Institute for Money, Technology and Financial Inclusion, at the University of California, Irvine in 2012–2014 provided me with yet another community of scholars and friends that pushed me to rethink the scope of this book. I thank Bill Maurer for pushing my thinking about the anthropology of money to the next level and for providing guidance in reframing my arguments in the book to speak to this fascinating literature. I also thank the members of Value and Money writing group, especially Ivan Small, Taylor Nelms, Beth Ready, Stevie Rhea for providing feedback and suggestions on earlier versions of the chapters. In addition, I benefited from conversations with and feedback by the faculty and graduate students of the Department of anthropology at UCI, especially Keith Murphy, Julia Elyachar, Tom Boellstorff, Kristin Peterson, Janny Li, Robbie Kett, Sean Mallin, Nima L. Yolmo, Nathan Dobson, Nathan Coben, and Nick Seaver. I am also thankful to Sean Mallin for a thorough copyediting of the manuscript before production.

Research for this book was funded by the National Science Foundation (DDIG #0753180), the Social Science Research Council, the Social Sciences and Humanities Research Council, the Council for European Studies and the Society for the Anthropology of Europe, The New School, and the Baker Award. Parts of the interviews and discussion in this book were published in "Tales from Albarado: The Materiality of Pyramid Schemes in Postsocialist Albania," *Cultural Anthropology* 26, no. 1 (2011). A section of chapter 3 was published in "Pyramid Firms and Value Transformation in Postsocialist Albania," *Ethnologie Française* 2 (2017). Chapter 1 was published as "The Magic of Pyramid Firms: Cosmologies of Speculation, Repertoires of Credit and Collapsed Finance" in *Ethnos* (2019). I thank these journals for granting permission to reprint these articles in this book. I have presented drafts of the chapters to various audiences and benefitted from the feedback of faculty and students at the SOYUZ meetings, the UCLA Culture, Power, and Society Colloquium Series, the Cosmoeconomics Workshop at the University of Bergen, the UCSD Socialism in Context Colloquium, and audiences at UCI and Ohio University.

I thank my extended family of fellow scholars, students, and friends with whom I crossed paths and drew much inspiration from during my time living in New York City. Among others, Elga Castro and Miguel Zenon, Hilla Dayan and Peter

Zuidhof, Carmen Ilizarbe and Juan Pablo Campana, Myrna Alejo, Rose Van Den Breemer and Anstein Gregerson, Sarah (Siddiqui) Wolek, Gabika Boçkaj have all marked the writing of this book through their friendship and intellectual stimulation. I am thankful for the solidarity and emotional support I received from them at the time, especially, Leilah Vanaina, Mateusz Hawala, Randi Irwin, YiYi Hsieh, Monica Fagioli, Ana Maria Ulloa, Zohar Rotem, Karolina Szamagalska (Follis), Charles Townsend, Kadija Ferryman, Gabriel Vignoli, Gregorz Sokol, David Bond, Emily Sogn. I also benefited from conversations with the growing community of Albanian American intellectuals based at the time in New York City; in particular, I enjoyed conversations with Brikena Hoxha, Ajkuna Hope, Elona Pira, Erjola Pira, Blerta Cela, Elidor Mëhilli, and Odeta Xheka. In addition to informing my thinking about Albania in the 1990s, Elidor Mëhilli provided insightful comments and suggestions to the introduction of the book.

During my time of teaching at Ohio University, I benefitted from a number of colleagues who supported me through the revisions of this manuscript. Among others, I benefitted from conversations and friendship of Diane Ciekawy, Haley Duschinski, Nicole Kaufman, Rachel Terman, Elizabeth (Liz) Lee, Stephen (Steve) Scanlan, Christine Mattley, Melissa Figueroa, Ziad Abu-Rish, Alec Holcombe, Assan Sarr, Nukhet Sandal, Myra Waterbury, Marina Peterson, Mariana Dantas, and Victoria Lee. At Cornell University Press, I thank editor Jim Lance for his enthusiasm about this book and I thank Ellen Murphy and Kate Gibson for seeing the book through production.

My family in Tirana, Montreal, and Baltimore is the gift that keeps on giving. I thank first and foremost my parents, Mimoza Musaraj and Vullnet Musaraj, for coping heroically with my and my brother's absence from their everyday life for many years now. I thank them and Penar Musaraj (with Florence Tremblay) for their love and support. In the United States, Susan and Barry Rosen have been a constant source of encouragement. I thank them for their genuine curiosity in my book and for their valuable insights. Last but not least, I thank Matthew Rosen for his inspiration, the intellectual partnership, and for his unfaltering support and confidence in my work. I owe the completion of this long journey to our mutual support, patience, and care as we juggle career, childcare, and life. My daughter, Simone, has grown up around my writing and discussions of this book. I thank her for being able to move seamlessly and enthusiastically across the different worlds of work and life that I have had to bring her along as I complete this long journey.

TALES FROM ALBARADO

THE TALE OF ALBARADO AND THE ANTHROPOLOGY OF FINANCIAL SPECULATION

In early 1997, Albania captured world headlines with images of angry protestors waving money bills and young men flaunting Kalashnikov rifles. The unrest that had gripped the country followed the collapse of a dozen pyramid schemes, locally referred to as *firma piramidale* (pyramid firms). These firms were all the rage in the early 1990s Albania, attracting 1.5 million investors, in a country of 3 million. By the end of 1996, the firms had accumulated nearly US$1.2 billion, or 50 percent of the country's gross domestic product (GDP) (Bezemer 2001, 8). When they collapsed in 1997, the country fell into anarchy and a near civil war. This book revisits these times of excitement and loss to gain a better understanding of how people from all walks of life came to invest in these financial schemes, which became intertwined with everyday transactions, dreams, and aspirations. Situated at the margins of post–Cold War Europe, the Albanian firms represent an economic reality that is endemic to capitalist economies: speculative bubbles and crashes. Through the study of the Albanian pyramid firms, this book takes an ethnographic view of speculative finance. More specifically, it traces how the Ponzi logics of accumulation, prevalent in the early 1990s Albania, were intricately connected to the significant political and economic transformations of the end of the twentieth century, namely, postsocialist transformations, mass migration, and neoliberal reforms.

I grew up in Tirana, Albania, and experienced many of the events and processes of transformation that I describe—from the slow and steady decline of late socialism in the late 1980s to the frantic experience of *tranzicion* (the transition from the command economy to the free-market economy) of the 1990s. Among

friends and family, I was considered lucky because I left to study abroad right before the chaos of 1997. When I returned to visit my family over the winter break
of 1997–98, the sounds of Kalashnikov rifles could still be heard routinely in the
city. On the night of December 31, I cautiously celebrated the coming of the New
Year in my parents' new apartment; the cheerful disorder of the fireworks intertwined with bullets, one of which had fallen on our roof and broke through the
ceiling. As the story of the bullet was retold to friends and kin, I heard again and
again how "this was nothing" compared to the number of bullets people had
dodged earlier that year. My absence in Albania during the infamous year of *nëntdhteshtata* (year ninety-seven) created a gap between me and my friends and
family. That gap continued to shape our relationships for years to come. That gap
also perplexed me on how this total collapse of the economy and of the state came
about and how the pyramid firms contributed to it.

In 2008, a decade after the collapse of the firms, I began my research on the
pyramid firms with former investors based in the cities of Tirana and Vlora. I was
curious to learn how investors were drawn to these firms and how they came to
trust them with their cash. These former investors referred me to the archives of
newspapers such as *Dita Informacion* (*DI*), *Koha Jonë* (*KJ*), *Gazeta Shqiptare*
(*GSH*), and *Albania* to find more information on perceptions of the firms at the
time of their boom. While reading through these newspapers on the dusty
shelves of the Albanian National Library, I ran into a column by Apollon Baçe,
entitled "Albarado." Baçe's writing stands out from the mainstream coverage at
the time for its critical attitude toward the firms. Writing in mid-1996, Baçe introduced the allegory of "Albarado"—a portmanteau combining Albania with
El Dorado, the fabled city of gold in the Amazon. In a grotesque cynical style,
Baçe described the economic logics and transactions that sustained the firms:

> Almost all citizens of Albarado inherited from the terribly red dictatorship an
> apartment, which the happily blue democracy gave to them as a gift.
>
> The value of the red-blue apartment is US$25,000. . . . Thanks to a terribly
> simple alchemic formula, the citizen, within three months, becomes the owner
> of four times US$25,000, in other words of US$100,000! This is just the begin-
> ning of infinite bounty! If he leaves the money in the charity [pyramid] firms for
> three more months . . . he becomes the owner of US$400,000. By the end of the
> year, [he will own] US$3.2 million, at the beginning of the new millennium, in
> 2000, he will become the owner of US$241 million. . . . And to think that there
> are fifty thousand apartments owned by the citizens of Albarado! (Baçe 1996)

Baçe's Albarado is both parody and cautionary tale: ridiculing the firms' promises of infinite gains and warning citizens against selling their apartments (ac-

quired under communism and newly privatized for cash) to buy into these firms. I borrow this allegory here as a way to capture the discourse of euphoria and the specific top-down and ground-up economic transactions that enabled the widespread participation in the pyramid firms.

Through the allusion to El Dorado, Baçe evokes the euphoria and excitement that permeated the daily reports, rumors, and firsthand accounts of quick and effortless accumulation of cash. Reading through the newspaper archives of the 1990s, I was, indeed, thrown back into a time filled with hope and excitement about the economic prospects of the free-market reforms of the early 1990s. What began to emerge from the pages was an ambivalent picture of the firms. Were these legitimate investment companies run by ambitious and brave local entrepreneurs, or were they fraudulent schemes profiting from government ties and the privatization reforms?

The allegory of Albarado is also notable for situating the boom and bust of the firms in Albania within a longer history of speculative financial schemes. Baçe describes participation in the Albanian firms through the metaphors of alchemy and infinite bounty, tropes reminiscent of the "euphoria" (Kindleberger and Aliber 2005) or "irrational exuberance" (Shiller 2000) of speculative bubbles that have emerged in other capitalist contexts. At the same time, he grounds the speculative activities of these firms in the specifics of postsocialist transformation—privatization reforms, housing-regime changes, and a cash economy.

These intertwined narratives of Albarado—the longer history of speculative bubbles and the specific economic transformations of the early 1990s—are central to my account. But rather than couching this narrative in terms of magical practices in an exotic and enigmatic country at the margins of Europe—a familiar trope in writing about Albania—I show how the firms emerged at the intersections of various pathways of wealth circulation, within Albania and across Southeast Europe.[1] I highlight the entanglements and disentanglements of these firms with local, regional, and global economic and social networks. Given the peculiarity of Albania's communism and postcommunism, I trace how the country's marginality was structured by the broader regional economic and political transformations of the end of the twentieth century. Besides, this instance of financial speculation is a good case study for thinking more broadly about the economic crisis and speculative finance in the context of ongoing neoliberal transformations in Albania and other parts of the world.

I do not aim to provide a comprehensive accounting of the financial transactions that took place through the firms. Since these transactions straddled the formal and informal financial spheres and given the lack of a system of bookkeeping and oversight, it is nearly impossible to provide accurate accounting on the financial transactions of the firms. The few official accounts that do so make it clear that their figures are estimates (Bezemer 2001; Jarvis 1999). However, ethnographic methods can provide unique insights into the patterns and strategies of investment, pathways of wealth circulation, and practices of value conversion mobilized by participants in the firms.

This ethnography of the Albanian pyramid firms addresses broader questions about how people from various walks of life get drawn to speculative Ponzi schemes. The book traces how participants viewed the pyramid firms in Albania, how they came to trust them with their cash, and what were the broader aspirations that informed their decisions to participate. Similar to other instances of speculative bubbles, participants in the Albanian pyramid firms saw these as legitimate capitalist firms investing in various economic sectors, including tourism, retail, agriculture, industry, and real estate. The legitimacy and hybrid nature of these firms were enabled by official institutions, political leaders, and media representations. These findings contribute to a broader understanding of speculative finance that goes beyond the tropes of "irrational exuberance" or "mania" but examines the economic and social contexts that make such speculative bubbles possible, credible, and legitimate.

The second set of concerns that I pursue relates to the materiality, sociality, and temporality of financial speculation. I ask what were the forms of wealth that circulated in and through the firms? What economic repertoires, capitalist or noncapitalist, were mobilized in and through them? What kind of economies and relations did these firms generate?

My research situates the activities of the firms within the economic and political changes of the early 1990s—the transformation from the command economy to free-market economy; the embrace of shock-therapy reform and structural adjustment policies; the implementation of deep privatization reforms; and the proliferation of a transnational remittance economy. I note that the firms became a critical "threshold of value conversion" (Guyer 2004) for different forms of wealth—cash in multiple currencies, privatization vouchers, kinship ties, and housing.

These insights resonate with other economic theories of bubbles and crashes. The trajectory of the firms I discuss parallels the critiques of neoliberalism that place crisis and bubbles at the heart, rather than the outside, of capitalist economies (Harvey 2010; Mirowski 2013). The Albanian firms emerged not from ignorance of capitalism but were enabled by some of the economic processes of the transition from the command to the free-market economy. This analysis also echoes neo-Keynesian theories of bubbles and Ponzi finance that emphasize the role of processes of economic and political transformation and periods of credit expansion as a catalyst of speculative financial practices (Kindelberger and Aliber 2005; Minsky 1982). I expand on these theories by taking a broader socioeconomic understanding of economic concepts such as value, wealth, and credit (Appadurai 1986; Guyer 2004; Hart 1986, 2001; Maurer 2006; Munn 1986; Peebles 2010; Roitman 2005). The economic and political transformations of the early 1990s Albania indeed brought about a credit expansion from the flux of international loans (Bezemer 2001). However, investors' stories bring into focus other forms of credit expansion that do not fit in the textbook definition of credit. The book focuses more specifically on two such sources of nonbank credit: remittance flows and privatized communist apartments.

By focusing on these two forms of nonbank credit, the book shows how the firms also built on financial repertoires that emerged from the ground up, in informal and semiformal economic spheres. These included rotating credit schemes, transnational remittance flows, savings in multiple currencies, and off-the-books trading of real estate. I refer to these repertoires as low finance, that is financial practices taking place outside formal banking systems, run by nonprofessional commercial actors, and mostly in cash (see also Guyer 2012; Musaraj and Small 2018; Narotzky and Besnier 2014). In Albania, the transactions that proliferated outside the formal banking system were crucial to the everyday workings and the expansion of the firms. These transactions were mediated by kinship ties and were used to accelerate the temporality of change from backward communism to European modernity. Taken together, these aspects of investing in the firms inform discussions about the materiality, sociality, and temporality of speculative finance (Hertz 1998; Ho 2009; Miyazaki 2003; Zaloom 2006). While literature in the anthropology of finance tends to privilege high finance, this account is committed to understanding the worlds of low finance. At stake here is how economic practices that take place outside banks circumvent and/or intertwine with official financial institutions.

The ethnographic account of the pyramid firms in Albania thus helps us understand speculative finance at the margins of global capital and Europe. It explains how these forms of speculation emerge at the interstices of official and unofficial, bank and non-bank, economic and cultural institutions and practices. Finally, this account helps us understand how Ponzi forms of accumulation and investment emerge in contexts of deep economic change and how they persist alongside neoliberal capitalism in Albania, as well as other parts of the global North and South.

Tranzicion and the Emergence of the Pyramid Firms in the Early 1990s

Like other sites of the former socialist world (Grant 1995), Albania's "short" twentieth century (Hobsbawm 1994) entailed a series of transitions—from the Ottoman Empire at the turn of the century, to a battleground of various competing empires during World War I, to a semicolonial regime during Mussolini's Italy in the 1930s, to a communist state after World War II, to a free-market democracy in the 1990s. The Albanian pyramid firms emerged in the early 1990s, a time of socioeconomic change in a country infamous for its extreme isolation (from both East and West) during the second half of the Cold War.[2] The transition to multiparty democracy in 1991 did not spark the kind of violence and unrest seen in other parts of the Balkans, but it nonetheless entailed a series of transformative events; namely, the storming of foreign embassies (in 1990) and the ensuing massive outmigration, student hunger strikes, and antigovernment protests.[3]

Tranzicion brought about deep economic reforms that led to the transformation from central planning to a free-market economy. The economic transformation went hand in hand with a political transformation from a one-party system to a multiparty democracy. These transformations were led by local movements and actors as well as by international institutions. In 1993, Albania welcomed the International Monetary Fund (IMF) and the World Bank (WB), eagerly accepting their loans as well as the conditions attached to them. Albania was not alone in embracing shock-therapy reforms and structural adjustment programs. Since the end of the Cold War, postsocialist and postrevolutionary contexts have been laboratories for testing the tenets of the Washington Consensus—a set of policies that include the liberalization of markets, strict monetary policy, and privatization of public services and infrastructure.

This set of policies, initially developed through neoliberal reforms in Latin American countries (especially Chile and Argentina), was soon exported to post-1990s Eastern Europe.[4] Albania was one of its most avid pupils among countries of the former socialist world.[5] Officially, the Albanian government complied with all IMF and WB directives, earning praise on the international stage as a leader in free-market reform. Meanwhile, the head of the first democratically elected government, Sali Berisha, came to power with an anticommunist and procapitalist mandate. Berisha's government heralded private entrepreneurship as an economic, political, and moral quest. Albania embraced shock-therapy reforms with unflinching enthusiasm. Berisha and the Democratic Party (Partia Demokratike [PD]) have not been the sole proponents of such neoliberal policies, however. All governments since 1991, whether led by the PD or the Socialist Party (Partia Socialiste [PS]), followed a similar neoliberal path.[6]

Albania's embrace of shock-therapy reforms was particularly problematic given the absence of basic market institutions and instruments possessed by other post-socialist countries. Most notably, by the late 1970s, the Albanian communist regime had abolished almost all kinds of private property—for instance, by this time, Albanian citizens could not own livestock, cars, or apartments.[7] Further, access to credit for individuals was extremely limited and in reality no credit market existed.[8] Finally, Albania went even further than its former allies in banning all means of making money out of money. Even some practices that were common in other former communist countries, such as government-run lotteries, were nonexistent in communist Albania.[9]

In the early 1990s, as these capitalist institutions and instruments were reintroduced, large numbers of people found themselves excluded from official financial institutions and opportunities because they lacked the necessary assets to acquire private property or gain access to credit. Many people lost their jobs with the closing of state factories and cooperatives. With this loss, they also lost proof of steady income. Most people did not have any savings given the scarcity of cash and capital; those who did lost their value following multiple and steep devaluations of the local currency. These factors made it difficult for people to take out loans for opening up a business or buying property.

On the national level, new market institutions were often adopted without regard for existing institutions but following formats and formulas from other so-called emerging economies. This resulted in unclear structures that enabled ambiguous forms of accumulation and investment. For instance, the private property regime that was introduced in the first years of tranzicion consisted of contradictory privatization laws. Thus, the first law on the privatization of state housing in 1993 gave ownership of housing to occupants; another law issued under the rule of PD gave ownership to ex-owners. As multiple privatization laws favored different constituencies—members of cooperatives or state enterprises, the politically persecuted, the ex-owners—conflicts arose over contradictory claims of ownership over the same home or land. By the late-2010s, the problem of property ownership remained unresolved in Albania.

Another significant gap in the financial architecture of the 1990s was the lack of commercial banking. Commercial banks were slow to be launched and regulated while the official banks followed strict regulations. Official state banks began to lend to individuals but they often required collateral or savings, which most Albanians lacked at that time. Unofficial financial entities such as the firms operated without any regulation regarding auditing, recordkeeping, income reporting (see Bezemer 2001). The lack of regulation on the firms attracted more investors.[10]

The pyramid firms were a mix of classic Ponzi schemes (whereby money is circulated from new investors to early investors) and joint-stock companies running increasingly on a Ponzi finance model (that is, promising exorbitant future returns on investments in other assets or economic activities, but in an unsustainable pattern) (Minsky 1982, 1992).[11] These firms had an ambiguous status—part formal, part informal. All were legally registered as either *kompani* (company/ies) or *fondacion/e* (foundation/s).[12] Kompani, registered as limited liability companies, had some investments in tourism, retail, construction, agriculture, and other industries. Fondacione had no assets or investments to their name and conducted a "purer" type of Ponzi scheme, circulating money from recent to earlier investors.[13]

While differing in legal form and the scale and scope of their activities, kompani and fondacione engaged in a financial activity widely referred to as *fajde* (from the Turkish for moneylending). "Fajde" is a term that refers to nonbank moneylending at an interest, most often lending from loan sharks. The term originated during the Ottoman rule and continued to be used through the 1940s (that is, before the establishment of the command economy) to refer to nonbank moneylending. As the practice of moneylending was banned during the communist regime, the term itself became obsolete and carried a negative ethical connotation. In the 1990s, the term re-entered public discourse, this time carrying a positive connotation and quickly being associated with the pyramid firms. This etymological history is explored in more detail in chapter 1. But here it suffices to say that the return of the term "fajde" in public discourse is not incidental. Instead, it signals the intertwined, overlapping, and interrupted financial histories and repertoires of the longue and short durée—in this case, from the Ottoman rule, to the interwar period, to the communist rule, and the postcommunist economy.

The firms claimed the legitimacy of their lending practices by citing the new legislation on moneylending in Article 1051 of the new Civil Code passed in 1993. Technically, Article 1051 referred to nonbank moneylending, typically from person to person. But the firms used this legal loophole to attract deposits by individuals, naming them as *kreditor/ë*, translated as creditor/s or lender/s but also used to mean investor/s. Besides borrowing from kreditorë, the firms also lent to individuals, to other firms, to organizations, and even to political parties.[14] The firms presented themselves as joint-stock companies toward kreditorë, describing the latter's deposits as investments. But even the kompani that did have legitimate investments (such as Vefa, Gjallica, Kamberi) promised interest returns that were clearly unsustainable. As such, these kompani operated by what Minsky (1992) described as Ponzi finance.

Although similar to other speculative financial schemes proliferating in postsocialist contexts (Borenstein 1999; Verdery 1996), the Albanian firms had unprecedented reach in economic, political, and social life in Albania. Over the six years, these firms attracted somewhere between one-sixth to one-half of the country's population as investors (Bezemer 2001; Jarvis 1999).[15] From the outset, they attracted depositors by offering high interest returns (8–10 percent) within periods short as three months and up to a year. By mid-1996, the growing competition among the firms drove the interest returns through the roof. By November of that year, some of the maverick firms offered up to 50 percent return on principle. Soon after these exorbitant interest returns went into effect, the state banks limited the amount of daily withdrawals, which restricted the firms' access to liquidity. Immediately, one after the other, the firms began to fold.

Up until late 1996, the firms seemed to complement the landscape of post-socialist transformations in Albania. The local buzz around the abundance (bollëk) from these firms seemed to replicate the international buzz around Albania's success in shock-therapy reforms. Indeed, IMF officials praised Albania for its rapid implementation of structural adjustment policies and hailed it as a success story of free-market reform (Camdessus 1995). Locally, the firms received broad support from public figures and political authorities. From 1993 to 1996, owners of major firms shared the national stage with leading politicians, appeared regularly on national television programming, threw lavish private parties, sponsored electoral campaigns and major cultural events, and gave interviews to local and international media. To investors, these public expenditures legitimized the firms; in public discourse, the firms' owners constituted an emerging class of entrepreneurs, the trailblazers of homegrown capitalism.

A visit by a team of IMF experts in late 1996 raised a red flag on the legitimacy of the firms. After two weeks of meetings with government officials, the experts expressed concern about the "nature of the pyramid firms" and recommended that the government audit them. At first, government authorities responded positively to this warning. The minister of finance, Ridvan Bode, suggested that the government had no choice but to audit the firms and the Albanian Parliament set up a Transparency Group to do so.[16] Days after Bode's words of caution, however, then president Sali Berisha issued a surprising public statement that contradicted Bode and openly defied the IMF. Berisha described the pyramid firms as "the big firms of the informal sector . . . with serious investments in the economy" (Hazizaj 1996b, 7). In his usual populist style, Berisha rejected allegations of money laundering by famously stating: "The money of Albanians is honest" (paratë e shqiptarëve janë të ndershme). This public statement became so iconic that, even a decade after the collapse of the firms, every kreditor I talked to repeated it verbatim.

With this declaration, Berisha exploited the blurred boundaries between formal and informal financial institutions (banks, pyramid firms, other informal lenders), as well as between licit and illicit flows of money (such as profits from arms and diesel trading with the war-torn former Yugoslavia, trafficking, and migrant remittances). Partly, such slippage was afforded by the inherently messy definitions of formal/informal economies (Elyachar 2003, 2005; Roitman 2005) and clean/dirty money (Peebles 2012). But these iconic statements had a performative effect: they delineated the limits of legitimate and illegitimate forms of finance. Blending descriptions of the unregulated communist black market with those of the postsocialist informal credit market, the statement declared the firms legitimate capitalist businesses, deserving of praise for their contribution to the national economy. In addition to a mark of legitimacy, these statements served as a sort of guarantee, a tacit promise that the government would back the firms and protect investors.[17]

State support and legitimization of ambiguous economic activities in the name of capitalism or national progress have not been limited to the pyramid firms, however. These ever shifting boundaries of private/public, formal/informal, licit/illicit boundaries, have come to constitute a mode of governance in postsocialist Albania. This form of governance is visible in many contexts: from the "legalizations" (*legalizimet*) of "select" informal homes (*shtëpi informale*) often used as a means of vote-buying, to the impunity of high-level officials accused of corruption. The study of the firms thus contributes not only to a record of the recent past but also to a better understanding of the continuities of specific economic logics and modes of governance in Albania beyond the collapse of the firms.

The Collapse of the Firms and Their Aftermath

The collapse of the firms in 1996–97 marks a crucial event in Albania's postsocialist history; it sparked a year of anarchy and violence that undid much of the progress made during the first decade of the country's economic transformations. The collapse began with the suspension of activities by the firms Sude (in December 1996) and Gjallica (in January 1997).[18] Other firms soon followed suit. The collapse of the firms quickly sparked protest and unrest, unleashing a political crisis and years of violence; these events constitute a crucial moment in the national historical imagination. The year 1997, locally referred to as *nëntdhteshtata*, is still remembered as a time of a "total collapse of the state" (Çupi 2005).

There is no consensus among former participants or outside observers on what precipitated the collapse of the firms. Some blame the end of the UN embargo against the former Yugoslavia and its effect on the illegal arms and oil trafficking from Albania (Abrahams 2015). Others point to the decision from the Bank of Albania in early January 1997 to limit the number of withdrawals the firms could make per day (Bezemer 2001, 10). This measure limited the firms' access to liquidity and credit from official banks. Once Sude and Gjallica went insolvent, bank-run scenario quickly engulfed all the firms.

Sude was the first of the firms to fold. It was a modest firm of thirty thousand investors, yet it played an important role in public representations of all firms after the collapse. Sude was the only firm run by a woman, Maksude Kadëna, who was once praised as a do-gooder (*bamirëse*) and later slandered as a "false Roma fortune-teller." Having no other assets or investments, Sude was deemed by the auditors to be a Ponzi scheme—it circulated funds from new investors to earlier investors. Sude suspended returns on deposits in December 1996 and, after a month of giving false hopes to its investors, Kadëna turned herself in to the authorities, admitting insolvency (the only firm owner to do so). Sude's collapse triggered peaceful protests in Tirana. Protestors were investors who had previously been waiting outside of Kadëna's apartment building in the hope of reclaiming their deposits. After weeks of waiting and hoping in vain, they took to the streets, addressing state authorities through the slogans, "we want our money back" (*duam paret tona*). The protests were crushed by violent beatings by the police and the Albanian secret service.

Gjallica was the second firm to fold. It was registered as a limited liability company based in Vlora and had the highest number of investors (144,000) and the largest deposits (US$690,000,000).[19] Gjallica's collapse sparked protests in Vlora, a city of about one hundred thousand and home to several firms. What began as a peaceful march soon turned into uncontrolled violence between protestors and police and, later on, between different bands that terrorized the city.[20]

For a few tense months, it seemed that this young democracy that had exceeded the expectations of the international community was suddenly turning back into an outright authoritarian dictatorship. The violence that erupted in Vlora quickly spread across other cities in the south. The army dissolved, police forces in various parts of the country did not function, and civilians (mostly young men) looted army storages that were mysteriously opened to the public. A general state of anarchy and instability plagued the country throughout 1997. President Berisha cast the protests as a communist coup and declared a state of emergency in March of that year, ordering the army to attack what he described as "rebels" in the south. Many army officers ignored this order, and many defected, thus preventing what could have been a bloody civil war. Soon after, Prime Minister Aleksandër Meksi resigned, and Berisha eventually stepped down in late spring of that year, thanks in large part to international pressure and a loss of support by many former allies, including the United States. In April of that year, the international peacekeeping forces of Operation Alba came into the country to restore order and maintain peace.

The collapse of the Albanian pyramid firms penetrated deep into the fiber of everyday life. Almost every household was affected by the loss of deposits at the firms. Alongside the violence and political anarchy that followed their collapse, an economic recession unfolded, isolating Albania once again from foreign investment and tourism. The lek depreciated by 25 percent in relation to the U.S. dollar, the country's GDP fell by 10 percent, inflation soared to 40 percent, and 150,000 families registered for unemployment assistance within six months (Bezemer 2001). The drop in foreign investments and the overall stagnation of the economy left an imprint on the country's economy for decades. It took Albania a long time to recover from the destruction, violence, and economic downturn of 1997. Since then, the country's economy has experienced slow but steady growth and the political system has become much more stable, though accusations of widespread corruption are endemic (see also Musaraj 2015, 2018). According to macroeconomic indicators, Albania is now a middle-income country. Nevertheless, it remains one of the poorest countries in Europe. Further, most other former socialist countries in the region entered the twenty-first century as members of the emerging political and economic regime of the European Union, while Albania remains a distant outsider.[21]

The collapse of the firms sparked significant political and economic reforms. The law on nonbank moneylending was changed to prohibit the taking of deposits en masse, new regulations on bankruptcy were passed, and many commercial banks were licensed to operate locally, enabling more bank loans to businesses and individuals and more banking supervision. The transition government of 1997 established an audit and supervisory authority on the firms—the Supervisory Group of the Pyramid Firms (Grupi Mbikqyrës i Firmave Piramidale; hereafter Supervisory Group). In the first year of existence, the Supervisory Group worked closely with the global consulting firms Deloitte & Touche and PricewaterhouseCoopers to audit the firms.

Despite the changes to the financial system, some of the iconic figures associated with the firms continue to be evoked in public discourse. Indeed, many of the political figures prominent in 1997 continue to dominate the local political scene today.[22] Iconic figures of the pyramid firms, such as Sude, are routinely used as a metaphor for bad financial planning. Besides being a symbol of fraud and poor accounting, the firms also constitute a business model that continues to operate in other economic spheres. Thus many lament that a similar "pyramid way" of accumulation and investment is replicated in other financial spheres such as in informal credit markets and the construction industry. A commercial banking sector has flourished following the firms' collapse. More than a dozen banks exist now—a high number for the size of the country—most of which are subsidiaries of foreign banks. The banking sector is highly regulated, in line with the

European Union banking regulations. Access to credit has increased, and more people have been financialized, taking more consumer loans and mortgages. Nevertheless, a black market in high-risk loans has proliferated, bringing back the term "fajde" into everyday discourse. Many businesses and individuals have turned to the black market of moneylending, taking on loans at very high interest from loan sharks. Other forms of financial speculation persist. Notably, former kreditorë draw an analogy between the firms and financing in construction, especially the practice of *klering*, a form of in-kind payment. This analogy hinges on the pyramid logic of taking money from Peter to pay Paul, the classic Ponzi scheme.

These persistent Ponzi logics of investment and accumulation are present not only in Albania; they are pervasive in other postsocialist and postrevolutionary contexts as well as other contexts where neoliberal economic policies dominate. As such, the Albanian pyramid firms present an important case for thinking more broadly about financial bubbles and crashes. The experience of gain and loss by the protagonists of this book speaks to a broader set of questions: How are financial bubbles made possible and legitimate? How are people drawn to such speculative financial ventures? What kinds of economies are made possible by such booms and busts, and how do these economies persist beyond the bust?

Bubbles, Mania, and Capitalism

When I began my research in 2008, the stock market had just crashed in New York City, sparking a global financial crisis. I had been living in New York City as a graduate student but managed to escape the crisis by being in Albania, which was not affected by the global financial meltdown, at least not right away. But the news of the global crisis permeated the mediascape in Albania through the ubiquitous satellite and cable television and the increasing presence of the Internet. My interviews with former investors into the Albanian pyramid firms took place as the world financial crisis was unfolding. I returned to the United States in 2009, as the country was slowly coming to grips with the devastating effects of the rising number of indebted homeowners. It was no longer possible to think and write about the Albanian firms as an isolated speculative bubble.

From the Tulip Mania of the Dutch Golden Age and the South Sea Bubble in eighteenth-century England to the subprime mortgage crisis in the United States, speculative forms of finance leading to a boom and bust scenario have been a staple of capitalist economies the world over. These have taken place in contexts of high as well as low finance and throughout the history of capitalism. Previous bubbles, such as the South Sea Bubble or John Law's scheme were attributed to an earlier stage of capitalism. Many of these events took place in economies that were either immersed in mercantilism or transitioning from mercantilism to national capitalism. Also, most of these bubbles were located in western European countries or European colonial empires. But recent bubbles have emerged in post-Fordist capitalist contexts, in the Euro-American world as well as in countries of the global South. A most notable recent example of a speculative bubble was the Madoff Ponzi scheme in the United States. Speculative schemes proliferating in the global South include pyramid schemes, such as the MMM scheme in Russia (Boreinstein 1999) and the Caritas in Romania (Verdery 1996), which were similar to the Albanian firms in that they emerged at the time of postsocialist transformations of the early 1990s and, at least in the case of Caritas, had a similar widespread popularity and impact on national economy and politics. Other sites located at the frontiers of global capital experienced similar scenarios of the search for a fabled El Dorado, such as the investment schemes of the Kalimatan mine in Indonesia (Tsing 2000). Finally, smaller-scale (but equally scandalous) Ponzi-type schemes continue to emerge in other places on the margins of global capital, such as the collapse of the U-Vistract scheme in the late 1990s Papua New Guinea (Cox 2018), the *el millionario* in 2007 in Guatemala (Nelson 2013), the DMG in Colombia (Ramírez 2014), or the ReDémare in Togo (Piot, Lachenal, and Mbodj-Pouye 2014).

Accounts of speculative financial practices in the media and scholarly work are typically fraught with words such as "bubbles," "mania," and "epidemics" (Ferguson 2005; Kindleberger and Aliber 2005; MacKay [1841] 2011; Shiller 2000). Such tropes suggest that speculative events stand outside the "real" economy and that participation in these events is driven by irrational decisionmaking. These are considered aberrations to the rational laws of the market (see, for instance, Greenspan 1996). Likewise, official and vernacular accounts of the boom and bust of the pyramid firms in Albania often posit mania, epidemic, or irrational behavior as tropes to explain the widespread nature of the firms. For example, official IMF accounts of the Albanian pyramid firms described them as an aberration from economic rationality, attributing their popularity among local investors to "unfamiliarity with financial markets" (Jarvis 2000, 46) and describing participants as caught up in the mania of Ponzi schemes.

I take a different approach to financial speculation. I consider such instances of boom and bust as being central to the capitalist, and more specifically for the recent examples, neoliberal economic transformations. By neoliberal economy, or neoliberalism, I refer to a set of economic policies that aim at the privatization of the welfare state. These include a wide range of measures including, monetarist economic policies that focus on the money supply, inflation, and exchange rates; privatization of welfare institutions such as health care, pensions, education; and the predominance of a specific form of subjectivity defined as an entrepreneurial self (Greenhouse 2012; Harvey 2005; Mirowski 2013; Muehlebach 2012). As neoliberal economic policies have spread from the United States and the UK in the 1970s to Latin American countries in the 1980s, to the postsocialist and postrevolutionary contexts in Eastern Europe, Eurasia, and Africa—so have booms and busts. As such, they constitute an important object of study for understanding the workings of contemporary forms of capitalism, at centers and peripheries of global capital. This approach echoes other schools of economic thought, of which I highlight three.

Since the world financial crisis of 2008, the field of behavioral economics has offered a persuasive critique of the efficient market hypothesis. Works in the genre include the precrisis account by Robert Shiller (2000) and postcrisis ones by Akerlof and Shiller (2015), as well as the burgeoning work by behavioral economists such as Richard Thaler (2015) and Daniel Ariely (2010). A behavioral approach to economic practices challenges the basic premise of neoclassical economic theory that everyone acts as a rational economic actor in the market. Behavioral economists blame the "irrational exuberance" (Greenspan in Shiller 2000) of market actors for the crashes that occur in the marketplace. While mainstream economists consider these psychological factors as externalities of the regular market operations, behavioral economists explore the central role that these forces play in economic decisions and practices. In other words, rather than presuming a universal economic rationality, behavioral economists take irrationality, peer pressure, and other emotional-psychological drives as key drivers of economic decisionmaking. One of the shortcomings of this approach is it substitutes one universal (the rational economic man) with another (human psychology), which does not allow for diversity in modes of thought and practice among different sociocultural groups.

Another important and more radical critique of the efficient market hypothesis spans a longer history that can be traced back to Karl Marx's opus on capitalism as an unsustainable social and economic system. In *Capital*, Marx proposes that commodities are of a fictitious nature. With money being the commodity par excellence, Marx concludes that interest-bearing capital is a fictitious form of value.[23] Building on this analysis of capital and capitalism, contemporary neo-Marxist approaches perceive crises as imminent to capitalist economies and especially to highly financialized economies (see Arrighi 1994; Harvey 1989, 2010). According to these approaches, crisis—embodied in loss of value, profits, and liquidity—is already foretold in a system where labor and wages are subject to a system of valuation dominated by the ultimate commodity: money. In other words, crises and bubbles are not external to capitalism but are crucial to the very essence of capital and its fetish character. Echoing this approach, I show how capitalist transformations in the early 1990s contributed to the rise of the pyramid firms and how speculative forms of finance continue to persist alongside an increasingly neoliberal type of capitalism in Albania.

The neo-Marxist critique of neoliberalism has found application beyond the centers of high finance. The anthropologists Jean Comaroff and John Comaroff (1999) note a direct connection between the emergence of speculative forms of finance in postsocialist and postrevolutionary contexts and the expansion millennial capitalism in the global South since the 1990s. This manifesto laid the ground for thinking about crisis and speculation as key elements of neoliberal presents and futures (Piot and Allison 2011). At the same time, Marxist and neo-Marxist approaches continue to maintain the rational/irrational divide in economics, positing financial speculation alongside other "enchantments" of capitalism.[24] First, this binary assumes a similar notion of universal economic rationality that is also at the heart of the market efficiency hypothesis. Second, the language of enchantments at the periphery makes the anthropologists uneasy. As Diane Nelson cautions, while writing about the pyramid scheme *el millionario* in Guatemala, "enchantment may hug near those considered modernity's others in a too-tight embrace, marking them the losers in the tribunal of reason" (2009, 206). In other words, by casting bubbles, Ponzi schemes, and other forms of speculation at the margins as enchantments, one risks denying reason and rationality to the participants in these schemes. Many participants in the Albanian firms engaged in elaborate practices that entailed calculation and strategizing. These strategies often amounted to forms of entrepreneurship and innovation. Rather than using the language of enchantment versus rationality, I propose we consider the financial activities of the firms through the lenses of multiple economic logics—a multiplicity of capitalist and noncapitalist forms of investment, conversion, and commensuration that intertwined with intimate relations of kinship and friendship. These practices help us trace how neoliberal economic formations emerge from a multiplicity of socioeconomic logics, affects, and life-worlds (see also Bear et al. 2015; Tsing 2015).

Neo-Keynesian approaches to bubbles and crashes constitute yet another critical approach to the efficient market thesis. This critique builds on the work of the economist Hyman Minsky (1986, 1992) on the financial fragility hypothesis. Minsky proposed that financial markets would inevitably shift from hedge and speculative forms of finance to Ponzi forms of finance as a result of credit expansions and the increase of money-manager forms of capitalism (such as hedge funds and pension funds). Advocates of Minsky's hypothesis studied other instances of economic bubbles and crashes through this framework. Charles Kindleberger and Robert Aliber's *Mania, Panic, and Crashes* (2005), for instance, build on Minsky's financial fragility hypothesis to develop an economic and historical explanation for the cyclical emergence of various speculative bubbles, from Tulipmania and the South Sea bubble to the asset and real estate bubble in 1990s Japan. *Mania, Panic, and Crashes* includes an entry on the Albanian firms with a telling heading: "Charles Ponzi is alive and well and living in Tirana," thus situating the Albanian firms within this longer history of financial bubbles.

Following Minsky, Kindleberger and Aliber take financial bubbles as symptoms of capitalism's inherent fragility (rather than its aberrations), as an effect of "displacements" (that is, economic and political change) and credit expansions.[25] Along similar lines, neo-Keynesian economists analyze the stock market crash of 2008 in the United States in light of the credit expansion in subprime mortgage markets (Ferguson 2005; Reinhart and Rogoff 2011; Roubini and Mihm 2010). A similar approach informed the most comprehensive account of the boom and bust of the firms in Albania by the neo-Keynesian economist Dirk Bezemer (2001). Drawing on Minsky's financial fragility hypothesis, Bezemer situates the Albanian firms at the heart of the macroeconomic policies implemented through free-market reform.[26] He points to a credit expansion in the Albanian economy, which he attributed primarily to the flow of international loans. Bezemer also points to the growing size of remittances as another source of this credit expansion. But given that they mostly circulate through nonbank infrastructures, remittances have received little attention in the financial accounts of the firms (but see Korovilas 1999). Also absent from these accounts are the nonmonetary forms of credit and debt (such as obligations among kin, friends, and neighbors) that mediated these remittance flows. Remittances and kinship networks were a key subject of discussion in conversations with former investors. Most kreditorë I talked to deposited their remittances at the firms, and every one of them pointed to friends or kin who had mediated their transactions. Taken together, these various forms of wealth and relations mobilized by participants in the Albanian firms point to gaps in economic understandings of bubbles and crashes.

Materialities, Socialities, and Temporalities of Speculation

The analytical approach to crisis and speculation that I advocate views instances of financial speculation as not only internal to capitalist institutions but also as intertwined with capitalist and noncapitalist forms of accumulation and investment. This book expands the study of financialization and financial speculation to contexts of low finance, where the bulk of financial activities occur outside official financial markets and are mostly in cash. It does so by exploring the discourses, materialities, socialities, and temporalities of financial speculation taking place through the Albanian pyramid firms.

Tropes of mania, epidemic, and folly abound in accounts of the pyramid firms' boom and bust in Albania. Many kreditorë also used this vocabulary to assess the firms retrospectively. In the newspaper archives, this mania and folly were predominant after the collapse of the firms, when media narratives shifted toward the discourse of the occult and hysteria, focusing primarily on Kadëna. By contrast, in the 1995–96 newspaper archives, I encountered representations of the firms articulated in terms of calculation, rationality, and entrepreneurship. These various representations of the firms constitute a good place to explore the unsettled boundaries of legitimate and illegitimate finance.[27] Rather than elements of universal human psychology, as behavioral economics would have it, these representations speak to conflicting discourses of postsocialist entrepreneurship. They serve as a means of legitimizing or delegitimizing particular financial institutions and practices, often through the language of gender and ethnicity. Thus, the shift in the public discourse around the firms in the late 1990s to the gendered representations of mania and hysteria delegitimized the firms that were once presented as the vanguard of postsocialist capitalism.

Discourse shapes the materials and practices of markets. The discourse of capitalist entrepreneurship and of "men of honor" helped legitimize the firms and formatted the materials of the market, such as cash, credit contracts, privatization vouchers (Muniesa, Millo, and Callon 2007). But the materialities of the market in turn shape the economic institution and the outcomes of their activities. Finally, people often use materials of the market in ways unanticipated by their producers, designers, or regulators. The materiality of financial speculation is a central theme in this book. Looking at materials of the market of fajde provides insight into the top-down and ground-up practices of value conversion across asymmetric regimes of value, the changing forms and functions of money in the 1990s, and the emergence of new financial repertoires—such as remittances, that have outlasted the firms and continue to play an important role in Albania's economy.

To trace the *social life* (Appadurai 1986) of the materials of the market of fajde, I follow various monetary and nonmonetary objects of wealth—such as remittances, houses, social and family networks, multiple currencies, and privatization vouchers. Kreditorë circulated these forms of wealth in and through the firms to generate new *forms of value* (Munn 1986), including capital, credit, immovable property, urban citizenship, and socioeconomic status. I work with the analytic of *thresholds of value conversion* (Guyer 2004) to capture the kinds of value transformation made possible by the firms. Jane Guyer (2004, 2012) developed the notion of threshold of value conversions in her study of economic patterns and transactions in societies of Atlantic Africa. Through ethnographic and historical research, she identified economic repertoires that have proliferated in a region historically situated at margins of colonial and postcolonial regimes. Her analysis underscored the multiplicity of scales of value that people located at these margins had to negotiate. Guyer highlighted the global and regional institutions that generate an asymmetry of values as well as the grassroots institutions and repertoires that proliferate at the interfaces of distinct value regimes. Though grounded in the specific history of Atlantic Africa, this analytic is useful to think about economic institutions and practices in other sites equally marginal and equally mired by asymmetry, volatility, and multiplicity of value.

Some degree of multiplicity and asymmetry in scales of value is present at any time and place, but contexts of radical sociopolitical transformation are particularly fraught with such multiplicities and asymmetries. The postsocialist transformations in the early 1990s Eastern Europe were also marked by a proliferation of different scales of value. As such, postsocialist contexts have constituted key sites for studying the processes of value transformation.[28]

Communist wealth consisted in collective or state-owned forms of property (apartments, public enterprises, and collective farms); in individual rights of access and entitlements to public goods and services (health care, childcare, food rations, jobs, education); and in social capital (kinship relationships, social networks, political ties, and connections) (Ledeneva 1998; Wedel 1986; Yang 1994). As many of these forms of wealth were devalued and revalued in the postsocialist context, the asymmetries between communist and capitalist forms of wealth generated key thresholds for possible value conversions (Verdery 1996, 2003; Truitt 2013). The privatization process in and of itself was a major site of value conversion across multiple (asymmetric) regimes of value. As such, it was—and, at least in Albania, continues to be—a prime site for speculation. This process favored many who had access to the communist networks of wealth. Katherine Verdery drew a similar connection when writing about the pyramid scheme Caritas that emerged around the same time in postsocialist Romania. Verdery notes the role of *entrepratchiks* (1996, 33, 199–200)—individuals who had been lower-level *apparatchiks* (members of the Communist Party) and economic managers in the state socialist enterprises. In the early years of postsocialist transformation, entrepratchiks were actively involved in buying state properties being privatized at a low cost through clientelistic networks. Similar patterns of wealth conversion and capital accumulation played into the formation of the Albanian firms; many of the firms' owners gained their assets (*asete*) through preferential access to the privatization of former state factories and other businesses (see also Musaraj 2011).

The materiality of money itself was crucial to the circulations at the firms. Money is a prime material of financial markets, but it too takes different forms and functions in different cultural and political contexts (Akin and Robbins 1999;

Bohannan 1959; Hart 2000; Maurer 2006; Parry and Bloch 1989). The shift from central planning to a free-market economy in Albania entailed a deep transformation in the forms and functions of money. This shift was particularly painful given that the country's authoritarian leader of nearly forty years, Enver Hoxha, remained a staunch disciple of Stalinism, maintaining a highly centralized command economy that focused on heavy industry and, since the 1970s, enforcing an extensive, highly moralized, and politicized ban on private property. This path diverged from other communist economies in the region that, to the contrary, moved toward more liberalized markets and allowed an (albeit limited) private economic sector. After breaking ties with the Soviet Union, Albania aligned with the People's Republic of China under Mao Zedong replicating a Cultural Revolution and adopting economic policies of self-sufficiency and isolationism. Until the late 1970s, Albania relied on Chinese aid and few exports for hard currency (Mëhilli 2017). By the late 1980s, the country accumulated a large foreign debt that put its economy at a disadvantage when Albania opened the doors to international markets in the early 1990s (Sandstrom and Sjoberg 1991).[29]

This peculiar economic history of communist Albania provides the backdrop against which changes in the forms and functions of money unfolded in the 1990s. Shock-therapy reforms were even more shocking and led to high rates of inflation and several devaluations of the lek, as well as the devaluation of other forms of wealth (savings, social services and benefits, housing).[30] Postsocialist transformations entailed a shift in ideas and moralities about money. During the communist economic regime, production was the source of value, whereas "with the new market emphasis, people [were] being asked to see commerce as a source of value" (Verdery 1996, 177). In addition to ideas about the morality of money, in Albania, the forms and functions of money shifted from serving primarily as a unit of account and means of exchange during communism to gaining the function of a store of value during the postsocialist transformations. During the post–World War II communist transformations, money significantly contributed to processes of disembeddeding and reembedding of social relations (Lampland 1995)—from kinship and clan-based social units to state and party mediated ones.[31] A similar process of disembedding and reembedding unfolded during the postsocialist transformations. The valuation and circulation of money, once dominated by the state, was now reembedded in social networks of friends, kin, and sekserë (brokers) as well as in authoritarian political networks (see also Bockman 2011). The early 1990s also saw a change in the need and quantity of money (as cash) in circulation. Money became both extremely valuable and scarce as unemployment soared and banks did not give out loans to people without collateral, which was the case for most Albanians (see also Bezemer 2001). People resorted to other sources of cash, and the firms were one such source. The firms, arguably, filled a gap between the need for money and the lack thereof. They acted as switchpoints between various flows of cash from formal and informal venues all the while mobilizing social ties and networks.

One way in which the firms acted as a threshold of value conversion was by absorbing, storing, and multiplying cash from migrant remittances (Korovilas 1999). The postsocialist transformations in Albania unleashed a mass migration to nearby western European countries. By the mid-1990s, migrant remittances sent in multiple currencies soon became one of the only sources of income for those who remained in Albania (King et al. 2005; Vullnetari and King 2011). The firms attracted these remittances by offering accounts in multiple currencies and high interest returns, options not available at the official banks.

To better understand the intertwined dynamics of remittance flows and investment in the firms, I pay special attention to the materiality of the cash circulated across these two different economic spheres. Investors often spoke about the large stacks and sacs of cash that they carried to or from the firms. This cash was primarily in the local currency but also in multiple currencies from other pre-Euro European markets. Given the multidirectional distribution of migrants, people living in Albania suddenly gained possession of currencies from several countries in Europe and North America. Migration patterns dictated the flows and amounts of currencies in circulation. The Greek drachmas dominated remittance flows, given the large number of migrants in Greece. Italian liras were followed by German and Swiss marks and the U.S. and Canadian dollars. Remittances thus acted as a sort of credit expansion that circulated outside the official banking system. Meanwhile, the firms provided a space that allowed investors to store, convert, and multiply the different currencies.

At the firms, investors sought alternative ways of storing wealth and expanded their "ability to convert" different forms of value (Guyer 2004; Villarreal 2014). In chapters 2 and 3, I note how this preference for access to multiple regimes of value and the ability to convert such values constitutes an enduring economic repertoire in postsocialist Albania. This repertoire emerged in the early 1990s as Albania loosened border and trade controls. It was a reaction to decades of economic and cultural isolation and official vilification of the "foreign" which, not surprisingly, had generated a fetishization of the foreign (see also Mai 2001; Musaraj 2012). This repertoire also emerged as a safety net in times of volatility and uncertainty. By gaining access to multiple forms of wealth, Albanian citizens sought to secure more durable value at a time fraught with currency devaluations and rising inflation. Finally, this repertoire continues to be a staple of the Albanian economy. As in other parts of the global South, remittances in Albania constitute a lifeline for many who cannot make ends meet.[32] Likewise, both the formal and informal financial sector operate in the dual currency system of lek and euro, with the former being the national currency and the latter being the preferred currency for savings and purchasing real estate.

Besides cash in multiple currencies, social ties also played an important role in mobilizing and mediating remittances through the firms. Most kreditorë invested through a third party—be that a *i/të njohur* (connections) or a sekser. These findings challenge the focus on top-down economics, on speculation as a form of abstraction of value, and on capital as having a purely fictitious character. Instead, the strategies and patterns of wealth circulation at the firms indicate how social ties and finance intertwine (see also Hertz 1998; Ho 2009; Zaloom 2006; Zelizer 1996). This Albanian story is not unique; social networks among migrant and minority groups were crucial to the original Ponzi scheme by Charles Ponzi as well as in the Bernie Madoff scam. Likewise, the *El Millionario* Ponzi scheme in post-conflict Guatemala mobilized Mayan kinship and community networks to draw investors (Nelson 2012). As such, the stories of the Albanian firms are key to understanding how financial speculation can take hold through highly personalized financial transactions rather than the abstraction of the social relations of production.

Housing was another important form of wealth circulated through the firms. The homes bought, sold, and desired constituted an important factor in the financial decisions for participating at the firms. These desires and decisions were shaped by the transformation of the housing regime and the dynamics of the emerging real estate market that began with the privatization of state-owned urban apartments in 1993. The transformation of the housing regime—from one of allocation to a real estate market—was one of the most dramatic changes of tranzicion in Albania, as in the rest of the postsocialist world (Fehérváry 2013; Zavisca 2012; Zhang 2010). This is precisely what Baçe captures in his allegory of Albarado: as housing became the only asset owned by most people, "the gift of the blue democracy," it represented a source of liquidity to invest in the firms. In 1996, people rushed to sell their recently privatized communist apartment for cash to invest to the firms. With the abolishment of the regime of allocation, housing also became a highly valued form of wealth that many hoped to purchase with the firms' gains. Coming out of a minimalist housing system, where the very cubic meters per person, or "living space" (Buchli 2000), were prescribed by government regulation, almost everyone felt a need for more spacious housing. Every kreditor I spoke to indeed claimed that they planned to buy or build a new home with the expected returns from the firms.

Interconnections between real estate bubbles and stock market bubbles are not uncommon. Kindleberger and Aliber (2005, 12) show how this is a recurring theme in the history of bubbles around the world. The interconnections between the world financial crisis in 2008 and the subprime mortgage crisis in the United

States are well documented. For Neo-Keynesian economists, the expansion of the mortgage market in the 1980s and 1990s caused a credit expansion that pushed financial transactions to a Ponzi form. Likewise, the financial speculation of the Albanian firms was in a sense intertwined with the expansion (or, rather, emergence) of a real estate market. But this intertwining was also distinct from other bubbles discussed in the literature.

A crucial point of difference between Albania and other contemporary bubbles is the absence of financialization or of other resource booms as sources of credit expansion (cf. Grant 2014; Ong 2011; Woodworth and Ulfstjerne 2016). Unlike the United States' subprime mortgage crisis, which was driven by a credit expansion of sub-par loans, postsocialist Albania had nearly no commercial banks to give out loans (mortgages) to people who were looking to buy new housing. Even those few banks that began to give out loans were very conservative as most people did not possess any assets that could be used as collateral. Further, people were not comfortable with the idea of paying monthly interest to banks. The firms, thus, provided (or, at least, promised to provide) an alternative source of financing real estate purchases: cash. Meanwhile, housing, such as communist apartments, became a source of liquidity for the financial activities at the firms. Housing, thus acted as a form of capital to invest in the firms. Many former kreditorë indeed recalled how brokers of the firms encouraged them to sell their apartment.

A focus on these intertwined economies of fajde and the emerging real estate market in Albania brings attention also to the temporalities of financial speculation. Here I approach temporality in two senses: (1) as the rhythm and scheduling of financial transactions, and (2) as a shared sense of being in time, vis a vis the imagined global temporality of progress.[33]

A defining feature of Ponzi schemes and Ponzi finance is the accelerated temporality of wealth making deemed as "unsustainable patterns of financial behavior" (Kindleberger and Aliber 2005, 28).[34] These accelerated temporalities of Ponzi types of finance emerge from the broader financial architecture of a given economic system. The Albanian firms emerged at a time of free-market reform that entailed the paradox of "very strict conditions on growth of the official financial sector [and] no regulatory impediments on those banking with Ponzi methods" (Bezemer 2000, 7). Many of the policies introduced and adopted in Albania belong to a broader repertoire of neoliberal policies that emphasize limited government, less financial regulation and monetarist policies; taken together, these policies embody a temporality of the long run. Shock-therapy reforms in Albania, thus, introduced new temporalities of finance and life that rubbed against those of the communist regime.

Communist time was officially meant to be linear and predictable, structured by the temporality of the five-year plan, the regular and reliable pay stubs.

However, in reality, time under the communist regime became increasingly irregular and unpredictable as people spent hours queuing for food essential and other consumer goods as well as "flattened and motionless" (Verdery 1996, 189) as not much seemed to change in the grand scheme of things. People in Albania and elsewhere in the former socialist world saw the free-market changes as a shift to the desired temporality of modernity: one of steady progress and knowable, predictable, and plannable future. This desired temporality, which Jane Guyer (2012) defines as a temporality of "near future," was shared, in theory, by both the capitalist and socialist modernities. Until the 1950s and 1960s, the two opposing sides of the Cold War reproduced this temporality in different ways: the Fordist and welfare state models in the West, the state-planned economies on the East. But since the 1970s, in the United States and the UK, and since the 1990s, in other parts of the world, new financial temporalities were also introduced due to the progressive dismantling of many of the welfare state institutions. These post-Fordist (and, I would add, postsocialist) financial temporalities are best captured in Guyer's (2012) dual neoliberal temporality of the long run and the punctuated present. As described earlier, monetarist policies inscribe a temporality of the long run. Meanwhile, the everyday life of people living under these policies is increasingly experienced as a temporality of a punctuated present, that is, of time that is "punctuated rather than enduring: of fateful moments and turning points, the date as event rather than as position in a sequence or a cycle" (Guyer 2012, 416).

Contrary to expectations, what people in Albania and elsewhere experienced during shock-therapy reforms was not the idealized predictable temporality of the near future, but the combination of the temporality of the long run and punctuated present. While official economic policy focused on the long run, everyday experience was increasingly marked by punctuated time. As state enterprises and cooperatives closed down, hundreds of thousands lost their jobs. This marked an end to the predictable rhythm of regular paychecks, social benefits, and access (albeit rationed and low-quality) to periodic basic consumer goods. Instead, in the 1990s, most made their living on short-term unsecured and unstable jobs, many borrowed from friends and relatives, and many more turned to remittances as a safety net. The latter came in sporadically and were subject to the unpredictable temporality of working under the table in low-skilled jobs, in construction, agriculture, and service industry.

The book situates the pyramid firms in Albania within these changing temporalities. Anthropologists of contemporary pyramid schemes and speculative bubbles have commented on the millennial and messianic aspects of the temporality of such speculative bubbles, which looks to a bright future, the second coming of sorts (Guyer 2012; Piot, Lachenal, and Mbodj-Pouye 2014; Verdery 1996).

This messianic spirit was also present in the promise that the Albanian firms would deliver an exponential amount of money that would change people's lives dramatically and quickly. In addition to the messianic time, I suggest that kreditorë sought the firms with the possibility for a temporality of the near future, which was no longer attainable through official financial institutions. By offering regular interest returns withdrawn as a sort of regular monthly salary, the firms promised a closer horizon for materializing a predictable economic life. By offering an accelerated path to buy the desired new homes, they also promised an accelerated path to the desired European modernity.

In their quest for new homes and subsequent decisions to participate in the firms, kreditorë were not just driven by euphoria, exuberance, or greed. They were also driven by aspirations toward European modernity. Housing constituted a crucial component of this shared vision of modernity. Kreditorë's desires for new homes echo those of many across the global South who look to housing as a means of ensuring access to a global middle class (Halawa 2015; Zhang 2010). In addition to class aspirations, longing for European modernity in Albania has a specific historical and cultural significance.

The trope of "Europe" signals a dual temporality in Albania's national imagination. On the one hand, "Europe" evokes a temporality of the past, a longue durée of cultural belonging to a European cultural space. These claims to Europeanness are often juxtaposed to other forms of undesired identities, such as the Ottoman (and implicitly Muslim) or communist other (see Sulstarova 2006).[35] On the other hand, since the 1990s, Europe also represents the temporality of the future; desired but not yet fulfilled (Mai 2001). With the opening of the borders in the 1990s, Europe—while forbidden but fetishized during communism— became attainable as a travel destination as well as a legitimate temporality of modernity to aspire to individually and collectively. Europe encompassed a wide range of symbols, materials, and tropes. Among others, homes came to represent forms of wealth that materialized this desired European modernity (Dalakoglou 2010; Dalipaj 2016). Reflecting on their success or failure to obtain the desired homes, kreditorë gauged their progress vis-à-vis their aspirations. In the 1990s, they thought it was possible to attain the desired new, post-1990s homes, often described as more "European," based on the spaciousness, design, and date of construction. This sense of the possible was fueled by expectations of spectacular and quick gains at the firms. A decade after the collapse of the firms, many lamented of "lagging behind" (kam/kemi mbetur mbrapa) this desired horizon of Europe. They often pointed to the quality of their homes as a sign of their lagging behind. These correlations between fajde, real estate markets, and the desire for a European modernity exemplify how the temporalities of finance intertwine with the temporalities of life (Guyer 2007, 2018; Miyazaki 2003, 2006). While the firms and their promises collapsed in 1997, I note, in the closing of this book, that similar temporalities of finance and life continued to be generated and negotiated in other economic spheres in Albania decades after the collapse of the firms.

An Ethnography of Speculation at the Margins of Global Finance

This book builds on ethnographic and archival research conducted over periods of extended and short-term fieldwork in Albania between 2008 and 2016. In 2008–9, I conducted fieldwork framed as an ethnography of multiple assessments of corruption in postsocialist Albania; the assessments of the firms' activities were one of many examples of corruption included in the original research design.[36] An internship at the Institute for Development and Research Alternatives (IDRA), a local research institute based in Tirana conducting national corruption perception surveys, provided an entry into some of the initial encounters and conversations I had about people's experience with the firms. My selection of the former kreditorë followed a snowball sampling method; in addition to my network of old and new friends, I drew on IDRA's geographically diverse pool of field interviewers (many of whom came from different regions of the country to study at the University of Tirana) to identify former kreditorë from different social and economic backgrounds willing to share their stories. Initial conversations with this first pool of informants provided further leads and contacts.

I continued to work on both the anthropology of corruption and on the pyramid firms throughout 2008–9, but it became increasingly clear to me that these were two separate projects. My research on the firms combined ethnographic and historical sources. I collected accounts of participation in the firms by former participants through casual conversations over extended coffee breaks, in-depth interviews with close to thirty former participants, and visits to the homes of key informants. Some of the interviews took place over multiple encounters. I followed up with key kreditorë in subsequent visits to the country in 2014 and 2015. In addition to talking to former participants, I also followed media stories of compensation of former kreditorë, prosecution of firms' owners, and public and internal reports on the administration of seized assets of the collapsed firms by the Supervisory Group. Some kreditorë shared personal documents that provided evidence of their activities at the firms, including credit contracts, books of accounts from brokers, and notices of subsidized housing to the families who lost their homes to the firms. I approach these various sources with an ethnographic sensibility; I am attuned to the moralities of exchange, the assessments of legitimacy and illegitimacy, as well as to the pragmatics, repertoires, and forms and functions of monetary and social currencies circulating in and through these firms.[37]

The bulk of this research took place in the cities of Tirana and Vlora—two major sites of pyramid-firm activity. Since being named the capital of newly independent Albania in 1920, Tirana has become the country's administrative, commercial, and cultural hub. Tirana's cityscape and population have undergone several radical transformations throughout the various "transitions" of the twentieth century. Since the outset of postsocialist transformation in the 1990s, Tirana's population has tripled; the city is now home to one-third of the country's people. Following the collapse of the communist command economy, hundreds of thousands of internal migrants left their disintegrating factory towns and collective farms and flocked to Tirana looking for employment opportunities and a more "European" lifestyle.

Vlora, by contrast, is a city with a longer history of urban settlement. It was a major port of the Roman Empire, an important administrative center during the Ottoman rule (1417–1912), and a hub for several national independence movements. It is also known as the city in which independence was declared in 1912, and it was a crucial base for the communist resistance against the Italian and German occupations during World War II. A major port, an important military base, and home to industrial complexes under the communist regime, the city of Vlora experienced rising unemployment since the collapse of the command economy in 1991. At the time of the boom in pyramid firms, Vlora became a source of migrants to Italy and Greece and a destination for internal migrants from rural areas. Thanks to its geographic location and its lax marine border patrol, throughout the early 1990s the city became a point of transit for all sorts of illegal trafficking, particularly to Italy.

Firms such as Vefa, Gjallica, Silva, and Kamberi established headquarters or major branches in Vlora, dubbed "the capital of fajde" (Sejdarasi 1996, 11). Locals took pride in these companies as homegrown business ventures. Given the widespread local participation in the firms, Vlora was the city that incurred some of the highest losses when they collapsed in 1997. For this reason, the city was also the epicenter of the bloody antigovernment protests that spread throughout southern Albania that year. Many of the former kreditorë based in Vlora noted that the collapse had been utterly devastating for the city since it was completely drowned (*i zhytur*) in these firms. Many of those I encountered there had lost all of their savings, remittance money, and stacks of cash with the collapse of the firms.

Being aware that these conversations were recorded after the collapse of the firms, I wanted to account for the temporal distance from the 1990s. I conducted research at the National Library newspaper archives, the state archives, and the

Ministry of Finance archives. I followed my informants' cues in navigating the newspaper archives. I found that, to a large extent, the newspaper coverage from 1996–97 confirmed much of the historical and political analysis presented in the oral narratives of the kreditorë. These archives also revealed important insights that were absent in the oral narratives.

Finally, I include here ethnographic research conducted during the summers of 2015 and 2016 that involved interviews and participant observation with various actors in the construction industry, including developers, subcontractors, and appraisers. Former kreditorë directed me to the construction industry, which they compared to the firms.

Organization of the Book

Sifting through newspaper archives and oral histories with former kreditorë, chapter 1 maps out local discourses of finance and entrepreneurship at the time of the firms' boom and after their bust. I note that these discourses were fraught with gendered and ethnicized undertones. A highly masculine discourse of entrepreneurship characterized press coverage and kreditorë's recollections of the firms at the time of their boom. This discourse served to legitimize the firms as virile entrepreneurs at the forefront of Albanian capitalism. By contrast, a feminized discourse that centered on the owner of Sude Kadëna delegitimized the firms as fictive fraudulent entities, their fraud thus attributed to occult practices and gender stereotypes. I take this discursive shift as a good place to explore the changing notions of legitimate/illegitimate finance and entrepreneurship at a time of dramatic free-market reform. I construct a genealogy of finance in postsocialist Albania in conversation with broader genealogies of finance in the global history of capitalism(s) (de Goede 2005; Ho 2009; Miyazaki 2006; Zaloom 2006). The chapter traces the similarities and continuities between communist and post-socialist cosmologies and repertoires of finance (such as fortune-telling, the black market, savings and credit circles, pyramid firms, remittance flows). Further, it underscores the use of gendered discourses of finance as a political act of legitimizing/delegitimizing the firms.

Chapter 2 explores the materialities of speculative finance. Starting off with accounts of "stacks and sacs of cash" that circulated at the firms, the chapter reviews the changes in the forms and functions of money (from serving primarily as a unit of account and a medium of exchange to gaining store of value functions) during the postsocialist transformations. Further, the chapter looks at how two forms of wealth—privatization vouchers and multi-currency remittances—point to top-down and bottom-up economic and social processes that enabled and sustained the firms. By being attentive to the materialities of fajde, the chapter considers how the pyramid firms played a role as thresholds of value conversion, enabling different forms of wealth to circulate and be converted across asymmetric regimes of value. I trace how the valuation and circulation of privatization vouchers—a new market device of the privatization reforms—impacted the acquiring of assets by various firms' owners. This trajectory speaks to the ways that firms were made possible by official financial institutions even as they operated outside these institutions. Second, I trace the circulation of remittances in multiple currencies through migrant networks. These circulations constitute a wider economic repertoire that was bottom-up and pervasive and that has become a staple of Albania's postsocialist economy. I argue that, by circulating remittances in cash in multiple currencies through the firms, kreditorë sought to accelerate processes of wealth accumulation while also seeking opportunities to access and convert wealth across different value regimes.

Chapter 3 looks at the intertwining of financial practices at firms with different forms of social ties. More specific, the chapter looks into the role of mediators such as sekserë and të njohur and the broader mobilization of migrant networks to attract deposits for the firms. The firms deliberately mobilized such social ties by offering incentives for sekserë and menaxherë to recruit their family members, neighbors, and friends. Further, the transactional pathways of circulation of migrant remittances through the firms were mediated by social ties of kinship and friendship. The chapter explores how social ties enabled the ongoing financial activities of the firms and how, in turn, transactions with the firms strengthened or weakened these social ties.

Chapter 4 turns to yet another important form of wealth: housing. I return to practices of selling/demolishing and building/buying/hoping to buy new homes to situate participation in the firms within broader transformations of the housing regime in the early 1990s Albania. This transformation—from a centralized regime of allocation to a free market in real estate—entailed a change in the very value and meaning of the home.[38] The home became a commodity and could be used as capital. At the same time, the chapter notes the continuities from the communist to the postsocialist context in the importance of the home as an object of transformation of the self (Humphrey 2005). Finally, I note how the home has come to constitute a crucial asset in postsocialist Albania as it is seen as an object that can materialize specific temporalities of the future. The chapter thus brings attention to the convergence of temporalities of finance and life (Guyer 2007, 2018; Miyazaki 2003, 2006) by exploring the intertwined economies of the firms and the emerging real estate market. For many kreditorë, who had no access to bank credit or cash, the firms provided a means of financing their desired homes. By offering an accelerated temporality of accumulation, the firms provided the promise of an accelerated temporality of European modernity. Alas, for those who lost the cash at the firms, these desired temporalities did not materialize, leaving kreditorë with a shared sense of "lagging behind."

Former kreditorë drew my attention to the construction industry by evoking an analogy between their modalities of financing and the accumulation at the pyramid firms. This analogy was captured in the expression "the pyramid way" (*mënyra piramidale*), referring to a particular logic of investment and accumulation whereby initial investment relied on an unsustainable future return. I explore these analogies in chapter 5. I specifically focus on a practice of financing in construction known as *klering* (in-kind payment). The term refers to nonliquid (noncash, nonbank) payment arrangements among developers, subcontractors, and buyers. Developers typically promised to pay subcontractors with apartments or other construction materials (such as concrete) rather than cash or credit. Often, these apartments were not yet built or finished. A stock of empty klering apartments in Tirana's peripheries in the late 2000s led to a crisis of liquidity (Çela 2009, 2010; Hoxha 2016). The financial practices in construction were often compared by former kreditorë and others to the financial logics of the pyramid firms. Following this analogy, I trace the *partial connections* (Strathern 2005) of these two different financial activities. I suggest that, like the firms, the construction industry relied on social networks and remittance flows as sources of financing, avoiding formal sources of credit and debt. First, here we have another form of speculative investment mobilized without recourse to official financialization (that is, bank loans). Second, homes once again served as a form of capital thus enabling a form of speculation without liquidity. Third, both activities thrive on the intertwined and blurred boundaries between formal and informal economies. Taken together, these analogies suggest that the Ponzi logics of accumulation and investment have become a persistent feature of postsocialist finance in Albania and of neoliberal capitalism more generally.

FAJDE, PYRAMID FIRMS, OR PONZI SCHEMES?

Gendered Discourses of Finance

> Precisely at the end of 1991, Albanians would bring out their old vocabulary the word, completely unknown, *fajde* [moneylending], a word to be now used at every hour, every minute, every second.
>
> —Edmond Laçi, *Revista Klan*, 1997

> Unlike in other countries, [in Albania, the pyramid firms'] phenomenon is entirely a private one and, except for the chance speculations, we can say that the money of Albanians is the most honest money there is. . . . The big firms of the informal sector have serious investments in important and profitable sectors of the [national] economy, from commerce, food processing and production, to tourism and mining.
>
> —Former president Sali Berisha, November 26, 1996

Most international media accounts of the spectacular collapse of the pyramid firms in 1997 in Albania center on the story of Maksude Kadëna.[1] A former worker in a communist shoe factory, Kadëna had established one of the most notorious pyramid firms (*firma piramidale*), Sude. Legally registered as a limited liability company (*shoqëri me përgjegjësi të kufizuar*), in 1993, Sude began to take deposits from a growing number of investors, officially referred to as *kreditor/ë* (creditor/s, investor/s). At the beginning of its activities, in 1993, Sude offered an interest return of 7–8 percent; by November 1996, the promised interest return spiked to 50 percent. Sude was the first of the seventeen firms to fold in early 1997. This ended the boom of what came to be known as the pyramid firms of the early 1990s Albania.

During my conversations with kreditorë, I learned about how they waited in line for their returns outside Kadëna's modest communist apartment in December 1996. Newspapers at the time reported their anxiety and frustration (Babaramo 1996a, 7). Kadëna suspended repayments of deposits but promised to restart business in a few weeks. But Sude's counters did not reopen. By the end of that year, Kadëna announced that she did not have the cash to give back to her kreditorë. She turned herself in to the authorities—the only firm owner to do so—and was eventually convicted and given a reduced sentence of five years in prison for defrauding her investors. In mid-1997, Sude's operations were taken over by the Supervisory Group for the Pyramid Firms (Grupi Mbikqyrës i Firmave Piramidale), which concluded the case on Sude's bankruptcy in December 2013.

Maksude Kadëna captured local and international news headlines in early 1997 as a "Gypsy fortune-teller" who "claimed to look into a crystal ball" (Andrews 1997). As the other firms followed in the footsteps of Sude's collapse, Kadëna became an icon of the fraudulent magic, or "occult practices" (Comaroff and Comaroff 1999), associated with *fajde* (moneylending), the practice of nonbank moneylending mediated by the firms. In 1997 the ethnicized and gendered depictions of Kadëna—propagated by locals and internationals alike (see Zogaj 1998, 139–45)—provided additional fodder for the claims that the firms in Albania were an instance of a "misreading of capitalism" in a country "new" to free-market institutions (*New York Times* 1997, 18). To mainstream economists and International Monetary Fund (IMF) policymakers, depictions of Kadëna as a Gypsy fortune-teller preempted harder questions about the benefits and short-comings of shock-therapy reforms implemented in Albania and across the post-socialist world during the early 1990s. These representations continue to circulate in current public discourse; they often serve as a metaphor for state-sanctioned fraud and derailment from sound economic policy.

Looking back at the archival record, and in discussions with kreditorë a decade after the firms' collapse, I encountered a much more nuanced vocabulary around the firms. For instance, although many reproduced the same gendered and ethnicized mockeries of Kadëna, reporters and kreditorë alike also used a familiar register of banking, investment, and credit, often describing their relation to the firms as that of investors or stockholders. To this day, many continue to call themselves kreditorë. In the course of conversations with former kreditorë, I began to notice how these distinctions in terminology also framed shifting understandings of legitimate/illegitimate forms of finance. For instance, when I asked one of the kreditorë to explain why he had trusted the pyramid firms, he corrected me: "[these firms] were not called pyramid firms [before 1997] but borrowing companies [*kompani huamarrëse*] because it is well known that with a pyramid firm you come out without a profit."[2] This distinction between solvent companies and speculative pyramid firms points to a shift in registers of legitimate and illegitimate finance from before to after the collapse of the firms.

Since their collapse in early 1997, these entities have become commonly known as *piramida* (pyramids) or firma piramidale; prior to 1997, however, they were widely referred to as fajde. Other common terms were *kompani* (companies), and *fondacione* (foundations).³ In this chapter, I flesh out the practices and moralities associated with these multiple terms as a way to explore the discourses of legitimacy that framed the rise and fall of the firms in Albania. More broadly, I am interested in understanding how speculative forms of finance become possible and legitimate through historically specific discourses of finance and how they draw on local financial practices and moralities.

I approach the discourse and language of finance and speculation not as a mere aftereffect of regulatory regimes and practices but as performative of such regimes (de Goede 2005; Hirschman 1977; Holmes 2013; Poovey 2008). In his account of the rise of capitalism in seventeenth- and eighteenth-century Europe, Albert Hirschman (1977) notes a shift from a language of "passions" to that of "interests," which led to a shift in attitudes toward the economic profession and served to legitimize and professionalize economics as such. Later works by Marieke de Goede (2005) and Mary Poovey (2008) analyze representations of finance in eighteenth- and nineteenth-century Europe and North America. In different ways, both works underscore the widespread use of gendered discourses to draw a line between legitimate/illegitimate forms of finance. For instance, de Goede writes that the feminine metaphors of *fortuna* (fortune) and hysteria were often used as a means of delegitimizing certain financial activities (such as credit or gambling) whereas masculine discourses of interest, rationality, and accounting served to legitimize others (such as market speculation). With few exceptions, these contributions focus on Anglo-American, European, and global centers of finance, and on official and professional spaces of finance. Similar registers of legitimacy/illegitimacy proliferated alongside the rise and fall of the firms in Albania, a country situated at the margins of global financial flows. This marginal location is important because it makes possible different histories and ontologies of finance.

I approach the discourses around the firms in Albania as "the very means through which the financial sphere was defined, shaped, and legitimized" (de Goede 2005, 59). I also examine the broader social and political implications of the shifting representations of the firms from their boom through their bust. Looking at the cultural connotations of these shifting representations, I underscore specific notions of legitimacy/illegitimacy, morality/immorality, and rationality/irrationality of finance that encompassed but also extended beyond the firms. Rather than dismissing the firms as fictive entities using cons and money magic, I propose that specific financial and economic institutions, sociotechnical arrangements, and discourses helped legitimize these firms as capitalist enterprises and their leaders as trailblazing entrepreneurs. More specifically, I examine the use of gendered and ethnicized representations of the firms and of their owners as a way to legitimize or delegitimize them. Further, I note the continuities and discontinuities of economic practices and moralities of late communist and early postsocialist local financial repertoires that were appropriated by the firms. I show how these discourses of finance and local financial repertoires interacted with one another contributing to the popularity and longevity of the firms; I also show how, in the aftermath of the firms' collapse, these discourses and repertoires of finance served to delegitimize the firms as isolated bubbles while absolving national and international bodies from any responsibility for their earlier proliferation and legitimacy.

The Ambivalent Moralities of Fajde

The term "fajde" stands out as a ubiquitous reference for the firms in the newspapers published between 1992 and 1996. The term appears alongside an emerging postsocialist economic vocabulary, which includes primarily English and Latin cognates, such as *democracia* (democracy), *tranzicioni* (transition), and *ekonomia e tregut* (the market economy). Unlike these terms, as Laçi reminds us in the epigraph, the term "fajde" reemerged from an old, forgotten vocabulary. Fajde derives from the Turkish *faide* and Arabic *fayde* (use) (Çabej 1996, 129); it refers to nonbank moneylending and was used widely during the late Ottoman rule and the short-lived monarchy of Ahmet Zogu. Although not unlawful, moneylending, especially when practiced by loan sharks, carried a negative connotation in Islamic ethics (as it had in Christian ethics as well).[4] During the communist regime, private, nonbank forms of moneylending became illegal. The terminology around moneylending and moneylender/s (*fajdexhi/nj*), took on additional negative connotations that emerged from a communist ethic of finance. Following Marxist and Leninist philosophies, interest-bearing moneylending practices (whether bank or nonbank) were categorized as predatory forms of capital accumulation.

Anthropologists of communist states have discussed the negative ethical symbolism in popular discourses around money, commerce, and moneylending in other parts of the Eastern Bloc. In communist Romania, writes Katherine Verdery, "money from 'commerce' and from 'speculation' was polluting, unacceptable, tainted with capitalist traces" (1996, 182). Caroline Humphrey describes similar attitudes toward money among Soviet citizens: "The habit of seeing all 'economic' activity as also intrinsically laden with political-ideological value is particularly marked and conscious among former Soviet people. . . . One aspect of this was the glorification of production/labor and the condemnation of commonplace trading for profit, called 'speculation' in Soviet parlance" (2002, 44). Indeed, petty trade was often frowned upon and, in a number of cases, was performed by and associated with specific ethnic minorities (Humphrey 1999; Pine 2002; Watts

2002) or women (Heyat 2002). Official and unofficial attitudes toward trading for profit or moneylending were likewise considered "speculative" among the Albanian public and among economists. For instance, in a comprehensive historical overview of the economic transformations in early communist Albania, the authors often referred to private trading as "speculation" (Fishta and Ziu 2004, 248–49).

This economic ethic had serious political implications in communist Albania. In the early years of the post–World War II communist transformations, moneylenders were categorized as "enemies of the people" (*armiq të popullit*), along with landowners, religious leaders, and political dissidents. This was a grave accusation that often led to imprisonment, persecution, limited rights to education and work opportunities. A passage from the autobiography of the notorious authoritarian leader Enver Hoxha (1981) captures how this ethic and these categories were framed in official discourse. Writing toward the end of his life, Hoxha recounts a highly curated version of the history of the formation of the Communist Party (later known as Partia a Punës së Shqipërisë [PPSH], or the Labor Party of Albania) during World War II. During the war, Hoxha was commander-in-chief of the communist resistance against the Italian and then the German occupation. Written retrospectively, the anecdotal accounts of the interactions with the "common people" (*njerëzit e thjeshtë*) during World War II serve to justify the class war (*lufta e klasave*) unleashed in the 1970s as part of the Albanian Cultural Revolution (*revolucioni kulturor*) (Blumi 1997). The following passage recounts a conversation between Hoxha and an imam (*hoxhë*) during World War II:

> ENVER HOXHA: Do you have evil [*të ligë*] people around here?
>
> THE IMAM: Yes, we have plenty. We have Bektash Cakranin and Rrapo Lelo. What about in your city, Gjirokastra, do you have these types of scoundrels?
>
> ENVER HOXHA: These types of scoundrels are everywhere [*hoxhë*]. Even in Gjirokastra we have plenty. We have gotten rid of the landowner [*bejlerë*] in Gjirokastra but we still have law enforcers [*agallarë*], moneylenders [*fajdexhinj*], and others like this. [He named a moneylender from Gjirokastra.]
>
> THE IMAM: Do you know him?
>
> ENVER HOXHA: I know him, of course. But how do you know him?
>
> THE IMAM: I know very well that fajdexhi. Because he has reached his nails all the way to our area as well. He and others like him have stripped our skin with fajde. (Hoxha 1981)

The narrative is unusual because it portrays a religious authority in a sympathetic light, which contradicted the antireligious policies and purges of Hoxha's regime.

Hoxha justifies this unlikely alliance by claiming that the imam did not seem too religious. The sympathetic representation of the hoxhë also points to a convergence between the Islamic and communist economic ethics, both of which pitched interest-bearing moneylending as an immoral practice. In his response to the imam, Hoxha lists moneylenders among the numerous enemies of the party, one notch down from the landowners. Both interlocutors shared a view of fajdexhi as predators, "reaching their nails" everywhere in the country and "stripping the skin" of the poor. The vignette advocates an anticapitalist ethic by appealing to popular religious sensibilities, reminding readers that, at least on some issues, such as the economy, the communist ethic was aligned with the (now banned) religious ethic.

This passage captures a particular economic ethic advocated by PPSH, which by the late 1970s maintained one of the most extensive bans on private property and eliminated interest-bearing loans and other financial instruments.[5] The negative ethical connotations of fajde and fajdexhi under the communist regime contrast with the enthusiasm with which the terms were treated in official and unofficial discourse in the early 1990s. This shift in the connotations of fajde constitutes a key site for tracing broader changes in attitudes and moralities around money and finance in postsocialist Albania.

Postsocialist Money and Finance

Because it condensed and translated so many connotations and ethical nuances, fajde embodies the broader ambiguities and contradictions of the financial institutions and practices that proliferated in postsocialist Albania. Also, because of its associations with the once-banned interest-bearing moneylending, in the early 1990s fajde became an icon of the emerging free-market institutions and of capitalism in its purest form. It is important to contextualize fajde within the broader push for shock-therapy reforms prescribed by the IMF and the World Bank and embraced with great enthusiasm by political leaders and Albanian citizens alike. Registered as companies with diverse portfolios and investments and engaging with finance capital, the firms that engaged in fajde performed, to a certain extent, some of the economic institutions and practices of shock-therapy reforms. I turn to these broader economic transformations in postsocialist Albania as a way to situate the firms as a part of—rather than an externality to—economic institutions at the time.

The shock-therapy reforms embraced in 1993 by Albania's first democratic government were a set of policies informed by the Washington Consensus and recommended to all countries of the former Eastern Bloc undergoing a transition to free markets. Some of the key economic reforms included "liberalization of price controls and of trade, tight fiscal and monetary policies and . . . a floating exchange rate" (Bezemer 2001, 3). Throughout the twenty-five years of the "transition" in Albania, governments from both major political parties equally implemented these policies. Postsocialist governments have consistently engaged in an ongoing process of privatization of former state property, liberalization of markets, and shrinking of the public sector. Shock-therapy reforms targeted primarily macroeconomic indicators and paid little attention to microeconomic regulations and practices. Framed after a utopian ideal of minimal government intervention, these policies echoed a global turn to neoliberal economic policies since the 1970s (Harvey 2005; Mirowski 2013). Rather than weakening the state, such policies have led to a transformation of the role of the state, from that of redistributive or allocative power (Verdery 1991) to that of a privatized form of governance (Hibou 2004). This transformation is not unique to Albania and the postsocialist world; it resonates with other sites of neoliberal transformation—from "advanced" liberal democracies (Barry and Osborne 1996) to postcolonial contexts (Bayart 2009; Elyachar 2005; Hibou 2004; Roitman 2004). Such transformations mobilized local histories and political structures in various (often unexpected) ways. Writing about the neoliberal transformation in Eastern Europe, Johanna Bockman (2011) argues that the implementation of liberalization and deregulation policies in postsocialist societies reinscribed highly hierarchical political relations, replicating—rather than undermining—the authoritarian forms of governance associated with communist regimes.

According to Verdery (1996), the transition of command economies to free-market economies has to be further specified as a transition into capitalist systems characterized by "flexible accumulation" (Harvey 1991) and the growing dominance of finance capital. International advisers, local economists, and political actors in various parts of Eastern Europe advocated this particular form of economic transformation, which Bockman reframes as a "dis-embedding and immediate re-embedding of markets in authoritarian neoliberalism" (2011, 2). In Albania, the country that staunchly held on to a Stalinist economic model under Enver Hoxha's rule, such dis-embedding and re-embedding of the market was one of the closest to the ideal type of shock-therapy transition advocated by international policymakers.[6] Berisha's increasingly authoritarian regime of the 1990s built on his embrace of neoliberal market ideology and the absolute support for shrinking the state and investing in private entrepreneurship. But, unlike in other former socialist contexts, it was not finance capital (foreign investment or expansion of bank credit) that played a major role in this process of dis-embedding the market in Albania. Rather, it was local firms, including pyramid firms, that took on this role by seeking to mobilize cash flows that circulated outside formal banking institutions.

Neo-Keynesian economist Dirk Bezemer (2001) provides a compelling analysis of how the financial infrastructure of the early 1990s enabled the emergence of fajde. Bezemer draws on the work of economist Hyman Minsky (1986, 1992) to argue that the firms were an instance of financial fragility inherent to capitalist markets rather than an externality or a bubble set aside from "normal" market logic. Writing in the context of Euro-American markets of the 1960s, Minsky argued that periods of credit expansion pushed different market actors toward more speculative, high-risk, and insolvent investments.[7] Bezemer noted a similar credit expansion underway in Albania. However, this credit expansion was not driven strictly by an expansion of bank credit (or financialization) but rather from the flow of bank and nonbank, official and unofficial financial wealth, including foreign capital (in the form of foreign aid and salaries for employees of international organizations), illicit forms of trade (in diesel, humans, drugs), and nonbank financial flows (such as immigrant remittances).

Berisha's infamous statement—that the firms were part of the informal sector—provides invaluable insight into the peculiar status of the firms at this time. The statement, repeated verbatim by every kreditor I talked to, reveals the continuities and discontinuities of late communist and early postsocialist moral discourses around unofficial (or informal) economic activities. The notion that fajde were an informal financial activity circulated among government offices prior to the IMF visit. A declassified correspondence between the Ministry of Finance, the Ministry of Interior Affairs, the Secret Services, and the Office of State Audit suggests that some form of inquiry and investigation into these firms had taken place in 1995–96. In memos sent to these offices, the Ministry of Finance defines the activity of "money by fajde" as an "informal financial market" (Ministry of Finance 1996, Nr. 872) and urges the other institutions to take steps toward formalizing these activities. Making reference to global financial regimes and to IMF and World Bank policies, these memos describe the firms as part formal and part informal. Here, formality or informality is determined based on a range of factors, including taxes paid on the profits from the activity, possession of a banking license, interest rates compared to those of the Bank of Albania, and allegations of criminal activity. Overall, in these correspondences, "informal" carries a negative connotation.

When describing the firms as "informal businesses," Berisha borrows this terminology but uses the term informal as a compliment to the firms. To understand this positive connotation of "informal," one needs to revisit late-communist discourses around finance. In the late communist context, informal/black market stood for an unregulated and often speculative form of free-market activity.

Because the black market during the late-communist regime was both illegal and utterly vilified as a representation of capitalist finance, activities associated with the black market (including moneylending) gained a positive connotation during the early postsocialist period. It is with this context in mind that, in Berisha's statement, "informal" is synonymous with "capitalist." The mistranslations of informal/capitalist/speculative were thus grounded in a particular economic history and informed by a historically specific moral discourse characterized by an important reversal: what was considered illegitimate and immoral by communist authorities was now automatically legitimate and ethical.

Such mistranslations were not symptoms of the fictions or misunderstandings of capitalism; rather, they were "productive" (Roitman 2004, 2005) of specific economic regimes, entrepreneurial subjectivities, and modes of wealth making. Representations of fajde/pyramid firms—in legal documents, in the media, and in political discourse—are a good place for analyzing how these economic regimes and entrepreneurial subjectivities emerged from a specific "framing" (Callon 1998) of the market through emerging legal institutions.

The Legal Framing of Fajde

In both the print media archives and in oral narratives from former kreditorë, fajde refers interchangeably to the *practice* of nonbank moneylending and to the *entities* that offered this financial service en masse, the pyramid firms. As with other market practices, fajde operated through specific market devices (Muniesa, Millo, and Callon 2007) and socio-technical arrangements that emerged in the broader context of a postsocialist economic regime. To understand the legitimacy of fajde at this time, one needs to take a closer look at the legal framings and discourses that shaped this practice and these entities. Indeed, the archival material and the oral narratives from kreditorë suggest that various legal technologies and discourses legitimated fajde.

Fajde served as an umbrella term for all entities taking deposits and promising interest on returns. As I mentioned above, other terms were used in official and vernacular discourse to distinguish between two categories of firms: *kompani* and *fondacione*. Kompani referred to fajde that were legally registered as limited liability companies (*shoqëri me përgjegjësi të kufizuara*). Some of the most well-known kompani were Vefa, Kamberi, Silva, and Gjallica. Kompani were some of the first entities to take deposits from people in the form of fajde and offered comparatively modest interest returns (4–5 percent until 1996 and 6–8 percent thereafter). They claimed to take "credit" (*hua*) from individuals following the provisions of the Albanian Civil Code (Kodi Civil 1994, Articles 1050 and 1051;

see also Elbirt 1997), which sanctioned the taking of interest-bearing loans from individuals, provided that the contract was signed in the presence of a notary public. The representatives of three kompani (Vefa, Giallica, and Kamberi) referenced these articles of the civil code when asked by the Ministry of Finance about the nature of their activity with fajde.[8] Moreover, as confirmed by the auditing process, kompani had investments in a variety of economic sectors (trade, tourism, the service industry, mining, and manufacturing).

Fondacione did not have any investments in other economic activities but alluded to having access to other sources of wealth (such as an inheritance from relatives abroad or ties to the government). The most notorious of these were Sude, Xhaferri, and Populli. Except for Sude, which started operating in 1993, fondacione were established in early 1996. Initially, they offered 8–10 percent interest returns, but by the end of the year their interests shot up to 30 percent (Populli). Economist Chris Jarvis (1999) describes the kompani as "hybrid pyramid schemes" and fondacione as "pure pyramid schemes." This distinction between these two sets of fajde was further reinforced during their audit after their collapse. The provisional government that took power in 1997 hired two global consulting firms to audit each set of fajde separately: Deloitte & Touche LLP for the kompani and PricewaterhouseCoopers for the fondacione.

Despite crucial differences in their legal status and in the nature of their business activities, kompani and fondacione were very much intertwined. For one thing, they all engaged in fajde—that is, accepting deposits from kreditorë in the form of a loan. In addition, many of the kreditorë invested simultaneously in both types of firms, often arbitraging their deposits and interests between fondacione's high-interest rates and kompani's more secure investments. Further, the firms lent money and adjusted their interest rates to one another. Despite important differences in their legal statuses and economic activities, both kompani and fondacione were legitimated by specific legal technologies and discourses of finance.

One such technology of legitimation was the credit contract (kontrata kredie), issued primarily by the kompani. Kreditorë repeatedly mentioned credit contracts to underscore the legality of the firms and to justify their own decisions to invest in them. To this day, the contracts are recognized by public authorities and used as a means of claiming compensation. Kreditorë continue to hold on to these contracts as evidence. Some still hope to retrieve their lost deposits from state authorities.

Credit contracts acted as a market device (Muniesa, Millo, and Callor 2007), framing the specific market of loans/deposits of fajde. Durim, a former kreditor and sekser (broker) to one of the major kompani, Gjallica, shared his credit contract, dated August 17, 1996 (figure 1.1). Per the contract, Durim had "loaned"

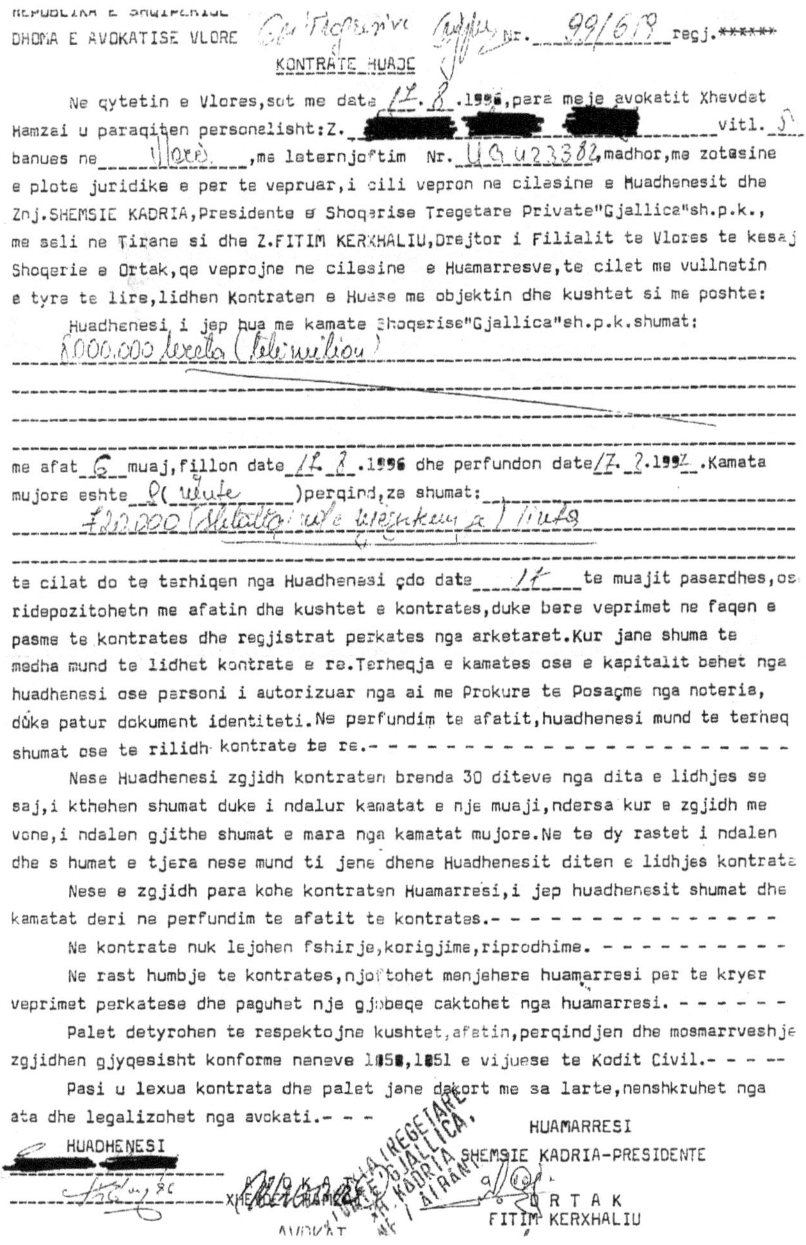

REPUBLIKA E SHQIPERISE
DHOMA E AVOKATISE VLORE [handwritten] Nr._____99/6/9_____regj.******
                                KONTRATE HUAJE

    Ne qytetin e Vlores,sot me date /7. 8 .1996,para meje avokatit Xhevdet
Hamzai u paraqiten personalisht:Z._____vitl. [ ]
banues ne___[Vore]___,me leternjoftim Nr._UG u23382,madhor,me zotesine
e plote juridike e per te vepruar,i cili vepron ne cilesine e Huadhenesit dhe
Znj.SHEMSIE KADRIA,Presidente e Shoqerise Tregetare Private"Gjallica"sh.p.k.,
me seli ne Tirane si dhe Z.FITIM KERXHALIU,Drejtor i Filialit te Vlores te kesaj
Shoqerie e Ortak,qe veprojne ne cilesine e Huamarresve,te cilet me vullnetin
e tyre te lire,lidhen Kontraten e Huase me objektin dhe kushtet si me poshte:
    Huadhenesi i jep hua me kamate Shoqerise"Gjallica"sh.p.k.shumat:
_1.000.000 lekela (kate milion)_____
_____
_____

me afat 6 muaj,fillon date /7. 8 .1996 dhe perfundon date/7. 2.1997 .Kamata
mujore eshte 8(tete)perqind,ze shumat:_____
_720.000 (shtateqind e njezetemije a) liata_____

te cilat do te terhiqen nga Huadhenesi cdo date____/7____te muajit pasardhes,os
rideposzitohetn me afatin dhe kushtet e kontrates,duke bere veprimet ne faqen e
pasme te kontrates dhe regjistrat perkates nga arketaret.Kur jane shuma te
medha mund te lidhet kontrate e re.Terheqja e kamates ose e kapitalit behet nga
huadhenesi ose personi i autorizuar nga ai me Prokure te Posaqme nga noteria,
duke patur dokument identiteti.Ne perfundim te afatit,huadhenesi mund te terheq
shumat ose te rilidh kontrate te re.- -
    Nese Huadhenesi zgjidh kontraten brenda 30 diteve nga dita e lidhjes se
saj,i kthehen shumat duke i ndalur kamatat e nje muaji,ndersa kur e zgjidh me
vone,i ndalen gjithe shumat e mara nga kamatat mujore.Ne te dy rastet i ndalen
dhe s humat e tjera nese mund ti jene dhene Huadhenesit diten e lidhjes kontrate
    Nese e zgjidh para kohe kontraten Huamarresi,i jep huadhenesit shumat dhe
kamatat deri ne perfundim te afatit te kontrates.- - - - - - - - - - - - - - -
    Ne kontrate nuk lejohen fshirje,korigjime,riprodhime. - - - - - - - - - -
    Ne rast humbje te kontrates,njoftohet menjehere huamarresi per te kryer
veprimet perkatese dhe paguhet nje gjobeqe caktohet nga huamarresi. - - - - - -
    Palet detyrohen te respektojne kushtet,afatin,perqindjen dhe mosmarrveshje
zgjidhen gjyqesisht konforme neneve 1050,1051 e vijuese te Kodit Civil.- - - --
    Pasi u lexua kontrata dhe palet jane dakort me sa larte,nenshkruhet nga
ata dhe legalizohet nga avokati.- - -   HUAMARRESI
    HUADHENESI   SHEMSIE KADRIA-PRESIDENTE
_____   _____
_____XHE[ ]   ORTAK
                                                  FITIM KERXHALIU

FIGURE 1.1. A credit contract (*kontratë huaja*) of a pyramid firm.

(Photograph by author.)

eight million Italian liras (roughly US$5,500) for a period of six months at an interest rate of nine percent. In other words, as stated in the contract, by the end of six months, Durim would receive a total interest return of 720,000 liras (US$491), which he could either collect or reinvest in the firms. The contract was signed by Durim and a notary public.[9]

The contract references Articles 1050 and 1051 of the civil code, which regulates the terms of moneylending from nonbank entities of individuals. In the aftermath of the collapse of the firms, there were different opinions on whether this application of Article 1051 was an accurate interpretation of the law. For instance, an economist at the Supervisory Group claimed that although the kompani were legally allowed to take up loans, the amount of interest offered within the short periods of time and the scale of "borrowing" from kreditorë were misapplication of that law. Yet the law allowed for such ambiguities. Article 1051 specifically states: "Unless otherwise agreed on by the two parties, the debtor must pay the creditor the interest [kamatat]. The interest must be paid annually unless otherwise agreed on by the parties of the contract." In other words, not only did the article legitimize nonbank moneylending; it also left unregulated the rates and terms of payments of the interest returns.

In addition to citing the provisions in the civil code, kreditorë recalled how the act of signing such contracts in the presence of a certified notary public added further legitimacy to fajde. Blerim, another former kreditor of Gjallica and Kamberi, justified his multiple deposits as follows: "Given that [pyramid schemes] were registered at the court, that they counted as a juridical person, you could not consider them as illegal [të paligjshme]. Given that you signed a contract in the presence of a notary public, you could not consider them as illegal."[10] For Blerim and many others, the legitimacy of fajde was twofold: first, kompani were private entities, legally registered as juridical persons; and second, the specific transaction of fajde was legitimate because it was performed in the presence of a licensed notary public. The credit contract thus constituted a market device insofar as it formatted a particular market in loans—the "informal credit market" as Jarvis (1999) defined it in his report on the aftermath of the firms' collapse. Further, the act of notarization made visible the socio-technical arrangements that made possible and legal both fajde and the firms. These arrangements involved a legal infrastructure and tools (the civil code and credit contracts), legal intermediaries (notaries public), and new kinds of financial entities that took loans from a broad public. Even though this socio-technical arrangement made fajde possible, it was permeated by shifting and ambivalent assessments of the legality and legitimacy of speculative finance.

"Albanian Money Is Honest"

Other crucial sources of legitimacy for the firms were political and state actors. Kreditorë repeatedly blamed the state and specific politicians who, they claimed, provided explicit or implicit (often false) guarantees for their deposits at the firms. Blerim, for instance, blamed government officials for feeding into his own assessment of the legitimacy of the firms and his decision to continue to invest in the firms:

> SMOKI: So, did you consider them as orderly [të rregullta] companies?
> BLERIM: Naturally. When you saw Alimuçaj [Vefa's President] besides Sali [Berisha], what else would you be thinking?
> SMOKI: I mean, even afterward [after November 1996], because then they were considered as illegal.
> BLERIM: Yes, later on the government came forth because it was no longer in their interest, the IMF came forth, everyone came forth saying that these were not orderly [të rregullta], that they were not legal [ligjore]. But still they let them go on. You cannot let such an activity go on for so many years.[11]

With regard to the moneylending that took place through the firms being legal, Blerim and other kreditorë blame key political authorities for the firms' legitimacy and, consequently, for their relative longevity. By "letting them go on" Blerim referred specifically to Berisha's infamous statement in support of fajde in November 1996. Berisha's full statement is worth revisiting since it encapsulates the official acts of legitimation of the firms as capitalist enterprises: "Unlike in other countries [in Albania] the fajde phenomenon [fenomeni fajde] is entirely a private one and, except for the chance speculations, we can say that the money of Albanians is the most honest [i ndershëm] money that can exist. . . . The big firms of the informal sector have serious investments in important and profitable sectors of the [national] economy, from commerce, food processing and production, tourism, mining etc." (cited in Hazizaj 1996b, 7).

In his typical populist style, Berisha addressed the masses of kreditorë anxious about the future of their deposits. The statement provides insight into the political discourse that helped legitimize the firms. By describing them as firms with "investments in profitable sectors of the economy," Berisha confirmed the view that they were serious and legitimate businesses engaging in legitimate financial activities. He sought to dispel widespread rumors of money laundering by saying that the money flowing through the firms was "honest" (të ndershme) and "clean" (të pastra). He affirmed the legitimacy of fajde by appealing to nationalist sentiments, on the one hand, and to the moral value of capitalist entrepreneurship, on the other hand.[12] If under state socialism fajde took on a negative moral connotation, under democracy the term was imbued with a positive morality. This moralization of the economy was continuous with the explicit ideological framing of the economy and of economic practice under the PPSH regime. Such moral framing and legitimacy of economic practices are not limited to communist contexts. Across the board, discursive acts of legitimation, often drawing on specific cultural norms and ethics, "actively create the conditions within which entrepreneurial and competitive conduct is possible" (Barry and Osborne 1996, 10). Berisha's statement had a performative effect through kreditorë's actions. Indeed, many kreditorë went on to invest more cash in the firms after Berisha's televised public statement, some even selling their recently privatized apartments for cash for the firms (see chapter 4). But legal and moral legitimations of the firms extended well beyond the official discourse; they permeated a wide range of media outlets and broader public culture.

The Bosses of Fajde

The local press is an important site for exploring how fajde and the firms gained legitimacy. Former kreditorë had directed me to the archives of two newspapers— *Dita Informacion* (Daily information [*DI*]) and *Koha Jonë* (Our time [*KJ*])—as a reliable record of the events unfolding during 1996–97. I relied heavily on the archives of these two newspapers to patch together a picture of the public discourse around the firms at the time. *DI* and *KJ* had been among the few voices to challenge the Berisha regime at the time when the firms began to fold. *DI* was run by the Nazarko brothers, both renowned journalists. The newspaper positioned itself on the left and was often critical of the Socialist Party for its compromises with the Democratic Party. *DI* was the only newspaper that refused to publish ads from the pyramid schemes, even when they were at the height of their popularity.[13]

KJ was known for its bold opposition to the Berisha government and for its nonpartisanship.[14] Many of the writers who were at *KJ* at the time are now prominent journalists and public intellectuals leaning on opposing sides of the political spectrum. Led by independent journalists who were fearless in their dissent, the newspaper was widely read as an independent voice of the opposition to Berisha's increasing authoritarianism. *KJ* became a beacon of independent and investigative reporting, especially during the tense months from January to May 1997, when protests involving thousands of kreditorë erupted throughout the country, leading to anarchy and nearly to civil war. At the height of the government's crackdown on protests in the south, *KJ*'s headquarters in Tirana was burned to the ground by Berisha supporters (CPJ 1998), and many of its reporters were threatened, beaten, abducted, and even tortured by the secret police.

It is because of these acts of courage and defiance in the face of state authoritarianism and intimidation that the kreditorë directed me to the pages of *KJ*. Yet, revisiting the archives of *KJ*, I also encountered a curious paradox. Unlike *DI*, which was critical of the firms from the outset, *KJ* held an ambiguous position toward them before their collapse. For one thing, *KJ*, like other newspapers of both sides of the political spectrum, ran ads of the firms through 1996 (figures 1.2a and 1.2b).

It also routinely published the interest rates promised by the firms on the same page as the currency exchange rates. These visual representations normalized the firms and presented them as joint-stock companies rather than speculative pyramid schemes. Finally, *KJ* covered the activities of individual firms in a normalizing and legitimizing register. A close reading of two articles published in *KJ* in 1996 (Godole 1996a; Sejdarasi 1996) provides a window into these legitimizing discourses. These articles capture the particular "historicity" (Koselleck 2004) of the term "fajde," reflecting the positive connotations associated with it up until 1997. Fajde here represents competitive capitalism rather than predatory lending. The new owners of fajde are portrayed as powerful "bosses" and leaders of

FIGURE 1.2A.   Vefa ad appearing in 1996 in Albanian newspapers. Courtesy of the Albanian National Library.

(Photograph by author.)

FIGURE 1.2B. Kamberi ad appearing in 1996 in Albanian newspapers.
Courtesy of the Albanian National Library.

(Photograph by author.)

postsocialist finance—a departure from the image of the bloodthirsty, exploitative moneylender in Hoxha's depiction.

In the first article, the economic journalist Bardhi Sejdarasi (1996) approaches *fajde* as serious businesses engaged in typical capitalist financial activities: "Colossal investments [*investime*] are 'financed' [*financohen*] by the funds of creditors [*huadhënësve*], but also yielding visible gains [*fitime*] that increase the citizens' interest in entering more loaning contracts [*kontrata huadhënie*] with lucrative compensations [*shpërblime të majme*]" (11). The vocabulary unmistakably points to a global register of banking and finance, combining English cognates of financial terms (*investime, financohen, kontrata*) with the Albanian terms for economic concepts of profit and credit (*fitime, huadhënës, huamarrje, shpërblime të majme*). Sejdarasi describes *kompani* as investment banks, investing the deposits of *kreditorë* in profitable areas of the economy: tourism, transportation, retail, and construction.

This is how some of the *kreditorë* described the firms as well. One *kreditor*, for instance, recalled his impressions of the firms prior to their collapse:

> SMOKI: Did you have any doubts about the firms before they collapsed?
> BLERIM: To tell you the truth, I did have some doubts. But it's like this.
> Even as Gjallica had started to collapse, I had money at Kamberi and there was a moment when I could have withdrawn my deposits because I needed to spend some money to open up my own office. So although this happened to Gjallica, I thought Kamberi was safe because it had so many investments. And the truth was that it had a lot of investments in the form of productive activities and I thought that it was generating funds.

Sмокі: So that's why you trusted this firm?

Blerim: Precisely because of this, because they had investments in the productive sectors of the economy, in tourism, agriculture, etc.[15]

These representations of kompani as investment banks were invoked repeatedly by the kreditorë. Most, like Blerim, recalled the firms' assets and investments as a way of justifying their decision to invest in the firms. A few others expressed even stronger support for the solvency of the firms at the time, insisting that, were they allowed to continue to operate without regulatory restrictions on their deposits and withdrawals from the official banks, they would have eventually been able to pay back their investors.

Media representations of the firms' owners further reinforced their legitimacy as cutting-edge capitalist enterprises. The article by Jonila Godole (1996a) captures these images. Written around the time of the IMF experts' visit, the article reads like a series of portraits of the owners of some of the leading firms, narrating the personal histories of their paths to financial success and describing their lavish lifestyles. What emerges from these profiles is an ambivalent image of these entrepreneurs. The bosses of fajde have aggressive and competitive masculinity in the marketplace and take every opportunity to display their newly acquired wealth through luxury cars, villas, and yachts. The tone of the article oscillates between admiration and cynicism toward this new business ethic and entrepreneurial type.

This ambivalent attitude is visible from the outset. The title of the article ("The bosses of fajde") is a pun on the novel title *Bosët e Dollarit* (*The bosses of the dollar*), the Albanian translation of *The Moneychangers* (1975) by U.S. author Arthur Hailey. *The Moneychangers* is reminiscent of Michael Lewis's bestsellers *Liar's Poker* ([1989] 2010) and *The Big Short: Inside the Doomsday Machine* (2010) on contemporary corruption and greed on Wall Street. Translated into Albanian in the late 1980s, Hailey's novel bypassed the rigid state censorship policies because it represented capitalism and the West through narratives of decadence, corruption, and exploitation. Yet, contrary to this intended morality, the novel became a symbol of what was on the other side of the Iron Curtain—readers were lured by the abundance and conspicuous consumption that permeated the lives of these investment bankers. The allusion to *Bosët e Dollarit* in Godole's article in 1996 reflects and further performs the ambivalent ethical assessments of fajde as legitimate capitalist entrepreneurs. Godole's descriptions of the "bosses" of fajde represent, to borrow a phrasing from James Siegel (1998), an entrepreneurial type that emerged in the early 1990s. This entrepreneurial type draws from various cultural repertoires of economic practice past and present and continues to persist in the business world in Albania to this day.

Postsocialist Entrepreneurs

In their public presentation, the firms embraced the nationalistic and moralizing capitalist ethic promoted by political figures. A full-page ad by Vefa on the firm's five-year anniversary exemplifies the kitsch business ethic advocated by the firms (figure 1.3). The ad lists Vefa's diverse investments in the economy: in transportation, construction and tourism, agriculture, culture, and marketing. Further, it lists Vefa's values as follows:

- The incarnation of humane capitalism
- Valuing national priorities
- Affirmation of stability and broad perspective
- Direct investment in the rapid circulation of money
- Dynamism and intuition
- Contemporary tendency in the field of the application of technology
- The accurate planning of pragmatic economics

The ad offers the image of a capitalist enterprise, competitive and charitable ("humane capitalism"). Vefa's activities were brought in line with the national project

FIGURE 1.3.   A five-year anniversary Vefa ad running in several Albanian newspapers in 1996. Courtesy of the Albanian National Library.

(Photograph by author.)

of free-market reform by way of references to "direct investments" in the national economy and contribution toward the development of capital markets ("the rapid circulation of money"—a reference to fajde). Further, the ad articulates a business ethic that combines a competitive spirit and entrepreneurial instinct ("dynamism and intuition") with rational calculation and planning ("accurate planning and pragmatic economics"). Finally, it points out connections with global business trends by emphasizing the company's "contemporary tendency" and the incorporation of "contemporary technology." Overall, the ad captures a historically specific register of entrepreneurship. It represents a capitalist ethic that combines aspects of Weberian discipline and calculation (Weber [1920] 2004), an instinctual financial acumen not unlike that of Wall Street traders and speculators (cf. Appadurai 2011; Ho 2009; Zaloom 2006), and a patrimonial communist economic ethos (Verdery 1996). This entrepreneurial ethic extended beyond the firms, encompassing postsocialist entrepreneurship at large.

In public representations of fajde, this postsocialist entrepreneurial ethic was articulated through a gendered discourse of virile masculinity, at the same time calculating, rational, and instinctual. Sejdarasi's article exemplifies the gendered dimension of this discourse. In the title, Sejdarasi paints foreign hard currencies as "the inevitable prey," "dominated" by the Albanian fajde. He continues with this metaphor of physical attack and overtaking of foreign currencies as follows:

> Vlora is attacking [sulmon] foreign hard currencies [valutat]. Day after day, the city of the south, renown for the large number of immigrants working abroad, for the excellent organization of clandestine emigration towards neighboring Italy, for the founding and developing of firms [firma] and companies [kompani] that represent the new image of the Albanian businesses and businessman, is now becoming "the capital of fajde." (1996, 11)

This triumphant image of Vlora as an emerging business hub again underscores the positive connotations of informality and the high regard for the firms as leading capitalist entrepreneurial ventures. This depiction of the city and its entrepreneurs is infused with images of aggressive masculinity as a source of entrepreneurial success. Sejdarasi describes the firms as competitive currency traders "attacking" and "dominating" the "inevitable prey" (preja e domosdoshme) of hard and soft currencies. Fajde and their owners are portrayed as powerful and virile entrepreneurs. These images of masculinity overlay representations of male honor, pride, and intrepidity that feature in cultural imaginaries of the Vlora. These cultural representations are invoked here to depict an image of Vlora as an emerging economic space, a trailblazer of Albanian capitalist entrepreneurship.

The metaphors of invasion, attack, and domination echo discourses of masculinity in global financial markets, past and present. As Marieke de Goede (2005) notes, finance as a profession has historically gained respectability when associated with more masculine traits. In the Euro-American cultural context, such discourse of masculinity has taken different forms; for instance, histories of finance in eighteenth-century England note the legitimation of speculation through metaphors of masculinity that entailed calculation, moderation, and accountability (2005, 34–36; see also Hirschman 1997). In more recent contexts, Caitlin Zaloom and Karen Ho underscore the ongoing performativity of masculinity among derivative traders (Zaloom 2005) and investment bankers (Ho 2009) in global centers of finance. On trading floors in Chicago, for instance, masculinity is expressed as an "economic instinct rooted in [a] conception of human nature rather than technical skill" (Zaloom 2005, 118).

The postsocialist entrepreneurial type, incarnated in the figure of the firms' owners, is portrayed through an image of masculinity that is similarly aggressive and instinctual. At the same time, representations of the firms and their owners infused these global entrepreneurial subjectivities with more historically grounded images of postsocialist entrepreneurship.[16] Thus, the fajde entrepreneur imparts some of the traits of what Verdery describes as *entrepratchiks* (1996, 33, 199–200). During communism, these low-level bureaucrats "spontaneously created their own profit-based companies from within the state economic bureaucracy" (33); in the early 1990s, many of them used their connections and inside knowledge of these enterprises to buy them as they were being privatized.

Indeed, many fajde owners had occupied such positions during the late communist regime. For instance, Vehbi Alimuçaj was a warehouse manager and Fitim Gërxhalliu, co-owner of Gjallica, was a former army captain. They had both procured a number of state properties privatized at low cost in the early 1990s (see chapter 2). In their capacities as managers or low-level administrators, entrepratchiks cultivated intricate social networks that operated through hierarchical relations of obligation and debt. Entrepratchiks provided access to resources to people without such access; in exchange, they accumulated credit to be collected in the future in the form of a return favor. These were patronage relationships infused with a specific kind of masculinity. Entrepratchiks acted as benevolent hegemons, breaking state rules to make favors using state resources and requiring loyalty and indebtedness in return.[17] A crucial aspect of this state-sanctioned form of masculinity in Albania was also a notion of "men of honor" that built on a longer cultural history.

Men of Honor and Fame

References to "men of honor" also emerged in accounts by (male) kreditorë. One of the few such accounts from persistent supporters of fajde owners came from Hektor, a former kreditor who also acted as a *menaxher* (manager, or recruiter) for Vefa. Hektor expressed respect and reverence for his former boss, Vehbi Alimuçaj. Among other things, he recalled a public event that involved Alimuçaj and the speaker of the parliament at the time, the former political prisoner Pjeter Arbnori. At first, I misunderstood how this event had played out. But Hektor was quick to correct me on the proper hierarchy of social status between Alimuçaj and Arbnori:

> HEKTOR: We celebrated Vefa's five-year anniversary at the Palace of Congresses, with the medal of Pjeter Arbnori, may he rest in peace . . .
> SMOKI: [misunderstanding the use of the pronouns] Pjeter Arbnori gave a medal of honor to Vehbi Alimuçaj?
> HEKTOR: No, no. [expressing some frustration] Vehbi is *honoris causa*, girl! He is a celebrity [*personalitet*]. It was Vehbi who gave the Medal of Honor to Arbnori. Why, who do you think [Vehbiu] is? [*cfarë e kujton Vehbiun ti?*][18]

Hektor's reverence for Vehbiu had persisted well beyond the collapse of Vefa and Alimuçaj's trial and imprisonment. Throughout our conversation, Hektor described Alimuçaj as a "big chief" (Sahlins 1963), exerting power through acts of indebting generosity and an implicit demand for loyalty by his subordinates. This depiction of Alimuçaj's status and power extended beyond the person and represented a particular entrepreneurial type that drew on specific notions of masculinity, as articulated in references to "man of honor."

Alimuçaj was praised for his hospitality, generosity, and honor, qualities that drew from a notion of masculinity that encompassed and exceeded the figure of the communist cadre/careerist. Hektor described Alimuçaj as "a man from Kurveleshi." He then proceeded to explain that this entailed being "a generous [*bujar*] man, with a big heart [*zemergjerë*]." Being a man from Kurveleshi carried a host of connotations. Kurveleshi refers to a geographic region in the south of Albania, one of the many highland areas subsumed under the broader umbrella of Labëria, a mountainous region, cutting across the administrative regions of Vlora, Tepelena, and Gjirokastra.

Being identified as a "man from Kurveleshi" implied being a man of honor (*njeri i besës*) and of the word (*fjala e dhënë*). As I was to realize in later conversations, Hektor (and other men I talked to in Vlora) assumed I read into the broader cultural connotations of "the man from Kurveleshi" given my own family ties to the region. As I often explained to my interlocutors during our introduction, my first name, Smoki, is an abbreviation of Smokthina, the birthplace of my grand-father. Smokthina is a cluster of villages located in the highlands of Labëria, just north of the Kurveleshi region. During these introductory conversations, I repeat-edly failed to convey my "halfie" identity (Abu-Lughod 1996; Gupta and Fergu-son 1997), my identification with Tirana as a cosmopolitan city, my Albanian American life story, and my general lack of knowledge of (and identification with) the Vlora highlands. On the contrary, at the first mention of my "origins," Smok-thina, it was quickly assumed that I shared in a particular cultural imaginary and set of values associated with the Labëria and Kurveleshi regions.[19] To my surprise, this form of "cultural intimacy" (Herzfeld 2005) cut across political lines, in and of itself highly polarized and polarizing in Albania, then and now. Though Hek-tor assumed we were on opposite sides of the political spectrum (my grandfather, Shevqet Musaraj, was a renowned writer of socialist realism, whereas Hektor had become a supporter of the Democratic Party since the 1990s), our presumed "cul-tural origins" became a common ground. In boasting about Alimuçaj as a "man from Kurveleshi," Hektor assumed I too would see the boss of the biggest fajde as a man of honor and courage, as a man of besa.

Besa means "oath, faith, trust, protection, truce, word of honor, or all of these together" (Tarifa 2008, 8). The concept refers to a social contract, a binding un-written oath, set on the given word of honor, the ultimate form of trust and ob-ligation. In Orientalist renderings, besa is the antithesis of disinterested market exchange.[20] Like other renderings of honor and shame throughout Mediterranean societies (Bourdieu 1966; Gilmore 1987; Peristiany 1965), in the anthropological literature on Albania, besa has been approached as a parallel (indigenous) nor-mative system that organized sociocultural institutions among a wide range of highland communities (Bardhoshi 2015; Durham 1910; Elsie 2011; Tarifa 2008). Besa was regulated by a common law known as *kanun* (law/norm).

Kanuns were more than a code of honor and shame. They regulated all sorts of social interactions, including property disputes (Bardhoshi 2012; Gjeçovi 1972; Tirta 2003). Kanuns were known to operate as parallel institutions under the Ot-toman rule and during various postindependence governments (1919–39). Soci-ologist Besnik Pula (2011) suggests that, despite being cast as a set of institutions that historically defied centralized power (be that of empire or nation-state), besa played a crucial role in the deployment of state power during the Ottoman rule as well as during the interwar period of nation-state formation. The first govern-ment of independent Albania (1919), writes Pula, actively used the institution of besa "to instrumentalize highland communal institutions in a way that gained the state direct influence over the population" (2011, 205). While the communist state engaged in an ongoing confrontation with besa institutions, with clan-based authority structures, and, especially, with kanun-prescribed property laws, a history of the actual use and incorporation of besa practices and relations within local and national administrative structures remains understudied.[21]

In the aftermath of World War II, given the broader nation-building project of state socialism, kanun was a target of the communist regime; to the communist state, it presented a rival system of a local authority and a source of legitimacy for a system of private property.[22] The various legal institutions of kanun were the target of much of the Albanian Cultural Revolution and the class wars (in particular, the kanun laws regarding property ownership presented a challenge to the reforms aimed at collectivizing and nationalizing private property in the 1960s).[23] Nevertheless, some of the social institutions of kanun, especially the institution of besa, were celebrated as a crucial part of Albanian cultural identity. Besa represented the ideal of generosity toward strangers, the keeping of tabs of gifts and counter-gifts (Bourdieu 1977; Mauss [1924] 1954), of keeping one's word, and of protecting national independence in the face of foreign invasions. As such, it was used to create a particular image of Albanian culture, despite it being at odds with many of the new social and moral values advocated in the broader context of the "new socialist man."[24]

Inspired by Soviet ethnography and its role as "missionaries of socialism" (Grant 1995, 76), Albanian communist ethnography took the remote regions of highland communities as an object of Othering and civilizing. Armanda Kodra-Hysa describes the paradoxical role of ethnography within the broader ideological framework of intellectual production in communist Albania as follows: "[ethnography] had to be the science of the nation's trajectory through history, and at the same time to contribute to the building of socialism and a socialist popular culture" (2011, 135). Through the Soviet influence, one of the founding fathers of Albanian ethnography, Rrok Zojzi (1972), for instance, worked within the frame of Frederick Engels's *Origin of the Family, Private Property and the State* (1884), largely influenced by the anthropologist Henry Louis Morgan's *Ancient Society* (1877) and his theory of developmental stages.[25] Following a historical-materialist approach to culture, ethnography made it its task to explore the roots of "national culture" (Kodra-Hysa 2011, 136).

Within this framework, the institution of besa was both an object of study of premodern Albanian culture (that needed civilizing) as well as a source of national pride and essential natural impulse for independence and equality. Besa was elevated to the status of national cultural heritage. Western ethnographers, such as Edith Durham ([1908] 2009; [1909] 2009), and romantic poets, such as Lord Byron ([1812–18] 2011), who sang praises to the Albanian codes of honor, also were included in the canon of the politically safe classics of foreign literature. In these exoticized and Orientalized images of Albania's "culture," besa played a similar role to that of honor and shame constructs applied and appropriated across Mediterranean societies. But further, besa and other traditional cultural norms became a target of state cultural purges as they were deemed to be obstacles to the emancipation of the proletariat.

By exoticizing besa and in portraying it as a temporal Other, academic and state representations ignored everyday realities of this enduring institution. They also ignored how besa relations of obligation and trust were either targeted by the state and/or mobilized by the state in its consolidation of power. Finally, these representations of besa overlooked the ways in which this cultural institution morphed through the establishment of state socialism and over the course of postsocialist transformations. Gendered concepts such as the "man of honor," continued to be the currency of masculinity in the communist context. Further, this notion of masculinity came into symbiosis with other forms of power and authority in the communist economic and political sphere.

This excessive generosity was an indebting form of generosity, a political strategy for ensuring political support as well as public trust. Hektor, for instance, described how Alimuçaj was not concerned with the thousands of lek he gave to politicians: "We told Vehbi, 'Look, they [the politicians] are taking all this money [from you].'²⁶ But he had made this calculation [hesap]: 'listen,' he told us, 'all the state officials, from the right and the left, have taken more than thirty million U.S. dollars. Thirty million dollars is an insignificant amount, so let us go on with our work.' There was plenty of money. What else could we say to him [Vehbi]?" Such "donations" reinforced relations between the business class and the political class; these relations extended well beyond the pyramid firms. Such relations continue to be entrenched in business practices in Albania to this day. As no gift is ever free (Mauss [1924] 1954), the generosity and benevolence of Alimuçaj and other firms' owners thus read as a particular business culture of clientelism that plagued Albania's free-market expansion. Similar practices that combined excessive expenditures and political rent were also reminiscent of those of state-enterprise directors, notorious for their private appropriation of public resources and their use of the state-owned enterprises as a way to access private wealth—in consumer goods as well as in social capital, including connections, loyalties, indebtedness (see also Ledeneva 1998; Wedel 1986). This form of authority and power was replicated in postsocialist business cultures. The firms' bosses made generous donations, expecting loyalty and favors from their subordinates or from political figures.

Both kompani and fondacione were the prime sources of sponsorship for television programs, cultural events, and even electoral campaigns. Kreditorë recall mockingly the purchasing of the globally renowned soccer player, Mario Cempes, by the so-called general (*gjeneral*) Xhaferri, the owner of the fondacion Xhaferri. As the popular anecdotes go, the Argentinean player was disappointed with his new home in Lushnja, where he arrived to coach a minor league team, compared to the lifestyle he had during his international career as a soccer player. Others recall Gjallica's widely advertised sponsorship for the prime television event of the year, *Miss Albania 1996*. These acts of sponsorship conflated a discourse of masculine generosity with that of capitalist largesse.

Hektor's accolades of Alimuçaj indicate how such notions of masculinity were absorbed into the discursive field that framed postsocialist entrepreneurship. These persistent cultural representations of masculinity and entrepreneurship, thus, helped bestow legitimacy onto Alimuçaj and his business activities. Altogether, these various discourses of masculinity—besa/honor, generosity and expenditure, patriarchal authority, and political rent-seeking—characterized a historically specific entrepreneurial ethic that was best embodied in the figure of the firms' owners but also extended beyond the firms and represented a successful and, most importantly, legitimate form of postsocialist entrepreneurship. Here, as in many other historical and cultural contexts, the gendered narratives served to legitimize these firms as emerging capitalist entrepreneurs.

A Savvy Accountant or a Fraudulent Fortune-Teller?

Beginning with the collapse of Sude in late 1996, public debate about the firms began to take a different turn. The undertone of media coverage of these firms shifted from the masculine representations of the new capitalists to feminized representations of fraudulent magicians. These representations proliferated, especially around the figure of Maksude Kadëna, the only woman to be the sole owner of a firm.[27] Depictions of Kadëna as a Gypsy fortune-teller with a crystal ball replicate the tropes of unpredictable, emotional, and hysterical behavior associated with speculative and fraudulent forms of finance (see de Goede 2005). This shift in register from fajde to pyramid firms, from the powerful and honorable "bosses" to the fickle and hysterical "Gypsy fortune-tellers" represents a familiar discursive practice in the history of capitalist finance. As de Goede notes with regard to the Euro-American context, "delusion and hysteria are the most salient and durable metaphors of crisis" (2005, 40). The media obsession with Sude as a fraudulent Gypsy fortune-teller constitutes a key site for tracing a shift in a local public debate around the nature of fajde from a legitimate to an illegitimate financial activity (figure 1.4). This shift is visible both in the newspaper archive as well as in recollections from former kreditorë.

FIGURE 1.4.   Collage with Masude Kadëna as the top of the pyramids. *Gazeta Shqiptare*, January 19, 1997, 1.

(Photograph by author.)

A passage from Zogaj's memoir illustrates how Sude was singled out from other firms and mocked for its fraudulence through an emphatically gendered and ethnicized discourse. Zogaj writes: "It is very possible that, in essence, the story of Sude is the story of the community 'Amaros Diva'" (1998, 140), the latter a reference to a Roma association in Albania. In contrast to other renowned firm owners, Kadëna's "portrait" in Zogaj's memoir is framed in terms of gender and ethnicity. The following are select passages from a longer section dedicated to Sude:

> The architect of this magnificent rebirth [of the ROMA community] is the honorable Sude Kadëna, the most well-known *daughter of the* Roma community in Albania, the *queen of goodness* accepted as such by the Albanian nation as well. (Zogaj 1998, 140–41; emphasis added)

> Soon after the departure of the IMF team of experts, Sude raised the interest rates from 12% to 16%. The global financial giant was challenged by a girl from the Albanian capital who may not have been good at fortunetelling but who had been able to involve in the pyramids not just the "Amaros Divas" [Roma] community in Albania but prominent women and men of [the highest class]. (Zogaj 1998, 154)

The passages are ridden with sarcastic remarks and grotesque representations of Sude, all couched in references to Kadëna's gender and ethnicity. Sude's activity is ridiculed, feminized, and made to seem irrational through a depiction of Kadëna as a fickle and fraudulent girl from the Roma community. It is crucial to note that the grotesque style of these passages assumes shared sexism and prejudice toward the Roma in Albania.

In my conversations about Sude in 2008–9, a decade after the firm's collapse, kreditorë repeatedly emphasized Kadëna's Roma identity. For instance, while talking about the reputation of the different firms, one of the kreditorë noted: "And then there was Sude, ran by an *arixhofkë* [a derogatory term for Roma or Gypsy]."[28] This characterization connected Sude's illegitimacy and fraudulence to Kadëna's ethnicity and gender. These indictments tapped into stereotypes of Roma women as simultaneously having supernatural powers of divination and magic and being prone to committing cosmological and financial fraud (Musaraj 2019).

Zogaj's description indeed reflects a broader trend in public representations of fajde after their collapse. Heads of other pyramid firms resorted to similar rhetoric as a way of distinguishing themselves from the "ghost firms." They contrasted with their own "investments" and "assets" and ridiculed Sude's style as that of a false fortune-teller whose fraudulence was repeatedly tied to her gender and ethnicity. As other firms began to fold, however, this particular characterization of Sude became representative of all fajde. The fajde phenomenon *(fenomeni fajde)* came to be characterized as "a folly," "an adventure," a sickness, a contagion, a virus, while pyramid firms' owners were compared to "false magicians" (Klan 1997).

These representations of Kadëna as a Gypsy woman overshadowed earlier representations of this "queen of fajde" that centered on her prior experience as a *llotari* (lottery or rotating credit association) organizer. Llotari were practiced by workers in state-owned enterprises. This was a tacitly sanctioned practice, widespread under the communist regime (see also Sulstarova 2005). Workers placed small amounts of cash from their meager monthly paychecks into a pool of money that rotated among members, usually coworkers. Llotari returns carried no interest and were evenly distributed. As such, the term "llotari" is a misnomer—in late communist Albania, it did not refer to a game of chance. Rather, this practice was more akin to rotating credit schemes ubiquitous in other contexts where people lack access to formal means of savings and credit (Ardener and Burman 1995; Banerjee and Dufflo 2011). Albania took exception even from other former communist countries (e.g., Romania), where traditional lotteries (involving chance, big wins, and loss) were organized by the state (see Verdery 1996). Still, the Albanian llotari retained some element of play and chance. Each member was assigned a number by a throw of the dice; the number determined the order of distribution of the collective fund.[29] Llotari represented an aspect of the communist informal economy. Many used llotari as a means of saving a large-enough sum of money to be able to purchase high-ticket items, such as furniture, appliances, or a television set. Individual loans were not available through banks for these types of purchases.

For Kadëna, who had no formal leadership role under the communist regime (that is, she was not an entrepratchik like Alimuçaj or Gërxhalliu), it was the prior experience with and access to the networks of her modest llotari that provided her with the resources necessary for running fajde. As the journalist Jonila Godole explains, "[Kadëna's] first clients were kin, neighbors from her apartment building and workers at the shoe factory" (1996b, 9). In fact, some of these early investors who had been participants in the llotari came to Kadëna's defense during the early weeks of her closing. These former kreditorë connected the story of Sude to that of the privatization and subsequent closing of the shoe factory. Like many other formerly state-owned factories, the shoe factory was privatized in the early 1990s only to be closed down soon after, leaving many workers unemployed. It was at this point that many of them turned to Sude: "In June 1994, when the Italian firm threw us into the street, Sude began its activities. Initially it was like a llotari, within the factory, but in January of last year [1995] it received a license. After us [the factory workers] our kin began to deposit at Sude and then other residents [of Tirana]. Sude fed 1400 workers of the factory owned and eventually closed down by the Italian firm, Filanto. We can't renounce [Sude]!" (Babaramo 1996b, 9).

These continuities between llotari and fajde contributed to Sude's credibility and legitimacy prior to its collapse. The factory workers recalled Kadëna's good record at managing the llotari. Even a few years after Sude's demise and her public shaming, neighbors still praised Kadëna for her accounting skills. They noted that she had completed high school with a specialization in economics and, hence, was "very good with numbers" (Rexho 2010, 1). Kadëna also made frequent references to her accounting skills. During the tense days of her suspension of activities in December 1996, she reassured investors: "I will pay back [shlyej] everyone, to the last cent. I know how to turn the pencil [di si ta vërtis lapsin]" (cited in Babaramo 1996c, 9). The ability to "turn the pencil" implied having dexterity in accounting. Further, speaking to the restless crowd waiting outside of her apartment building, Kadëna reminded investors that, "for four years [she had] been accountable [korrekte] towards [her] clients" (cited in Babaramo 1996c, 9). These various representations of Kadëna draw on yet another entrepreneurial type and another set of economic repertoires (Guyer 2004). Kadëna evoked the women entrepreneurs active in aspects of the informal economy in Albania. Both women and men had been active in various informal economic activities—from petty trade and redistribution of rationed goods to organizing and managing llotari. Although a systematic study of these practices and their gender dynamics is lacking, anecdotal evidence shows that women predominantly engaged in such informal practices, often cultivating networks of friends and family and a system of favors (Ledeneva 1998; Yang 1994) as a way of accessing scarce resources. Women's presence in petty trade and in running the llotari also resonates with other market niches dominated by women (Heyat 2002) as well as with a widespread practice of rotating credit associations across the global South also primarily run by women (see Ardener and Burman 1995; Schuster 2015; Villarreal 1994).

The use of the language of lottery and of "the game" (*loja*) in the context of Sude suggests continuity between the communist llotari and the postsocialist fajde. In a Ministry of Finance inquiry earlier that year, Kadëna was cited as having described Sude as a llotari (Ministry of Finance 1996, Nr. 872). In communications to the public, too, Kadëna invoked analogies to the communist llotari. During the first days of its suspension in early December 1996, Kadëna explicitly referred to Sude as a llotari and promised to open up a new one after settling the accounts of the first one (Zili 1996, 7). Days before it ceased its activities, Sude had announced "a new game" (*një lojë e re*) that offered 50 percent interest on new deposits. As one of the newspapers explained, investors could "deposit 100,000 lek [US$100] today and withdraw 200,000 lek [US$200] in two months" (Godole 1996b, 9). This language was familiar to former llotari participants who invested in different cycles of rotating credit.

A fundamental difference existed in the economic logic behind the communist llotari and the fajde. In the former, investors collected the same amount of cash they had invested (in other words, no interest or capital gains); in the latter, the investors were promised exorbitant returns on their initial investment. At the same time, the analogies between llotari and fajde were a crucial source of legitimacy for the latter activity. This analogy was not simply a discursive mistranslation; it also indicated continuity in repertoires of informal financial practices. Unlike those used by former entrepratchiks, these informal practices were more diffuse and used by people (mostly women) with no official title in the party system or in state enterprises; rather, this constituted yet another entrepreneurial type characterized as savvy (*i/e shkathët*), resourceful, and with an ability to network (rather than as a symbol of honor, for instance). This entrepreneurial acumen was also gendered. But the gendered associations contributed to ambivalent ethics attached to such entrepreneurs. The transformation of Kadëna's public image exemplifies this ambivalent ethic of entrepreneurship.

Women of Magic and Fraud

I found the mention of Kadëna's Roma identity ubiquitous in the newspaper archives and in conversations with kreditorë. I found references to Kadëna's fortune-telling skills to be less frequent during the time of the firms' boom. I also found these representations to have intensified after Sude's collapse.

As mentioned earlier, in their recollections, kreditorë repeatedly emphasized Kadëna's Roma identity and alluded to her fortune-telling abilities. Although it expanded during the transition to a free-market economy, fortune-telling was also a common way of making money under the table during the communist regime. The practice was part of the broader informal economy that, while officially banned, was nonetheless widespread. Roma were integrated (deliberately or by force) into the national economy and social infrastructure. However, they participated widely in a range of informal economic activities—from playing music for money in weddings to trading illicit goods within the country and abroad (Dalipaj 2012; Vullnetari 2012b).

During the communist regime, Roma communities in Albania received mixed treatment. On the one hand, they were considered by party leaders as victims of centuries of oppression and were therefore provided with residence, employment, and full communist citizenship rights. On the other hand, in addition to being displaced and often forced to work in low-skill jobs, the Roma continued to be a target of ethnic stereotypes and other forms of discrimination (see Dalipaj 2012). While being afforded some leeway in these informal/underground activities, Roma communities also occupied a liminal position—much like communities of traders elsewhere, including the figure of the Jewish trader/financier (Simmel 1950) and Muslim women in Azerbaijan (Heyat 2002). Their liminality afforded them freedom of movement that others lacked but, as was the case for the aforementioned groups, liminality also presented a set of dangers, such as distrust and moral indictment. The stress on the identity of Sude as a *magjype* or *arixhofke* (both local terms that refer to Gypsies) needs to be read as an act of delegitimation of Sude in particular and of fajde more generally.[30]

The use of gendered or ethnicized rhetoric as a way of delegitimizing certain financial practices in times of crisis has a long history that parallels that of global capitalism. Literary theorists and feminist historians have noted the use of gendered metaphors, especially that of hysteria, to distinguish between legitimate and illegitimate forms of finance (de Goede 2005; Ingrassia 1998). De Goede (2005) explains how the use of the language of hysteria as a metaphor for crisis serves a political purpose. She notes that "the argument that situates financial crisis in the realm of delusion and madness simultaneously produces a domain of 'normal' market operations" (42). In other words, such binary gendered representations draw boundaries between legitimate and illegitimate forms of finance in different points in time.

Indeed, a similar act of delegitimation through gendered and ethnicized representations is evident in the shifting public discourse around fajde in Albania. The feminized and racialized depictions of fajde *after* their collapse contrast with their masculine representations during the time of their boom (1993–96). This shift in public representations of fajde through the figure of Kadëna, underscoring her untrustworthiness by way of her ethnicity and gender, has gone unnoticed in public discourse about the Albanian firms.

Conclusion

Scholars from various disciplinary backgrounds have noted how gendered representations of finance serve to legitimize or delegitimize some financial practices over others (de Goede 2005; Hirschman 1977; Ingrassia 1998; Poovey 2008; Zaloom 2006). Other scholars, especially economic anthropologists, have explored the wide range of local financial repertoires and cosmologies of capitalism in different places and times (Chu 2010; Guyer 2004; Parry and Bloch 1989; Sahlins 1994). In this chapter, I showed how these two processes combined and played out in the course of the boom and bust of the firms in the mid- to late-1990s Albania.

When writing about gendered discourses of finance as a way of drawing the boundaries of "normal" markets, de Goede (2005) reminds us that representations of finance are political acts. They are crucial strategies for creating legitimate spaces for particular market practices. Indeed, as Janet Roitman (2013) argues with respect to narratives of crisis relating to the recent financial meltdown in the United States, such breakdowns in financial systems should be approached as a product of state agencies and infrastructures rather than as aberrations from market principles. The shift in representations of the Albanian firms that I traced in this chapter—from that of male capitalist entrepreneurs to that of fraudulent female magicians—constitutes an important political act of delegitimizing certain practices while leaving unquestioned other supporting institutions and practices. Fajde were first legitimized as the leading firms of homegrown capitalism before being delegitimized as the workings of false magicians. Noting this shift highlights two important points about the anthropological study of finance.

First, the boom of such firms in the early 1990s Albania constitutes a case in point for how speculative financial practices become legal and legitimate. Discourses of legitimation of the firms during the time of their boom built on legal, political, and cultural repertoires of entrepreneurship and historically specific notions of speculation and informality. One cannot account for the popularity and effectiveness of the firms without attending to these repertoires of finance and to the historical imagination that has shaped them. The various articulations of the firms' legitimacy that I teased out in this chapter provide a counternarrative to theories of mass mania and exuberance as drivers of financial bubbles in peripheries as well as centers of global finance. The legitimacy of the firms in Albania owed a lot to a strong national discourse of capitalist entrepreneurship and a widespread tolerance (if not a celebration of) informal economic practices that, during late socialism, were considered capitalist practices. I showed how these perceptions and framings of informality persisted through the early 1990s.

Second, discursive acts of legitimation and delegitimation of financial practices often draw on specific cultural repertoires of economy and finance. In the specific case of Albania, gendered representations of fajde reinforced the legitimacy of the firms while painting an image of their owners as the new entrepreneurial type that would dominate the postsocialist business landscape. This process of legitimation was performed through the different genres of masculinity invoked in the images of the bosses of fajde that circulated widely in public discourse and that had persisted a decade after the firms' collapse. This is an important observation to make not only for the purpose of historical record but also to highlight particular business cultures and entrepreneurial types that came to dominate the Albanian business world in the 1990s and beyond. Indeed, the masculine representations of the firms discussed above extended beyond the business world; representations of firms' leaders reinforced particular forms of masculinity and power (the men of honor and plenitude, political and business collusion) that persist in the broader public culture in Albania to this day.

Gendered representations of speculative finance also point to strategies of distinction and delegitimation of the speculative market from the "normal" market. These practices of delegitimation and isolation also draw on gender and ethnic constructs. I highlighted the turn to feminized and ethnicized representations of one of the firms, Sude, when it began to fold in early 1997. I also pointed out how representations of Sude and Kadëna as the Gypsy fortune-teller looking into a crystal ball became an icon of all the firms and of fajde. Such representations, widespread both locally and internationally, led toward a framing of the fajde phenomenon as an instance of "occult practices." These registers of hysteria, occult, and fraud around Sude built on a local historical imagination that associated women with less-rational forms of entrepreneurship and the Roma with fraudulent and occult entrepreneurial practices.

In sum, taken together, these various discourses of entrepreneurship and of speculative finance served simultaneously to legitimize certain policies and institutions while framing the failings of these institutions as externalities, speculative bubbles, or crises. In these processes of legitimation and delegitimation, various cultural discourses were mobilized, pointing to social entanglements of finance to begin with. As such, these discourses provide insight into the specific genealogies and histories of finance and in different historical and cultural settings, expanding our notions of financial repertoires deployed in various capitalist contexts, at centers and peripheries of global capital. In the following chapters, I continue to explore these diverse financial repertoires by looking at the forms of wealth and value that circulated in and through the firms. I also trace the entanglements of the firms with other markets that emerged at this time as a consequence of privatization reforms, transnational migration, and housing transformations. I bring attention to the everyday monetary practices, processes of value conversion, and temporalities of investment that took place in and through the firms.

2

"MONEY FLOWED LIKE A RIVER"
Materialities of Speculation

Just like you stack newspapers today, that's how stacks of dollars
filled up rooms then. Yes, there were stacks of cash; I saw them with
my own eyes.

—Former kreditor, Vlora, July 2008

During my conversations with *kreditorë* (creditors/investors) in the late 1990s, I
was struck by the repeated accounts of abundance (*bollëk*). Kreditorë from all
walks of life reminisced about the stacks of cash in the firms' coffers, the bundles
of cash they carried around, the unbridled consumption of food and drinks in
cafes and restaurants, and the excessive wealth of firm owners. "It was a time when
even the dogs ate *petulla* [homemade donuts]!" proclaimed Hektor. To shake off
my silent skepticism, he continued, "There was so much money! I saw it with my
own eyes." Like Hektor, other kreditorë emphasized the concrete presence of the
wealth generated by the firms. These accounts came from winners and losers alike
and were often told with a tinge of nostalgia for the lost good times.

I talked to Hektor at an outdoor coffee shop at the center of Vlora on a lazy
weekday afternoon. We were joined by Bardhosh, an anthropologist based in
Vlora, and my friend and research assistant, Rozi. Bardhosh had insisted that I
meet Hektor, and I soon found out why. Hektor was a big man in his mid-forties,
with dark hair and a pronounced mustache. He had a deep voice that commanded
our attention during his stories and kept us chuckling with his ironic remarks
and exaggerated gesticulations. When talking about the firms, Hektor's eyes lit
up and his lips curled into an ironic smile. Besides his larger than life personal-
ity, Hektor also possessed the invaluable experience of working closely with one
of the firms. Hektor had worked as a *menaxher* (manager/broker) for Vefa, the
most trusted of the firms. He spoke with ease about his close relationship with
Vehbi Alimuçaj, the owner of Vefa who was serving his prison sentence at the time
of our conversation. In recollections of his participation in the firms, Hektor did

not hide a sense of pleasure about his experience. His nostalgia for the lost times of abundance was common among other former kreditorë.

I struggled to make sense of these recollections of the abundance during the time also known for multiple currency devaluations, rising unemployment, and economic dispossession. To be sure, most of the kreditorë who shared these stories had experienced the economic strain of varying degrees. Hektor, for instance, was not gainfully employed at the time of our conversation and struggled to make ends meet for his wife and two kids. A former army officer during the communist regime, he was laid off in the early 1990s. He joined a polyphonic singing group through which he met Alimuçaj. Alimuçaj hired him as a menaxher for Vefa. Menaxherë and sekser/ë (broker/s) were tasked with recruiting and managing money from depositors. The former typically managed a larger pool of money and were more directly involved with recruiting than the latter.

As a menaxher for Vefa, Hektor recruited his soj e sorollopi—that is, his close and distant kin, friends, and acquaintances. Hektor initially managed other people's money. He claimed that at one point he deposited as much as 150 million dollars under his name. This money was accumulated from at least 115 other kreditorë, who had pooled smaller amounts of money informally from their friends and family. Hektor estimated that he was representing the money of close to one thousand investors. He eventually invested his own money too. Lacking savings or immigrant remittances, he sold his one-bedroom apartment and deposited the money at Vefa and other firms. For four years, these firms sustained Hektor, his family, and his singing crew. At the time of the collapse, however, he lost his deposits and his hope of buying a new home. Despite his losses, Hektor continued to be thankful to Vefa and insisted that the firm continued to possess millions of dollars saved in foreign bank accounts. Hektor's trust in the firms' wealth was an exception. Most kreditorë I talked to had no doubts about the insolvency of the firms. Some reported that they did not think the firms were solvent even at the time they deposited their savings. Many confessed that they thought they would be able to withdraw their money just in time. Kreditorë also shared firsthand and secondhand accounts of the stacks and stacks of cash in circulation; in conjunction with these narratives of abundant cash, kreditorë also emphasized the abundance of food, consumption, and firms' assets.

These accounts of abundance contrast with stories of virtual and illusory wealth that allegedly fuel the "madness of the crowds" (MacCay 1841) and the "irrational exuberance" (Shiller 2000) behind widespread participation into speculative bubbles. They underscore the materiality and concreteness of financial speculation rather than abstraction and illusion.

The trope of the "bubble" used to refer to events such as the collapse of the Albanian firms entails a fictitious value, an illusory form of wealth, or an error in

calculating future profits. Neo-Marxist and neo-Keynesian economists have provided an alternative account to these prevailing narratives of bubbles and crises.
The Marxist critique takes bubbles and crises as a manifestation of the inner contradictions of capitalism (see Harvey 2010, 2011). Neo-Keynesian economists
relate them to periods of credit expansion and the introduction of new mediums
of wealth and credit as well as new financial innovations. Both lines of analysis
share a view of speculative bubbles as intrinsic to or intertwined with markets
rather than as externalities or errors.[1]

This is one of the running themes in the classic work, *Mania, Panics, and
Crashes*, by the economic historians Kindleberger and Aliber (2005). Among other
examples, the authors discuss, for instance, two of the earlier bubbles: the 1720s
South Sea Bubble in England and the Mississippi Bubble in colonial France. They
argue that these "were related, and stoked by monetary expansion in the two
countries" (59). Run by private joint-stock companies tightly linked to state banks,
these bubbles were intricately connected to other market operations. They were
concomitant with the expansion of paper money and banknotes—monetary
technologies adopted and advocated by state financial institutions. The Mississippi Company, for instance, benefitted not only from owner John Law's ties to
French royalty and the Banque Royale but also from issuing an overabundance
of paper notes, a financial innovation at the time.

Writing about the financial "crisis" of 2007–9, Janet Roitman (2013) pushes this
critical perspective on speculative bubbles and crises even further. Roitman shows
how particular forms of risk were valued or commodified through the introduction of specific financial tools, or "market devices" (Callon, Millo, and Muniesa
2007), and through a process of knowledge production and validation by a distributed network of agencies, professionals, market institutions, and market actors (in
this case, FICO scores, Fannie Mae and Freddie Mac, banks).[2] In other words, institutions, practices, and discourses of finance co-constitute the definitions of
value, wealth, risk, credit, and debt that underlie a so-called bubble or crisis.

These perspectives resonate with the rise and fall of the firms in Albania, which
were affected by a credit expansion that took place alongside the economic transformations of the early 1990s. But this credit expansion was not led primarily by
an expansion of bank credit, otherwise known as financialization.[3] Instead, most
people gained access to nonbank forms of money and credit.

Looking at the materiality of transactions of the firms this chapter identifies
monetary repertoires that cut across official and unofficial infrastructures of finance. By infrastructures of finance, I refer to the various institutions and
channels—state and nonstate, discursive and material, official and unofficial—
that help define, shape, and mediate financial transactions (Elyachar 2010; Maurer, Nelms, and Rea 2013). My notion of monetary repertoires takes after Jane

Guyer (1995) who describes these as economic practices, institutions and norms with distinct cultural histories, not solidified into official institutions yet enduring and generative of other institutions and practices through the course of historical transformations. I use these two analytics jointly to talk about the official and unofficial financial institutions and practices that shaped and were, in turn, generated by the speculative financial activities of the firms.

The chapter is organized into three parts. First, I explore the changes to the forms and functions of money taking place alongside the postsocialist transformations noting a shift in the functions of money—from serving primarily as a medium of exchange, payment, and unit of account during the communist regime to acquiring more store of value functions in the early 1990s.[4] Second, I trace the connections between money and other forms of wealth emerging at this time. Specifically, I discuss the top-down process of privatization through *letra me vlerë* (privatization vouchers) as a pathway of value conversion that generated a bifurcated path of dispossession for many and accumulation for a few. Third, I explore the bottom-up monetary repertories of wealth accumulation mediated by the firms. The ubiquitous presence of cash in the kreditorë's recollection is not only symbolic of the tensions between the token and commodity functions of money (Hart 1986); it is also indicative of emerging financial repertoires and performances (Guyer 2004) and changing forms of value and wealth (Munn 1986) at a time of significant economic and political transformation. I suggest that the firms provided an additional infrastructure of finance that mediated between the formal banking system and the emerging multicurrency cash economy, and enabled forms of value conversion not available through official channels. This financial infrastructure was enabled by the postsocialist privatization process and the remittance economy. Kreditorë used the financial infrastructure provided by the firms to create more diversified and enduring forms of value.

Stacks and Sacks of Cash

A recurring narrative about the general atmosphere during the time of the firms is that of stacks of cash circulating in broad daylight. Hektor, the former Vefa recruiter, reminisced about that time:

> HEKTOR: Look, there was plenty of money.
> SMOKI: But, where did you think all this money was coming from?
> HEKTOR [SPEAKING WITH IRONY]: What did I think? I thought what Vehbi used to tell me: to not give a damn because there is as much money as you want. And so we came and deposited . . .

Sмokı: Did you ask him where the money came from?

Нектоr: "Stay in your place," [Alimuçaj] would say. "Do you have enough to eat and drink for yourself?" [impersonating Alimuçaj's mocking Hektor's questioning] "Where is the money? Do you want to see the money? Come along to see the money." He would grab me by my neck and bring me to see the stacks of cash. Just like you stack newspapers today, that's how stacks of dollars filled up rooms then. Yes, there were stacks of cash; I saw them with my own eyes.[5]

Hektor was one of the few kreditorë who talked about having seen the stacks of cash "with his own eyes." As a member of Alimuçaj's inner circle, he had access to the fabled coffers filled with cash. He described his conversations with Alimuçaj with pathos and exaggerated gesticulations, drawing imaginary shapes of the stacks of cash. The signs of intimacy with Alimuçaj provided further proof of the integrity of Hektor's eyewitness accounts of the stacks of cash. His storytelling was impressionable—and this was intentional.

Another former kreditor, Ermira, who worked as a cashier for one of the branches of Cenaj, described with a similar nostalgia her "pleasure" of working at the firm at a time when "money flowed like a river." A mother of two in the mid-forties, Elmira moved from Fier to Vlora after the collapse of the firms. Our conversations took place at her modest one-bedroom apartment in Vlora, where she lived with her husband and youngest son. In contrast to Hektor, Ermira showed deference and distance from the owners of the firm she worked for. She spoke of them as her bosses. She respected them and defended them as good administrators of the firm. She spoke to Rozi and me in a motherly way, given that her older daughter was about our age. And though her storytelling style was more subdued and less exuberant than Hektor's, she too described with a bit of nostalgia the times of the firms' boom. Unlike Hektor, however, Ermira was overwhelmed by the large amounts of cash that she had to keep track of every day. She recalled her feeling of sickness (*e kisha si sëmundje*) from touching money because of the stress she felt about keeping track of all the deposits and withdrawals.

Despite their differences, both Hektor and Ermira emphasized the physical presence of stacks and bundles of cash as evidence of the firms' wealth. And both drew a parallel between the abundance of cash and a culture of generosity and giving. "There was a lot of humanism (*humanizëm*), then," stated Hektor, with a slight hint of irony. Likewise, Ermira described how she benefited from the generosity of her clients, who gladly rewarded her with tips: "It was no problem for [the kreditor]. For instance, one would come to pick up their interest once a month. Only in interest they would collect one million or two million [old lek, or 100,000 [new] lek, equivalent to US$1,000], and would leave a ten or twenty [thousand old lek, or US$20] without a problem. But 20 here 20 there, it became like a second salary for me." What was nothing to the kreditorë, noted Ermira, made a significant difference to her, given her salary of 30,000 lek (around US$300) a month.

Other kreditorë reported the physical presence of sacks of cash in their movements around the city to deposit and transfer money to and from the firms. Some recalled carrying large amounts of cash in sacks or plastic bags. For instance, Dalipi, a former sekser and kreditor, described the difference between the 1990s and the mid-2000s as follows: "Frankly, Smoki, this was a time when people moved around with sacks of cash and nobody bothered anyone. Whereas today, if you're carrying even 30,000 lek, they would mug you right away."

Another kreditor, Muhedini, recalled the anxiety he felt the night he withdrew his deposits from the *fondacion* (foundation) Populli, only days before it froze its accounts:

> Muhedini: The night government authorities announced the news about the firms' bankruptcy, Populli was open for just two hours. I went there. There were tons and tons of people waiting. They [Populli's staff] were distributing only certain due dates. The young woman at the cashier's counter would ask: "What is your date?" Luckily, my due date was included in her list. I gave the receipt. I took the money in a plastic bag. There were many bills. People around me looked lost and confused. Everyone was losing their minds. I jumped on my bike with the bag of cash. I biked in the horrible rain. I arrived home; my wife opened the door. I took the ball of money and threw it to her yelling, "Here you have it, your damn money!"

When I talked to Muhedini and his wife, Violeta, they were living in New York City. I met both of them while teaching ESL courses at a New York college. Muhedini and Violeta had immigrated to the United States in 1998. They recalled their experience with the firms in vivid detail. Muhedini blamed his wife for encouraging him to participate in the firms. When he invested in the firms, he was also running a small business and did not need the money to cover everyday expenses, but he said Violeta kept lamenting about their neighbor's new house purchased with the firms' money. Violeta did not dispute the account, but neither did she assume responsibility for the losses they had experienced at the firms. "I don't regret it," she said, "because we came close to even." They invested 1,000,000 lek at Sude and 500,000 lek at Populli, which they lost, and gained 1,200,000 lek from investing at a third unspecified firm. So overall they came out with a loss of 300,000 lek. Given their other sources of income and their luck with winning the U.S. green card lottery, Muhedini and Violeta did not feel set back by this loss. Others were less fortunate.

Stacks and sacks of cash were often invoked in accounts of disappearance and loss of wealth. Among other stories, some verging on conspiracy theory, I heard several iterations of eyewitness reports of the disappearance of bags of cash from Gjallica on the night before it froze its accounts. Versions of this story, told by several former kreditorë, speculated that bags of cash transported out of Gjallica's headquarters in unmarked minivans ended up in the hands of notorious foreign political figures. The list of the alleged beneficiaries ranges from former U.S. presidents George H. W. Bush and George W. Bush to the renowned Palestinian leader Yasser Arafat and Libyan dictator Muammar Gaddafi.

These vivid descriptions of the stacks and sacks of cash embody the intimate experiences with gain and loss at the firms told to someone like me who had not lived through (*përjetuar*) those times. But they also speak to a crucial aspect of the firms—that they attracted and mediated flows of unbanked cash. As such, the firms represent an interesting case of speculative finance taking place outside formal banking institutions and global currency markets and not directly and solely tied to financialization.

Mediating the Cash Economy

The proliferation and bust of the firms in Albania were contemporaneous with the global expansion of finance capital, virtual money, and digitization of currencies. They were also contemporaneous with the integration of Albania's isolated monetary system into the global economy. The free-market reforms of the early 1990s Albania had "a strong monetarist flavor" (Muço 1997, 22). The banking reforms entailed, among other things, the implementation of a flexible exchange rate and tight control of monetary instruments. Up until 1996, however, no private banks operated in Albania, leaving the state banks to serve as the sole mediators of financial exchanges and the sole official sources of credit. At this time, formal lines of credit were limited for people seeking to set up new businesses or needing to finance new housing.

The firms were connected to the formal banking system—they had accounts at state banks where they made frequent deposits and withdrawals. But their transactions primarily took place outside the formal banking system and were not counted in official accounts of financial institutions and transactions.[6] These firms operated across various financial regimes, both official and unofficial, thus participating and contributing to a "pluralization of regulatory authority" (Roitman 2004, 18). Participants in these firms also sought opportunities for gain and accumulation—in money as well as other forms of wealth such as socioeconomic status and housing—across asymmetric value regimes (Appadurai 1986; Guyer

2004)—from communist and postsocialist forms of value and property to local and transnational currency markets.

The ubiquitous presence of stacks and sacks of cash speaks to an emerging cash economy in Albania in the 1990s. That decade was a time of changing monetary policy, of several devaluations of the national currency, and of flux of foreign currencies through migrant remittances. Everyday transactions were mostly unbanked and in cash. The firms channeled these unofficial flows of cash by providing a bridge between the official banking system and the cash economy. This proliferation of unbanked cash in postsocialist Albania replicates financial landscapes across various sites in the global South (Banerjee and Dufflo 2012; Rutherford 2011). The poverty line typically defines cash economies. Cash also becomes prevalent in contexts in which people are excluded from official banking infrastructures for various reasons—among others, high bank fees, distance from banks, or lack of trust in banking institutions.

This abundant cash in people's everyday transactions points to a radical change in the forms and functions of money in Albania at a time of economic and political transformation. As such, it provides insight into a peculiar monetary history that is interrelated, yet distinct, from the Western history of money.

Changing Forms and Functions of Money

Since Aristotle, scholars have distinguished between four functions of money: store of value, unit of account, means of payment, and medium of exchange. They typically see these functions developing in an evolutionary way, with money in more industrialized economies achieving more functions and becoming more general purpose—that is, having more convertibility across a wider range of incongruent spheres of value. Anthropologists of money have challenged this analysis on several counts. First, some have noted that the historical record does not conform to the evolutionary transformation from barter to money to credit (Graeber 2011; Humphrey 1985; Humphrey and Hugh-Jones 1992). Second, ethnographic studies across different cultural and historical contexts suggest that the functions of money (and of different kinds of money) are more expansive. These functions are subject to market and state regulation (Hart 1986, 2000), cultural norms of signification and differentiation (Appadurai 1986; Keane 2003; Zelizer 1997), and performances by people using money in their everyday transactions (Guyer 1995; Maurer 2006). Finally, these functions of money may change and combine in different ways over time and across different contexts (Guyer 2014; Humphrey 1985; Truitt 2013).

Without putting into question the insolvency of the firms and the fraudulent intent of their owners, here I am interested in how the transformation from a command economy to a free-market system affected the flows and value of money circulating through the firms. The postsocialist transformation entailed an important shift in the functions of money—from serving primarily as a unit of account and medium of exchange and payment to gaining more importance as a store of value. This process, which unfolded differently across the former socialist world, constitutes a distinct trajectory of the history of money from the concept of the "ascent of money" (Ferguson 2009) prevalent in Western intellectual history.

The Western history of money of the nineteenth and twentieth centuries is marked by what Milton Friedman describes as a rise in "the demand for money as an aspect of wealth/asset theory" (cited in Guyer 2012, 2214). This development, notes Guyer (2012), is a recent innovation. It is also not a universal one. Guyer traces a different trajectory of money in Atlantic Africa. Her ethnographic and historical research suggests a bifurcated history of money, whereby African currencies were "largely contained within the medium of exchange and mode of payment functions" (2012, 2219), all the while European currencies gained more store of value functions. These differentiations were shaped by specific rules of trade, exchange, and convertibility of currencies, dictated by colonial regimes. The history of money in the former communist space represents yet another trajectory of money forms and functions.

Scholars of Eastern Europe analyzed the postsocialist transformations of the 1990s through the lens of what Karl Polanyi (1965) has famously described as "the great transformation" from embedded to disembedded markets (Hann and Hart 2009; Verdery 1996). Polanyi used the term in reference to the formation of market economies in nineteenth-century Europe (see Hann and Hart 2005). A closer look at these societies provides a more complex set of dynamics that make it difficult to talk about stark embeddedness or disembeddedness of the market. Socialist and communist economies do not fall neatly into Polanyi's categories of economic systems—reciprocity, redistribution, and the free market. They straddle elements of redistributive and market economic systems.

State socialism was a kind of redistributive economy insofar as consumption was governed by state-regulated norms of rationing rather than the free market. In her theorization of communist economies, Katherine Verdery (1996) notes that these states did not value money and markets but placed primary importance on the "allocative power" of the state. Verdery's analysis of the communist system, which draws on her extensive fieldwork in Romania, is apt for the Albanian experience as well. While the economy was controlled by the allocative power of the state production, consumption, and redistribution, significant processes of disembeddedness also took place in these economies. The values of Polanyi's three fictitious commodities (land, labor, and money) were not subject to market forces, and hence not entirely disembedded from the social. At the same time, because of the centralization of ownership through the state and the forced industrialization of the economy, these fictitious commodities were disembedded from one set of social ties (networks of kin and clans) and re-embedded in another (party structures, work communities, cooperative communities).

Studies of Hungary and the former Yugoslavia, two state-socialist economies that implemented market socialism, especially in the 1970s and 1980s, have provided unique examples of these processes of disembededdness of the market.[7] Given its staunch commitment to a Stalinist economic ideology, Albania differed dramatically from these Eastern European peers. Processes of disembedding and reembedding also unfolded in Albania during the consolidation of the communist regime.

In particular, the collectivization of land and cattle constituted a process of disembeddedness of these commodities from kinship and clan networks and their reembeddedness in the social ties organized around party-state networks. By the 1970s, for instance, rural residents were restricted from relying on the subsistence economy. They were allowed to own only 200-square-meter gardens for private use and one piece of livestock—everything else was state property (see Lelaj 2015; Muço 1997). These restrictions ensured that everyone relies on the state redistributive economy for their basic goods. Likewise, the commodification of labor ensued from the processes of industrialization and collectivization. Jobs were provided only by the state, and work was a source of money, benefits, housing, and other forms of wealth.

Money contributed significantly to these processes of disembeddeding and reembedding. The economic transformation of post–World War I Albania resembled postcolonial transformations in other parts of the world, which entailed the creation of national currencies alongside processes of state formation (Helleiner 2003). The National Bank of Albania (Banka Kombëtare e Shqipërisë [BKSH]) was established in 1925 following the independence of the country from the Ottoman Empire and the subsequent transfers of governance between various European powers during World War I. During this time, the newly formed nation-state experienced a multicurrency regime, with various currencies circulating. The BKSH was the first to issue Albanian currency (the Albanian gold franc [franga ari] and the paper lek), though the currency was issued and in large part controlled by an Italian financial group. The BKSH circulated the national currency and issued credit primarily to Italian businesses that established themselves in Albania in the interwar period and to local businesses with ties to Italian businesses (Krisafi 2012, 37). The end of World War II was celebrated by the communist state as a national victory over the semicolonial regime of the 1930s under the de facto administration of Italy's Mussolini government.[8] In this transformation to a communist nationalist regime, money was a crucial symbol of national identity and sovereignty. The BKSH was nationalized and renamed the State Bank of Albania (Banka e Shtetit Shqiptar [BSHSH]), the bank reserves were brought to Albania (they were in Italy until 1943 and briefly in Germany during 1943–44), and Albanian money was issued and controlled by Albanian government authorities. The making of the communist state was enacted through the making (Mitchell 2002) of the communist economy.

Following World War II, the Albanian financial system was severed from the Italian government and business community; Italian businesses were nationalized without compensation. Foreign banks were not allowed to operate in Albania, and no foreign currencies were in circulation. The value of the Albanian lek was kept at a fixed exchange rate. Following the Bretton Woods agreement, the peg to gold was eliminated as was the Albanian gold franc. Bank credit increasingly favored state enterprises and agricultural cooperatives rather than businesses or individuals.

As discussed in the previous chapter, money carried a negative connotation in communist morality. In Albania, this vilification of money was not just a discursive formation. In the new communist national economy, money was limited to performing the functions of unit of account (it enabled the redistribution of state-controlled goods and services), means of payment (in the redistribution of salaries and payments of taxes and contributions to the state), and means of exchange (used to purchase state-distributed commodities). Money, to use Keith Hart's (1986) formulation, was designed to serve more as a token rather than a commodity. Although it lost its function as a store of value, money played an important role in disembedding economic relations from kinship, clan, and patron-client networks and reembedding them in the party-state governmental and social structures.

With the unfolding of collectivization and the command economy, money penetrated social life more than ever as more people were integrated into state payrolls (given the full employment policy) and the rationing system. Centralization and redistribution entailed more commodification (see also Lampland 1995)—people were now buying everything with money at state-owned stores.

The loss of the store-of-value function of money was also the result of sustained efforts at devaluing money as a form of wealth. Those who had wealth in money (or gold) before the communist regime were expropriated in the early decades of the communist regime. Also, it was impossible to save money. Wages and prices were strictly controlled by the state and kept to levels of equivalency (salaries were barely able to cover all the consumption needs, which were regulated by the rationing system). Further, interest-bearing financial products were strictly limited; credit was available mostly between state firms, but individuals could not borrow from the banks and banks could not generate money from lending (there were no capital markets). Finally, money could not secure access to other highly valued forms of wealth, such as jobs, education, or housing. Rather, access to these forms of wealth was best secured through the vagaries of the rationing system, political capital, and social networks (Ledeneva 1998; Yang 1994). As was the case in other command economies, this particular configuration of money and markets led to chronic crises of liquidity and a widespread barter economy that, in some cases, persisted long after the collapse of the command economy (Humphrey 2000; Woodruff 1999).

After the political and economic transformations unleashed by the fall of the Berlin Wall, money (much like land and labor) underwent key transformations. Former socialist economies that embraced free-market reform quickly shifted to floating exchange rates. Many of these countries experienced drastic devaluations; Albania experienced several between 1990 and 1997. By September 1991, the Albanian currency was devalued 250 percent vis-à-vis the U.S. dollar and another 100 percent by the end of the year. As was often the case in similar contexts, one aftereffect of such devaluations was the necessity to transact in large bundles of cash.[9]

Most important, the desire for cash reflects the changing function of money—its gaining of status as a store of value. Money was not only a form of wealth but also provided access to other desired forms of wealth, including abundance in food, drinks, and luxury goods. Indeed, the kreditorë who raved about the pleasures of circulating large stacks of cash also reminisced with both nostalgia and regret about their reckless expenditures in newly opened restaurants and cafes. Kreditorë and firm owners were equally implicated in these acts of conspicuous consumption.

Eat, Drink, and . . . Circulate: Abundance and Scarcity at the Time of the Firms

After listening to Hektor's tales of the piles of cash and his praise for Alimuçaj, my research assistant could not contain her skepticism toward Hektor's enthusiastic portrayal of Vefa, especially given her background in economics and experience as an accountant for a local market-research center. Without hiding her skepticism, she prodded Hektor:

> Rozı: In other words, are you saying that the *fajde* [moneylending] phenomenon was a positive phenomenon?
> Hektor: The period of the pyramids is considered an excellent period. The period is considered as follows: even dogs were eating *petulla*

[Albanian donuts]. In other words, there was abundance [bol-lëk]. . . . We menaxherë were eating, drinking, singing, and . . . cir-culating [*xhironim*].

Hektor's use of "eating, drinking, singing, and . . . circulating" was a play on the popular saying, "hani, pini, dhe këndoni, sa të rrojë Lala Gjoni" (eat, drink, and sing, as long as Lala Gjoni lives), which refers to the pleasures of consuming lib-erally thanks to a benefactor (Lala Gjoni being a generic name for "uncle" Gjon). Hektor implied that the abundance of consumption of food, drinks, and his op-portunities for singing were enabled by Alimuçaj's generous giving as well as by circulating Vefa's cash.

Accounts of excessive consumption and expenditures, by the firms and the kredi-torë alike, appear in the archival record as well. For instance, the journalist Bardhi Sejdarasi (1996) drew a similar connection between the abundance of cash from the firms and the increased consumption in restaurants and cafes: "Vlora is boiling in money, people flock toward the city even from neighboring regions. . . . Vlora's res-taurants are full any time of the day or night. Life can be enjoyed even with fajde money." Sejdarasi does not hide his cynicism toward the sources of funding that sustain these forms of conspicuous consumption. The cynicism aside, his account resonates with descriptions of everyday life at the time by the kreditorë as well.

Accounts of abundance in food and drinks make a sharp contrast to the de-cades of rationing, scarcity, and shortages in consumable goods that plagued countries of the former socialist block (Kornai 1980; Verdery 2002) and especially Albania, given its increasingly isolationist economic policies (Aslund and Slojberg 1992; Pashko 1993). Kreditorë remembered the decades of queuing and ration-ing, and they took pleasure in the abundance that was made possible by the firms. But in retrospect, kreditorë contrasted the abundance of their expenditures with other forms of dispossession and scarcity that were unleashed by postsocialist transformations.

Manjola, for instance, contrasted the increased outings and expenditures at res-taurants with a drop in productivity and rise in unemployment: "The [time of the firms] was the most fatal period. Women would withdraw their interests and shop in abundance, and they did not realize that this was our money; we were consuming our own money. If it were my money in my hands, I would not spend it like that. I would spend it with thriftiness (*nikoqirllëk*). Whereas then, lunch at home, dinner at Amerikani or Radhima."[10] Manjola's description of the 1990s as "the most fatal period" echoed the sentiments of many other Vlora residents I met through the course of my research who looked back at the early 1990s as a time of great dispossession. This gloomy picture of the past referred in particular to the increasing rate of unemployment, which followed the closing of factories that provided jobs in Vlora—among others, the Sodium factory (Uzina e Sodës), the PVC Factory, and the Cement Factory. Coincidentally, I had just passed by the said factories on my way to meeting Manjola. I missed the bus stop to her office and stayed on the bus to the Sodium factory where I spent some time with the bus driver and ticket collector. Both were laid off officers who had taken up these low-paying jobs, and both commented on the now dilapidated factory and the lack of employment that continued to plague the city.

Manjola contrasted practices of conspicuous consumption by kreditorë, including herself, with the overall scarcity that plagued the nation following the closing of state factories, decollectivization, and migration abroad. In retrospect, she lamented her careless expenditure of the firms' interests into the newly opened restaurants in Vlora's prime locations. The restaurants and locations she listed were prime destinations for local tourists—Amerikani (the American), a nickname for the New York Hotel and Restaurant, and the bay of Radhima, a newly developed area south of Vlora. The proliferation of these restaurants and cafes fed into a collective imaginary of the city as the "undiscovered" pearl of the Mediterranean waiting to be developed into the next tourist destination. The proliferation of these restaurants was rumored to be sponsored by trafficking money— the adjacent bay of Radhima, in particular, was known at the time as a hub of the rubber boats illegally shuffling back and forth to nearby Italy.[11]

Conspicuous consumption was also a feature of the public life of firm owners. In addition to the donations mentioned in the previous chapter, firms threw lavish parties that became the subject of media attention. In his memorable recollections of the rise and fall of the schemes, journalist, poet, and politician Preç Zogaj described in a similar grotesque style an exclusive Vefa reception at the inaugural party of Iliria Island, an entertainment center built on a pier on the popular beach of Durrës:

> Entering "Iliria Island" [Ishulli Iliria], grateful to be invited, Nazarko and I, as we admit to one another later, feel as though we were part of a burlesque opera. The waves swayed the motorboat "Vefa" near one of the island's legs; a "Vefa" race car appears a little further as the trophy of national capitalism; the long lines of politicians and beauty pageant contestants who eat and smile with confidence and grace; the speech given with pathos by [minister] Mr. Titani in the name of [Vefa] president Alimuçaj "for the government that we love and loves us"; the parade of local comedians, their very warm jokes that not only do not upset the ministers and members of parliament present, but, on the contrary, that entertain them, just like in Europe; contemporary music, the sparkling glasses of drinks, the clicking sound of the toasts. (Zogaj 1998, 35)

The celebration of Alimuçaj's new asset brought together politicians, business-men, and beauty pageants as well as excessive displays of typical luxury items—a yacht, a racecar, and a helicopter. Such forms of wealth represent a global cur-rency of the newly rich and corrupt officials (see also Osburg 2013). The gro-tesque style of Zogaj's description of this event evokes this global culture of con-spicuous consumption. Often, such forms of conspicuous consumption are linked to forms of illicit wealth. In the Albanian context, several authors and kreditorë point to the channeling of illicit wealth through the firms—specifically, the trafficking taking place through Vlora and the state-mandated breach of the UN embargo (Abrahams 2015; Bezemer 2001; Jarvis 1999). Another major source of wealth for the firms was the state-sanctioned privatization process. This pro-cess entailed the conversion of values (Guyer 2004, 2012) across distinct (asym-metrical) regimes of valuation.

Guyer's expanded definition of value conversion is useful for thinking about the different processes of value transformation that unfolded during the time of the pyramid firms in Albania. For Guyer, the notion of conversions refers not merely to currency exchange but more broadly to "transactions between spheres of exchange" where "a fundamental incommensurability is recognized and pre-served" (2012, 2216, 2215). In her ethnographic and historical study of mone-tary repertoires in Atlantic Africa, Guyer defined "conversion" as a transaction that "adds, subtracts or otherwise transforms the attributes of exchange goods in a way that defines the direction of future transactional possibilities" (1995, 30). The conversions of value and wealth enabled in and through the Albanian firms promised the potential for redirecting future transactional possibilities, both for the firm' owners and kreditorë.

The conversions taking place through the firms cut across different scales of value—local, national, and transnational markets; communist and postsocialist forms of wealth. The transactions of the firms were intertwined with the priva-tization process, itself mired in conversions of incommensurables. In addition to money and its changing functions, other objects of value that changed hands in the process of postsocialist transformations included former state property and privatization vouchers. The site of Alimuçaj's infamous party, Iliria Island, is a case in point for how such conversions unfolded.

Firm Assets and Privatization Vouchers

Iliria Island was built on a pier on the beach of Iliria, Durrës, in the late 1980s by communist state authorities; it was privatized by Vefa in the summer of 1996. As a child at the time the "island" first opened up, I remember the buzz around what seemed to be a new entertainment center at the nearby Adriatic Coast. The concrete structure that, from above, resembled a flower, was bustling with new cafes and restaurants at a time when the modest tourism industry catered to locals. In the early 1990s, before it became overshadowed by myriad other luxurious developments, Iliria Island held symbolic cachet. It represented a more modern approach to tourism. It was because of this symbolic meaning that Alimuçaj purchased the site through the public procurement process. By late 1996, Alimuçaj flaunted Iliria Island in Vefa's ads and postcards (see figure 1.3, lower left corner). The property became the icon of Vefa's wealth.

Indeed, key firms accumulated assets through the process of postsocialist privatization. A closer look at these practices of accumulation of former state properties points to important processes of devaluation and reevaluation of communist to postsocialist forms of wealth. Between 1995 and 1997, ninety-seven small- and medium-sized factories and enterprises (SMEs) were privatized through the Mass Privatization Program. Many of these, including the famed Iliria Island, appear on the list of seized assets of the major *kompani* (company/ies) by the Transparency Group (the Group for the Transparency of the Pyramid Schemes). In other words, the firms accumulated their assets from this first wave of public procurement of state properties.[12] For instance, by 1996 Alimuçaj owned two chicken farms, four beer factories, several medium-sized factories (*kombinate*), as well as hotels, bars, restaurants, and apartments in several towns in Albania (Tirana, Durrës, Berat, Pukë, Shkodër, Krujë). According to the rules of the public procurement process, state property could be purchased only through letra me vlerë to prevent access to foreign companies and provide an opportunity for local entrepreneurs.

Letra me vlerë were introduced in 1995 as a means of transferring ownership of state-owned companies over to the private sector.[13] The Mass Privatization Program initiated in 1995 entailed two simultaneous processes. On the one hand, letra me vlerë were distributed to all Albanian citizens over the age of eighteen (Mema and Nevruzi 1999). On the other hand, the process of privatization of state-owned SMEs was set into motion. Privatization vouchers could be used to purchase these SMEs. This privatization model—also known in Albania as the "free-market model" (Mema and Nevruzi 1999, 2)—was implemented in other postsocialist countries, most notably in Russia.[14] In both places, privatization vouchers could be traded in the market, and their value was subject to two distinct valuation regimes: the arbitrary scheme of putting a price tag on state properties (the nominal value) and the informal currency exchange market (the market value). Thus, as their market value depreciated, the nominal value remained the same. Thus, at one point in 1996, letra me vlerë with a nominal value of 40,000 lek had a market value of 800 lek (figure 2.1).

FIGURE 2.1. *Letra me vlerë.* Issued by the Bank of Albania (Banka e Shqipërisë) with an expiration date of December 1999.

(Photograph by author.)

Muhamet, a former kreditor and a beneficiary of letra me vlerë, explained to me how these circulated among various official and unofficial markets and how they intersected with the circulations of the firms. Muhamet had invested in four firms, including the kompani Vefa and Silva and the fondacione Populli and Xhaferri. Originally from Vlora, Muhamet was based in Tirana at the time of our conversations. During one of my visits to his home, Muhamet's wife, Lavdie, also joined in. Both were retired at the time and, besides the meager pension and Muhamet's sporadic jobs as a driving instructor, the couple depended on remittances from one of their children who had migrated to the United States. Muhamet shared his experience with obtaining letra me vlerë in the early 1990s, and weighing his options for how to use them:

> It was said at the time that Albanians would become co-owners of the wealth [*pasurisë*] that had been created over the years. And they found a way to give the so-called letra me vlerë. These were distributed at the work centers [*qendra pune*]. It was a beautiful shiny paper like the praise let-

ters [*letrat e lavdërimit*] from school. There has been a terrible abuse with these. I tell you how. These letra me vlerë ended up selling at 2 percent of their [nominal] value. They were purchased at great discounts. . . . And many of these former state enterprises were sold with letra me vlerë. These "experts" [*ustallarët*] knew and pretended as though everyone could buy them [the SMEs], but only those with connections could buy these enterprises.

Like Muhamet, many others laughed at letra me vlerë because of their quick devaluation and the loss of wealth that they entailed. These were paper objects meant to redistribute communist wealth evenly among a large number of people and thus provide a means for former workers in the system to set up small businesses. Their very design evoked national pride—the somber image printed on them is a drawing of the uncontroversial national hero Skenderbeu, a warrior and leader who challenged the Ottoman Empire in the fifteenth century—and translated communist value to postsocialist value.

Letra me vlerë served as a market device (Callon, Millo, and Muniesa 2007). In practice, however, only a few were able to use letra me vlerë for their intended purpose—to purchase state-owned property. Most sold them for quick cash in informal currency exchange markets. Because they were also exchangeable for cash, letra me vlerë quickly depreciated. Muhamet recalled his dilemma about how to use his letra me vlerë:

> Sмокı: But, why were people selling letra me vlerë, given their low market value?
>
> Muhamet: Well, of course, they did. Instead of keeping them at home as a piece of paper, they'd rather sell it. . . . Now, someone who had letra me vlerë [worth 50,000 lek] would go and sell them for 1,500 lek. Do you understand what this meant? [The kompani owners] would buy these letra me vlerë and use them to buy the SMEs. How this wealth [*pasuri*] was misused, I just don't know! I, for instance, with my letra me vlerë, I was not sure that I could even buy a kiosk at the periphery. Those who were able to buy the big SMEs had the assurance [*sigurinë*] that they could buy this wealth [*pasuri*]. They had access. Who are they?! Officials and their kin.

Muhamet's experience echoes that of hundreds of thousands of others who also found that letra me vlerë alone did not secure access to the new forms of postsocialist wealth. His account also suggests that kompani owners straddled the informal market of letra me vlerë and connections to state authorities in charge of privatization tenders.

Muhamet's experience highlights the limitations of letra me vlerë as a market device; their use and purpose limited and redirected by emerging repertoires of asset accumulation and informal finance. This account corroborates critiques of the Mass Privatization Program from local and international development economists. According to Childress (2009), the privatization of formerly state-owned enterprises through tradable vouchers favored the emergence and quick enrichment of an elite group of connected officials. This scenario reflects a broader pattern of uneven distribution of communist wealth through privatization schemes across Eastern Europe.

In practice, this scheme of privatization through letra me vlerë translated into a process of wealth dispossession (Elyachar 2005). State-owned wealth (such as SMEs) was turned into tradable commodities through the mechanism of letra me vlerë; the latter were exchanged and devalued in currency exchange markets (letra me vlerë were sold for 2 percent of their nominal value); and were finally exponentially revalued. This process led to rapid dispossession for some and rapid accumulation for others. Those who possessed letra me vlerë but had no access to key government employees were further dispossessed as they exchanged them for cash; and those who bought letra me vlerë at market value (firms' owners and other entrepreneurs) accumulated new private assets (SMEs) at low cost.

Given the nominal value of letra me vlerë, their rapidly depreciating market value, and the highly questionable process of assessing the value of the SMEs, possibilities for speculation and arbitrage abounded. Others have already underscored the interrelations between postsocialist transformations and the emergence of speculative financial entities, such as pyramid schemes (Verdery 1996). However, Muhamet's account points to market devices such as letra me vlerë that enabled and shaped this correlation. It further points to the regulatory regime that enabled these particular forms of dispossession. Finally, it indicates anticipated and unanticipated practices and performances with these devices that created opportunities for speculation and dispossession of different groups of people.

In addition to having access to the political networks governing the privatization of state-owned enterprises, kompani benefited from the cash that kreditorë received in exchange for the vouchers. They "borrowed" the cash to purchase more letra me vlerë and used the latter to purchase more SMEs. This chain of transactions represents a "pathway of value conversion" (Guyer 2004) whereby asymmetries in the values of different forms of wealth (SMEs, letra me vlerë, lek) were maintained over a significant period of time that encompassed and exceeded the life cycle of the firms, as privatization through letra me vlerë continued a decade after the collapse of the firms. This pathway of value conversion enabled the accumulation of assets by kompani (famed SMEs and buildings of special significance) and generated more cash that kreditorë proceeded to invest in the firms.

Muhamet's conversions are a case in point. As a worker in a state factory (he was a mechanical engineer), he was able to obtain letra me vlerë. With the nominal value of these vouchers and without connections, Muhamet would not be able to purchase a business that would provide income. He then sold his letra me vlerë for cash at the currency exchange markets. But the cash he received was so meager that he decided to then deposit it at the firms, in the hope that it multiplied. When he lost his deposits at the firms, he had thus also lost the meager value of letra me vlerë and the hope of starting his own business.

The privatization scheme through letra me vlerë was just one way to circulate cash through the firms. Another more prominent source of cash was the growing remittance economy of the early 1990s Albania. The mass migration of Albanians to neighboring European countries, especially Greece and Italy, played a crucial role both in the quantity and quality (denominations, exchange rates, symbolic cachet) of the cash that flowed through the firms. I use this other pathway of value conversion as a way to highlight specific financial repertoires—saving in multiple currencies and converting currencies—that were pervasive at the time of the firms and that continue to be a feature of everyday financial transactions in Albania to this day.

Durim's Book of Accounts

I first realized the extent of the use of multiple currencies through the firms when Durim presented me with the book of accounts he had kept when working as sekser for Gjallica. Durim began to work for Gjallica in 1996, at the peak of the firm's activities. At its inception in the early 1990s, Gjallica was registered as a currency exchange business. Starting in the mid-1990s, when the fajde phenomenon had taken hold of hundreds of thousands of kreditorë, Gjallica started soliciting deposits under the banner of fajde and invoking the articles of the new civil code of 1993. By 1996, the peak of pyramid firms' investments, Gjallica was a growing kompani with investments in tourism, industry, and construction. At the time of its collapse in 1997, Gjallica was estimated to have served 170,000 kreditorë and to have accumulated US$800 million in deposits.

Gjallica was perhaps the second most important firm, after Vefa. It was especially entrenched in Vlora. Fitim Gërxhalliu, Gjallica's co-owner, was a former army captain and used his army contacts—now unemployed—as sekser and menaxher.[15] Many kreditorë, sekserë, and menaxherë I met in Vlora worked as army officers during the communist regime, lost their jobs in the 1990s, and eventually joined the ranks of Gjallica or Vefa. During the communist regime, Vlora had served as a crucial military base, hosting an infamous submarine center that was once co-owned with the Soviet Union and served as a strategic point in the Adriatic Sea. The militarization of Vlora accounted for the city's high number of army officers and their move toward the firms in the 1990s after drastic layoffs.

Like Hektor, Durim served as an army officer during the communist regime. Because many of his family members were politically persecuted, he was assigned to serve in the northern city of Shkodër, where he had no family relations. Like Hektor, Durim was laid off in the early 1990s. He had returned to Vlora to be close to his extended family. There, he tried working at a farmers' market, then at the informal money exchange (*kambizmi*), and finally at the firms in mid-1996. After the collapse of the firms, he enlisted as an officer once again. He continued to serve in the army to increase his pension, which was fast approaching. At the time of our conversation, he was also working as security personnel at an internet cafe.

I met with Durim at an outdoor coffee shop in Vlora, and Rozi joined our conversation. Unlike Hektor, Durim did not talk with much reverence about Gjallica or its leaders. He did not have a close relationship with Gjallica's owners, and he had decided to join the firm after trying out other jobs that had not provided him with much income. Through these various jobs, Durim was able to give a detailed account of the strategies of wealth accumulation and circulation at the firms. At the end of a long conversation, Durim walked back home and fetched an accounting book he had kept to keep track of the deposits, withdrawals, and interest returns of his clients (figure 2.2).

The book of accounts reveals crucial details about the circulation patterns of cash through the firms. The book lists kreditorë who deposited money through Durim. As Durim explained, he managed only his kin's money. Many of the kreditorë listed in the book were close relatives living in a nearby village. Durim acted as a broker to the firm, making monthly deposits and withdrawals per the instructions of his kin. This particular pattern of investment was common among kreditorë. Many of the sekserë were relatives or connections (*të njohur*). As such, family and social relations played a crucial role in mediating transactions with the firms. These networks of kin and acquaintances were a key social infrastructure (Elyachar 2010) that mediated deposits to the firms.

Another feature of the book of accounts that drew my attention was its separate columns indicating deposits, interest, and withdrawals in multiple currencies: the Albanian lek, the U.S. dollar, the Greek drachma, the Italian lira, the German marks. The list of currencies is of itself a relic of a bygone multicurrency regime of western European countries before the euro (see also Peebles 2011). The list thus contains a "memory bank" (Hart 2001) of monetary regimes no longer in place at the time of my research. The list contained a record of the circulation, valuation, and earmarking of different currencies as they related to the

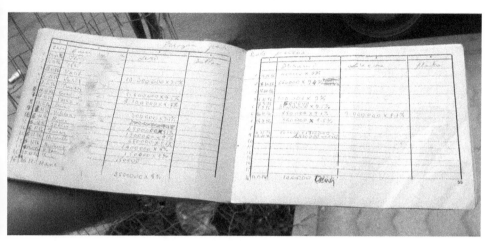

FIGURE 2.2. Durim's book of accounts, listing the sums of deposits in multiple currencies (from left to right, lek, dollars, drachmas, liras, and marks) for each of his clients. Vlora, September 2008. Last names are blurred to protect the identity of the listed kreditorë.

(Photograph by author.)

migration patterns of Albanian migrants in the early 1990s. Besides the lek, the drachma stands out as the most used foreign currency for deposits to the firm. Durim explained that some of the firms (mostly the kompani) accepted deposits in multiple currencies and even returned the interest in those same currencies. This pointed to a crucial aspect of the firms' financial transactions: the firms enabled savings and interest gains in multiple currencies, something not possible at official banks.

In further conversations with other kreditorë, I became more attuned to the discussion of these multiple currencies. Kreditorë spoke of their deposits and withdrawals of the lek, drachma, and lira at specific firms. Ermira, the accountant at another firm, talked about managing accounts in multiple currencies: "The bookkeeping and cash reserves [of the firm] were in all the hard currencies [*valutat*]—from francs, liras, dollars, in other words, all kinds of currencies I had to have in various denominations so I could give back the change. I kept them all separate. The lek was in massive quantity, it was a mountain peak." This abundance of multiple currencies was itself celebrated as a form of wealth. Accessing multiple currencies in a context where, until 1990, anything foreign (let alone currencies) was strictly forbidden and highly moralized represented a gain in wealth, status, and belonging to a global community. Ermira told me: "Yes, there was the dollar, but we had all kinds of dollars—the Canadian dollar, the U.S. dollar.

Then the Swiss franc and the German mark. I had never seen some of these currencies before! There was liras . . . Everything, girl!" I joked with Ermira comparing her operations with that of international banks. She laughed with amuse-
ment and pride and responded: "I don't know any other bank in the world to hold
as many hard currencies. But these were brought by the immigrants. From wher-
ever they were, the poor souls [*të shkretët*]." Even with the losses of migrant remittances and other forms of wealth, the time of the firms had been a high point
of the postsocialist transformations for many, in part because of this sense of
inclusion in a global community through access to various currencies. In other
words, rather than nationalist aspirations, these desires for multiple currencies
speak to hopes for European and cosmopolitan futures (see also Grant 2010; Pelkmans 2003).[16]

The circulation of multiple currencies through the firms makes visible monetary repertoires that emerged early on during the postsocialist transformations. The very presence of the currencies in Durim's book of accounts and other
kreditorë's narratives constitutes a trace of the geography of Albanian migration
at the time. Migrants sent their remittances in the currencies of their host
countries—drachma from Greece, the country with the most Albanian migrants,
lira from Italy, with the second most number of migrants, followed by currencies
from other European countries hosting a smaller number of migrants, such as
Germany, Switzerland, and Austria. These accounts also trace the practices of valuation and value conversion that people on the ground sought to perform
through the firms. Most kreditorë preferred to keep their remittances in foreign
currencies, which they indiscriminately referred to as valuta—the officially recognized hard currencies (the U.S. dollar, the Swiss franc) as well as formally recognized soft currencies (the Italian lira, the Greek drachma).

The high value of hard currencies was not just based on their market value
but also cultural and symbolic value. As foreign currencies were forbidden and
vilified during the communist regime, possessing such currencies carried additional political and cultural capital. During the communist regime, for instance,
dollar bills would be displayed in glass cases (alongside other valuables, such as
china, pottery, souvenirs) as a mark of distinction. But a second, more pragmatic
yet equally important aspect of the value of foreign currencies at this time was
their durability.

As mentioned earlier, people participating in the firms had experienced several devaluations and lost their savings in lek. They then sought to keep their remittances in the hard currencies as a way of storing wealth in the long run.
Kreditorë differentiated between currencies in ways that did not conform to global
currency exchange values and the general purpose versus specific purpose or hard
versus soft currency designations by global financial standards. The "hardness"

or "their capacity to hold value over time" (Guyer 2012, 2214) of these currencies was subject to people's access to them and their ability to use them for different purposes.

Drachmas were accessible to kreditorë with family members who had migrated
to Greece. Hence, they appeared often in kreditorë's accounts of deposits and
withdrawals. They dominated Durim's book of accounts. Other hard currencies,
such as the U.S. dollar, were less accessible and less desirable. Durim recalled that
when he worked at the currency exchange, he did not want to deal in dollars but
preferred liras and drachmas. He noted that a lot of counterfeit dollars circulated
at the time, which made this currency "riskier" (më e rrezikshme). The abundance
of and familiarity with liras and drachmas, by contrast, made these currencies easier to work with.

The earmarking of different kinds of money has a long history in the global
North (see, for instance, Zelizer 1994). However, the coexistence of different currencies and money-objects is especially prevalent in colonial and postcolonial
contexts (Akin and Robbins 1999; Guyer 1995; Hart 1986), in sites located at the
margins to global financial flows (Maurer, Musaraj, and Small 2018; Villareal
2014), and in sites undergoing short-term or long-term economic transformations (Peebles 2011; Truitt 2013).[17] The proliferation of a multicurrency regime
in Albania emerged in a context of economic and political transformation. The
persistence of this multicurrency regime through the present speaks to the enduring state of volatility and devaluation of the local currency.

The earmarking and use of different currencies are essential transactions in
the economic lives of those located at the margins of global economic flows. Jane
Guyer called for studies of soft currencies precisely because "limitation to exchange functions can ensure the restriction of their zones of use and make sud-
den shifts in purchasing power more likely, in turn ensuring their restriction to
those people with little or no choice (that is the national citizenry at the poor end
of the wealth hierarchy)" (2012, 2215). In other words, considering how soft currencies are valued and how they circulate within and outside formal banking
infrastructures provide us with insight into the inclusions and exclusions experienced as forms of structured inequality (see also Maurer, Musaraj, and Small,
2018).

The circulation of multiple currencies through the firms in the early 1990s Albania speaks to the emergence of a new "currency interface" (Guyer 1995) that
has persisted through the present. The broader context for this currency interface was a progressive softening of the local currency—that is, its limited purpose
and convertibility—and a flow of remittances in multiple soft and hard currencies. The firms mediated and exploited this currency interface. By accepting multiple currencies and by offering interest returns in these currencies, the firms

enabled kreditorë to save and profit in these currencies. Kreditorë's strategies of circulating and converting multiple currencies through the firms belong to a broader financial repertoire that emerged in the 1990s—a time of increased marginalization by official monetary regimes and practices—and that persist to this day. Durim's experience of moving across the different sites of money circulation and conversion gives us insight into the tension between top-down financial infrastructures and bottom-up financial repertoires.

Mediating a Multicurrency Regime

Kreditorë, sekserë, and menaxherë actively arbitraged currencies across various financial infrastructures. Durim described such strategies of arbitrage that he witnessed while working as a *kambist* (moneychanger).[18] Before becoming a sekser, Durim had spent a couple of years exchanging currencies at Vlora's informal currency exchange market, Kapelja (the Hat). He had started to work as kambist soon after being laid off from the army. This work exposed him to other menaxherë from Vefa and Gjallica who eventually convinced him to become a sekser for Gjallica during its last three months of existence. When I asked him about the decisions by former kreditorë to deposit in foreign currencies, Durim shared the following story:

> SMOKI: Did people think that it was better to deposit in drachmas or dollars, perhaps because they were winning double, that they were also winning on the higher value of the hard currencies [compared to lek]?
>
> DURIM: There was something peculiar then: much fluctuation in the value of the lek. The fluctuation began a week before the [1996] elections. There was a hard blow to the lek then, in fact, I incurred a very high loss, there was a drastic depreciation of the hard currency. I, for instance, lost 80,000 lek [roughly US$800]. At the time I was "playing" [*lozja*] with 100,000 lek [US$1,000], just to be able to feed my family, I had withdrawn this money [as a loan] to buy a new house and since I withdrew it, I had bought hard currencies and planned to sell it the next day.
>
> SMOKI: Which hard currency did you "play" with?
>
> DURIM: Mainly with drachmas and lira. And I kept postponing it. I thought I would exchange it today or tomorrow and then I ended up having an 80,000 lek loss. That's when I turned to the firms. I saw these menaxherë that were playing this game then. They would return 24 percent now and 6 percent later. And you know what they did?

Because menaxherë did not have liquidity in lek, they would come
to us, the kambistë, and they would take a loan from us, say, for a
couple of hours and give us one percent back. And that's how I min-
imized my loss to 30,000–40,000 lek [US$300–400].[19]

Durim's story of loss and arbitrage outlines the entanglements of the firms' stacks
of cash with official and unofficial monetary regimes and the various opportunities for speculation and arbitrage that emerged therein. These regimes included
official monetary policy, transnational currency regimes, local official and unofficial currency exchange rates, and firms' rules on accepting multiple currencies.
The experiences as kambist and sekser provided Durim with unique access to how
these intertwining processes took place on the ground. His reference to the fluc-
tuation in the value of the lek following the contested 1996 elections points to
the direct impact of official monetary policy and politics on the everyday wins
and losses at the currency exchange.

Further, Durim's details on the monetary circulations by the firms' menaxherë speak to strategies of arbitrage that the firms engaged in, thanks in large part
to their access to stacks of cash in multiple currencies. In other words, the firms
made use of the deposits from migrant remittances to create liquidity (in lek or
otherwise). These entanglements between the firms, informal currency exchange
markets, and migrant remittance flows constituted crucial thresholds of value creation and conversion.

The firms and their menaxherë were not the only ones that tried to bank on
the asymmetries and fluctuating value of different currencies. Kreditorë with access to remittances in various currencies also engaged in acts of arbitrage as most
kreditorë deposited in more than one firm. Manjola invested in both Gjallica and
Vefa, as had Durim and Hektor; Blerim invested in Gjallica and Kamberi. Hektor
described his movements of money among different firms:

We worked with all the firms. Mostly we worked with Vefa because we
thought it was most guaranteed and we received 10 percent interest there.
Then, when we received large sums, we would take this to Gjallica. For
instance, one time I received 100,000 lek. I took it and brought it over
to Gjallica; they used to give you back 33 percent on the spot. I took the
33 percent and deposited right back in. When I made a lot of money, I
took 10,000,000 lek and brought it to Cenaj. I received 33 percent in
hand. I took the 33 percent and brought it to Vefa.

This pattern of diversification and arbitrage repeatedly emerged in conversation
with other kreditorë. Many sought to have money in multiple firms. Many also
moved the interest received from a kompani to a fondacion, hoping to make profit

quick while keeping some of their deposits in the more stable and guaranteed kompani. Overall, kreditorë sought profits at the margins of promised interest returns and the timelines for those returns offered by the different firms. Kreditorë also tried to hedge risk, spreading their deposits among the kompani and fondacione. Kompani offered more credibility and long-term security for deposits and accepted higher amounts of deposits but offered more modest interest (5 to 8 percent). Fondacione offered much higher interest returns in shorter periods but accepted smaller deposits. For instance, on October 8, 1996, the interest returns of the firms ranged from 8 percent (from kompani Vefa and Gjallica) to 25 percent (from fondacione Xhaferri and Populli).

Given these variations in terms of deposits and interest returns at different firms, kreditorë also tried to bank on the marginal differences between the firms. We can think of kreditorë currency exchanges and movements of pyramid firm deposits as ways of creating "marginal gains" (Guyer 2004), taking advantage of and working against the thresholds of value conversion in the formal and informal currency markets.

Access to multiple currencies during the postsocialist economy constituted a source of more enduring value over time. It introduced stability in the face of the uncertainty and dispossession unleashed by the economic realities of transition. Possessing foreign currencies enabled a diversification of sources and stores of value for those located at the margins of emerging socioeconomic geographies (Guyer 2004; Villareal 2014). As I describe in the following two chapters, such strategies of wealth accumulation are also strategies of negotiating relationships, of "gaining time" (Guyer 2012, 2220) and of arbitraging personal and national futures (Miyazaki 2013).

In the Albanian context, the firms played an active role in creating a space of possibility for such arbitrage opportunities. They accepted foreign currencies from unbanked and unregulated sources; they engaged in currency exchange in unofficial local currency exchange markets; and they deposited parts of their liquid assets in national banks. They bridged official and unofficial financial infrastructures. The firms were uniquely positioned to enable value conversions and wealth accumulation not accessible through other institutions and infrastructures. By enabling such conversions, the firms provided (or promised to provide) a means of socioeconomic mobility for many who had no access to other forms of wealth.

Conclusion

The proliferation of the pyramid firms in Albania coincided with similar financial schemes in other parts of the world. As Comaroff and Comaroff (2000) note, this proliferation of speculative finance in various parts of the global South is re-lated to the expansion of neoliberal market reforms since the 1990s. How such financial speculation at the margins intertwines with global flows and regulation of capital is not a straightforward story. Looking at the specific materialities of wealth that circulated through the Albanian firms helps us understand how changes to top-down monetary policies, forms and functions of money, and official and unofficial infrastructures of finance made possible certain pathways of value conversion that enabled the firms and were in turn enabled by the firms. This account also provides insight into financial repertoires that emerged from the bottom-up. Not only are these two sets of forces crucial for understanding how the firms emerged, what they enabled, and how they affected participants but they also provide insight into the monetary regimes and financial repertoires that persist in Albania. In particular, the firms channeled migrant remittances, en-abling people with no access to formal financial institutions to have access to multiple currencies. This practice constitutes a persistent feature of low finance in postsocialist Albania.

The market reforms of the early 1990s shook the foundations of the financial structure that had prevailed during fifty years of an extreme form of the com-mand economy. Postsocialist transformations entailed profound changes in the forms and functions of money. Money, which had been limited to perform-ing exchange, payment, and unit of account functions came to constitute a prime store of value, a means of accumulating new forms of wealth—from everyday con-sumer goods to housing. These changes in the functions of money from the top-down and global to local level increased the pressure on local people to seek more cash as a means of socioeconomic and cultural mobility. But this demand for wealth in cash came at a time of limited access to formal banking institutions by a vast majority of people who lost other sources of wealth (such as employment or savings). The firms, hence, served as an alternative banking system for the ma-jority of the (unbanked) population in Albania. The suggestion that the firms acted as banks came up repeatedly in my conversations with kreditorë. Some re-called the various public claims by former firm owners that their firm had ap-plied for banking licenses (according to official sources, only one firm had done so).

Another opportunity for speculation that led directly to the wealth accumula-tion of the firms was the privatization scheme through letra me vlerë. Like other forms of privatization vouchers, letra me vlerë were a market device intended to convert state-owned wealth into privately owned wealth. In Albania, letra me vlerë were also tradable for cash in the informal currency exchange markets. This dual aspect of letra me vlerë—as a fixed unit of value in state property (their nominal value) and as a floating value as currency (market value)—quickly led to their depreciation. In practice, letra me vlerë were traded by the firm owners to accumulate state wealth at low cost while yielding meager wealth in cash for those who traded them in currency exchange markets. This in turn led to a dual process of rapid dispossession for a majority of citizens and rapid accumulation for a small group of entrepreneurs. The pattern constituted a bifurcated pathway of value conversion that was central to the accumulation of wealth by the firms. Other entrepreneurs also built their initial wealth through the same process of value conversion from state-owned to privately owned wealth through letra me vlerë.

In addition, the firms mediated other pathways of value conversion that emerged from bottom-up financial repertories. The emerging cash economy and the flow of remittances in multiple currencies were key sources of wealth channeled through the firms. Attention to these bottom-up practices brings forth a more complex picture of financial speculation in neoliberal times. Among other things, these practices underscore the mutual imbrication and co-constitution of processes of formalization and informalization of the economy (Guyer 2004; James 2015); the multiple entanglements of capitalist economies with other logics and practices of accumulation (Gibson-Graham 1996; Tsing 2015); and the new monetary practices and repertoires that emerge at the interstices of these logics.

By their design, the firms intermediated various conversions of value across different currency regimes. They also provided the possibility (albeit short-lived) of accumulating wealth of more enduring value. In offering to transact in multiple currencies, the firms provided a means for vulnerable kreditorë to store and circulate their remittances in currencies of varying softness and hardness, and hence of different durability over time. As such, the firms tapped an emerging unofficial economy and capitalized on local desires for saving in multiple currencies as a means of hedging the risk of further devaluations and dispossessions.

The preference for multiple currencies continues to constitute a highly valued form of wealth in Albania. The cash economy dominates exchanges and financial transactions even though banking has expanded its reach, and more people have access to and make use of formal financial services. Although not as diverse in the kinds of currencies in circulation (due primarily to the advent of the euro), the Albanian currency regime is still dominated by multiple currencies. For instance, home values in contemporary Albania are calculated in euros, and home purchases are often made in euros. Some companies pay their employees in dollars or euros, and people often carry around multiple currencies in their wallets. Sharing a cab with a friend in the summer of 2015, I noticed she paid the driver in euros and accepted the change in lek. Many hotels and bed and breakfasts in the south of the country where I conduct my current research advertised their rates in euros and accepted euros (but not dollars) as payment. When I offered to pay in lek, they converted their rates from euros to lek.

The presence of this multicurrency regime is caused by various factors, some of which emerged and persisted since the early 1990s, others emerged after the creation of the European Union. Despite these changes, what has remained consistent over the first twenty-five years that followed the collapse of the communist regime is a multicurrency regime that permeates all spheres of economic life. This preference for multiple currencies has economic, social, and cultural significance. Access to various currencies constitutes a form of wealth with more durability over time. Further, different currencies carry different cultural and political histories and symbolic meaning. Given Albania's isolationist and nationalist monetary policies during the later period of the communist regime, gaining access to multiple currencies expresses the desire for a cosmopolitan and European identity and future.

3

"WORKING THE MONEY"

Migrants, Remittances, and Social Ties

> The worst was that we were working the money [*e punonim paranë*],
> we would deposit the interests back into the firms. So that it would
> multiply [*shtohej*] even more. . . . It was the sweat of my and my
> husband's labor, both husband and wife we suffered migration [*e
> hëngrëm imigracionin*] and then came here and threw it all into the
> firms [*e hodhëm te firmat*].
>
> —Former kreditor, Vlora, 2008

Media reporting and policy analysis of the firms—the pyramid schemes prevalent in Albania in the 1990s—emphasize illegal sources of cash, from the breach of the UN embargo against former Yugoslavia to the illicit trafficking of humans, drugs, and arms. These explanations do not account for all the cash that circulated through the firms, nor do they capture the number of people involved. For instance, the flow of remittances to Albania, which have been estimated at $700 million annually between 1993 and 1998, accounted for the quick rise of the firms (Korovilas 1999). These macroeconomic estimates are corroborated by the *kreditorë*'s (creditors/investors) recollections. Indeed, stories of migrant remittances lost to the firms abound, particularly in southern Albania, from where hundreds of thousands of young people went to Italy and Greece in search of employment and a better life. Of the kreditorë I interviewed in Vlora, the famed "capital of fajde [moneylending]" (Sejdarasi 1996, 11), everyone had migrant kin abroad or had been a migrant worker at some point in the 1990s. This is another aspect of the rise of the firms in Albania—albeit one that has received too little attention.

Manjola had one of the most telling stories of losing her migrant remittances to the firms. At the time of our conversation, Manjola was in her mid-forties and worked as an accountant for a local municipality in Vlora. She commuted from Narta, a nearby village. She lived with her in-laws and her two children while her husband remained "in migration" (*në imigracion*) in Greece, as did all of her immediate and extended kin. Manjola had migrated to Greece in 1992 and returned to Albania four years later. Upon her return, she invested her savings (estimated

94

at US$80,000) to Vefa. In early 1997, when Vefa suspended all transactions, Manjola had only a couple of months to go until her returns were due. She lost all her money when the firm collapsed.

Remembering this loss a decade after the collapse, Manjola exclaimed with frustration: "that was the sweat of me and my husband's work, both husband and wife we suffered migration [*e hëngrëm imigracionin*] and then came here and threw it all to the firms [*e hodhëm te firmat*]." Manjola's feelings are shared by hundreds of thousands who spent years working low-paying jobs as migrants in Greece or Italy only to see their savings vanish overnight when the firms collapsed. Manjola's life story speaks to the mass movement of people and money in Albania at the end of the twentieth century. Her decisions to migrate and then to participate in the firms echo investment repertoires that many Albanians mobilized in the early 1990s as a means to gain wealth and to achieve a good life.

According to Manjola, she did not only lose monetary value to the firms; most important, she lost the fruits of her labor as a migrant. Manjola's trajectory brings attention to another pathway of value conversion: the circulation of remittances to the speculative firms. This pathway of value conversion, I note in this chapter, also points to a set of investment repertoires that intertwined with the circulation of money at the firms. Here, I approach the notion of repertoires as economic practices with particular cultural histories that emerge, go dormant, and reemerge at different times, and are generative of new economic realities but are not yet solidified as institutions (Guyer 2004, 97–99, 116). I focus on social networks and the remittance economy as two investment repertoires mobilized to create new forms of wealth. First, I look into the use of intermediaries to invest in the firms. One type of intermediary were the *sekser/ë* (broker/s) and *menaxherë* (managers) who were paid by the firms for bringing in deposits. Another type was *i/të njohur* (connection/s), more familiar intermediaries who facilitated deposits for kin and friends either for free or as a favor. Both types of intermediaries played an essential role in establishing the public's trust in the firms. Second, I explore the transnational migrant networks as a key conduit of cash to the firms. These networks of intermediaries constitute a key site for exploring how monetary transactions at the firms intertwined with the social ties among kin and transnational migrant communities.

By looking at how the firms tapped into social networks and remittance flows and at how kreditorë channeled their remittances to the firms via kin, this chapter engages in a broader discussion about the intertwining of finance and social ties (Zelizer 1996, 1997), especially in the case of speculative finance (Hertz 1998; Ho 2009). I suggest that social ties enabled and fueled the financial speculation of the firms. The firms generated more deposits by actively mobilizing social ties between kin, connections, and migrants. At the same time, by participating in the firms, kreditorë sought to transform their social worlds.

Of Money and Social Ties

A long tradition within economic theory and moral philosophy juxtaposes money and social ties. Money transcends, depersonalizes, and commodifies transactions between people. As sociologist Georg Simmel (1967) puts it, it is credited with rationalizing and depersonalizing relations while also enabling people at farther distances to connect. According to Karl Marx ([1867] 1990), through this depersonalizing quality, money veils the social structures of inequality at the heart of the capitalist mode of production, distribution, and consumption. These perspectives on money have informed the work of anthropologists studying the social transformations in various locations undergoing industrialization and expansion of the capitalist economy.[1] At the same time, key anthropological studies have also questioned this dichotomy and provided accounts of a more complex relationship between money and social ties.

The pioneering works by Malinowski ([1922] 2008) and Mauss ([1925] 1954) were an effort to critique economic theories that separated markets from social relations. Decades later, landmark edited volumes by Appadurai (1986) and Parry and Bloch (1989) reset the conversations within economic anthropology—dominated until then by the formalist versus substantivist debate—emphasizing the calculative dimension of the gift (see also Bourdieu 1977) and the social aspects of market exchanges. Parry and Bloch (1989) note that the moral suspicion toward money was a cultural construct, informed primarily by a tradition of moral philosophy prevalent in Western European thought and practice. This philosophy, they argue, was not universally shared by other cultural traditions. In the Anglo-American context, this dichotomy has been challenged by the sociologist Viviana Zelizer (1997), who meticulously traces various practices of earmarking different kinds of money used for different social purposes and relations. Zelizer's observation that money and social ties combine in different ways resonated with others working across various cultural contexts and encountering different configurations of money and social relations (Halawa and Olcoń-Kubicka 2018; Kwon 2015; Villarreal, Guérin, and Kumar 2018). Anthropologists of finance note that social networks and rituals are central to the everyday operations of financial markets (Hertz 1998; Ho 2009; Zaloom 2006). Finally, social relations such as kinship and forms of identity such as race, gender, and nationality are crucial to economic institutions from property to finance to trusts (Humphrey and Verdery 2004; Maurer 2000; Vevaina 2014).

Kreditorë's patterns of investment underscore the complex interplay between money and social ties. For kreditorë, social ties ensured more trust, more confidence in the firms. They often pointed to social ties as the reason for their participation at the firms. Kreditorë thus resisted the image of abstract and impersonal finance, grounding their financial dealings instead in the personal nature of their relationship to the conduit, be that a sekser or të njohur. These patterns of investing at the firms reveal a concept of money that is always already personal, intimate, and social.

Money Mediators: Sekserë and Të njohur

Intermediaries known as sekserë and të njohur featured prominently in the stories of recruitment of the kreditorë. Often, when asked about the initial decision to deposit into a given firm, kreditorë would mention that they "had a të njohur at Gjallica" or handed the money to "someone that was a sekser, a relative of [their] wife." In other cases, the intermediary was "a neighbor who collected money from the building," a "trusted i njohur," or a relative.

The first category of intermediaries, the sekserë, referred to individuals who were either hired by the firms or gained a commission, often an additional cut on the interest returns of the kreditorë.[2] Sekserë were ambiguous social figures: some kreditorë blamed them for their losses, while others described them as close connections that were equally victims of the firms. The term "sekser" refers to a broker that carries out a financial transaction on behalf of another, and was used in the mid-1990s to refer to individuals that mediated deposits and recruited investors to the firms. The term continues to be used to refer more generally to brokers of legitimate or illegitimate business deals. These transactions span real estate sales to bribing public officials (see also Musaraj 2018). In the context of the firms, sekser/ë (and menaxher/ë) referred to brokers paid by the firms to recruit kreditorë. Often, sekserë were close or distant relatives; in other cases, they were acquaintances or total strangers.

The other category of intermediaries, i/të njohur, refers to someone "in the know" who provides access to scarce or forbidden goods, services, or favors.[3] A i njohur could be an acquaintance, a close friend or relative, or a work colleague. "Sekser/ë" and "i/të njohur" would sometimes overlap. But they also differ in important ways. Both terms refer to third parties that are trusted based on social connection and familiarity. Often, the sekser who mediated a deposit at a firm was a i njohur. But sekser also implied a more business relation than a connection. Sekserë usually gained a material benefit from the transaction, whereas të njohur did not necessarily receive a payment. Instead, the "payment" was rendered as social capital or favors to be cashed in later. Seksërë was an ambiguous professional category. Like brokers in other financial realms (such as stock markets), seksërë were paid for investing other people's money. Unlike stock market brokers, seksërë were not licensed; most had no training in accounting or finance; and they invested their own money too at the firms.

Another critical distinction between sekser/ë and i/të njohur relates to the genealogy of these terms. The term "sekser/ë" belongs to the postsocialist era and is used to refer to different kinds of brokers who mediate a transaction between two parties for a commission. By contrast, "i/të njohur" was a widespread term pre-1990s. During the communist regime, të njohur facilitated access to government privileges or scarce goods (see Musaraj 2009, 159–64). The term is synonymous with the Russian *blat* (Ledeneva 1998) or the Chinese *guanxi* (Yang 1994), both referring to the use of social networks to obtain goods and services in the communist economies of shortage (Kornai 1979; Verdery 1996). In the postsocialist context, transactions with connections continue to imply a relationship mediated by gifts and favors, an exchange that does not necessarily entail monetary gain, but that often entails mutual obligation and trust. Building up and maintaining such networks of të njohur then and now constitutes an investment repertoire in and of itself.[4]

Making and Breaking Social Ties

Kreditorë emphasized social ties as a source of trust in their financial transactions with the firms. They repeatedly referred to seksërë and të njohur to emphasize their relationships with the firms. They went out of their way to show that they did not invest their money in an abstract and distant entity but with someone they knew and trusted, someone who had reassured the kreditorë of the stacks of cash in the coffers of the firms or who had invested their own money. By emphasizing social relations, trust, and familiarity with the firms, kreditorë thus insisted on a personalized and socialized rather than abstract and disembedded finance.[5] These transactions also strengthened social ties. Participation at the firms brought people closer together. Deals with the firms were a source of excitement; kin engaged in passionate conversations about future investment plans or enjoyed acts of conspicuous consumption (lavish dinners in restaurants, hosting feasts) thanks to the firms's returns.

The firms' collapse impacted social ties. Some blamed seksërë for inciting people to participate or for misinforming them about the terms of their contracts with the firms. Ermira, a cashier at one of the firms, noted that "in Vlora, seksërë did a lot of dirty things [*bënë shumë pislliqe*]." Like Ermira, many others described how some sekserë took a significant cut from the interest returns from the kreditorë they represented, often without the latter's knowledge. For instance, Skënder depicted sekserë as untrustworthy people, "who committed fraud." He noted that he deposited his money himself every three months but that this entailed waiting in long lines. One day, he ran into a friend qua sekser who told him: "I have a të njohur here that finishes up the deal quickly." He told the sekser he wanted to "lock his money" for three months but, instead, the sekser "locked it" for one year without Skënder's knowledge. There was a significant difference in the interest applied to these two timeframes. Three-month deposits accumulated 5 percent interest, whereas yearlong deposits accrued 10 percent interest. The sekser would give him a small amount of cash every three months, "pretending the account was locked for three-month deposits." One day, when he went to the firm directly to withdraw his interest, the teller of the branch told Skënder that, according to their records, his account was locked for a year. From his calculations, the sekser had made around US$6,000 on his money. The one-year contract cost Skënder his entire deposit because he was not able to withdraw the money before his due date, which was set past the date the firm collapsed. Although this was beyond the sekser's control, Skënder could not help but blame the sekser for his losses.

In Skënder's case, the sekser was a distant acquaintance, so it was easy to cut ties. But in other instances, when the sekser was close kin, the negotiation of relationships was more complicated. Some kreditorë reported chilled relationships with sekserë and të njohur; others maintained contact and relationality despite the losses. I asked Durim how his relatives reacted after they lost their deposits. He said: "Look, when I took the money from my brothers and sisters and others, I made it very clear that, as long as the firms are concerned, I take the responsibility for the money, but if they fall, they fall for me as for everyone else." He said that he had not experienced any animosity from relatives when the firm he brokered for went bankrupt. Likewise, a kreditor I call Muhamet shared the story of his dealings with a relative who had acted as a sekser to one of the firms. The relative had borrowed money from Muhamet to make a deposit at one of the firms and take a cut from the returns. However, he lost the money and could not pay his debt to Muhamet, and migrated to the United States after the collapse of the firms. Although Muhamet lamented the loss of the money and did not forget that he was owed a debt, he still maintained a good relationship with his relative.

What emerges from these various stories are testimonies of financial investments intertwined with and facilitated by social ties. Such patterns of investment were not exclusive to the firms; they continue to be a standard way of doing business in Albania. As such, they provide insight into enduring forms of entrepreneurship that have emerged through the course of postsocialist transformations.

The trajectories of transactions by kreditorë suggest a multidirectional relationship between money and social ties, whereby each impacts the other, often in unpredictable ways.

Throwing Remittances to the Firms

In Vlora, in particular, I heard repeated accounts from kreditorë whose primary source of cash for the firms were remittances. The city's location—across the Adriatic Sea from Italy and a few hours' drive from the Greek border—and its rising unemployment in the early 1990s led to mass migration, which continues to this day. Vlora was also a hub for a number of the firms as well as a key node of trafficking activities (of drugs, arms, humans). It is not surprising then that a number of the stories involving remittances and pyramid firms' participation come from residents of this city.

Manjola was one of many Vlora residents whose migration story intertwined with the history of the rise and fall of the firms. Everyone in Manjola's village had kin that migrated to Greece. Everyone, noted Manjola, invested at the firms. Under the communist regime, Narta was one of the few villages that had received recognition of being a Greek ethnic minority (*minoritarë*).[6] Manjola grew up speaking Greek at home and in the village and started to learn Albanian only in the first grade. When the borders with Greece were opened in the early 1990s, almost all inhabitants of Narta received recognition of their Greek nationality (but not full citizenship) and right to employment—a privilege that most other Albanian migrants in Greece lacked at the time (see also Barjaba and King 2005; Bon 2017). This status was significant as it implied that Narta residents had an easier time, both legally and socially, finding work and residing in Greece.

After they returned to Narta in 1996, Manjola's husband took up a job as a taxi driver while Manjola was not officially employed but busied herself with administering her family's cash deposits to the notorious firms Gjallica and Vefa. Manjola recalled her transactions with these firms in great detail:

> I managed the money of everyone, my brothers, my sisters, my brothers- and sisters-in-law. . . . If you had over 10,000,000 lek [about US$100,000], you would get 10 percent interest whereas, for less than that, you would get only 8 percent. So maybe because of the interest or of the human greed to get more, we pooled it all together. Also, because everyone else was abroad, it was easier for me to withdraw the interest in one lump sum.[7]

Manjola had played the unofficial role of sekser since she collected the additional interest on the large sum of cash she had deposited at the firms. Her role as an intermediary was contingent on the social ties to her migrant kin. Manjola's operation represents a typical pattern of participation at the firms: namely, the mobilization of transnational migrant networks and of remittances as sources of cash. For most kreditorë, depositing money at the firms became a family affair. It was a topic of everyday debate and decision making among close and far away family members.

These decisions did not go uncontested. Many kreditorë recalled arguments with their partners or relatives, and final decisions that were at times unanimous, at times not. Some kreditorë, for instance, blamed their spouses for their decision to invest at the firms. Others blamed themselves and regretted not having listened to their wise spouses. Still, others refused to place the blame on a single person, insisting that theirs was a joint decision. In Manjola's case, it seemed that this was a unanimous decision dictated by the circumstances (all the other family members were abroad) but also spurred by specific incentives from the firms (the allure of the additional interest on the higher deposits).

Manjola's bundling of kin remittances to deposit at the firms illustrates an important pathway of value conversion mediated by transnational social networks. This pathway of value conversion builds on monetary repertoires that emerged from the bottom up and that take place primarily outside the official banking system. The circulations and conversions of migrant remittances constitute an enduring investment repertoire in Albania's postsocialist economy. This is an investment repertoire that had a longue durée in Albanian history while also being specific to the context of postsocialist transformations and changing geopolitical configurations in the European political space. This investment repertoire fueled the firms and persisted well beyond their collapse. Finally, this investment repertoire by definition proliferates by intertwining social ties with monetary transactions.

Great Escapers and Remitters

Migration was a widespread phenomenon in Albania before the communist regime—from the Ottoman era, through the country's independence, until the end of World War II (Bon 2017). Vlora and the Bregu region (the southern coast), in particular, have historically experienced migration. Before the establishment of the communist state, Albanians migrated to nearby Greece, Italy, and Turkey, and as far as the United States and Australia (King, Mai, and Schwandner-Sievers 2005; Tirta 1999). These earlier migration patterns were known as *kurbet* (from the Turkish *gurbet*, or "going to a foreign land"). The communist regime portrayed kurbet as a symptom of a sick society, and it sought to prove its own healthy state by seeking to ban travel and movement at all costs (see also Vullnetari 2012).[8]

The isolation and highly politicized nature of travel became one of the most draconic (and much derided) policies of an increasingly paranoid communist regime. Citizens of Albania were not issued passports unless they were traveling abroad with government permission (granted only to those who had ties to authorities). Going into exile was considered an act of treason, with dire consequences for the family members left behind. For instance, my grandmother's two brothers went into exile around the 1960s. This caused a rift within the family. The closest kin (the immediate family of one of the brothers and their mother) were persecuted and shunned as people with a "bad biography."[9] The children of the brother in exile were banned from higher education and professional jobs. Meanwhile, my grandmother had to choose between her kin and her immediate family. Choosing the latter protected her children from the possible implications of a "bad biography"—no right to higher education, potential relocation to remote regions, hard labor. Such choice also entailed cutting ties with her mother, brother, and sisters. She chose the children over her mother and suffered the consequences in silence for many years. It was not until the early 1990s, at the age of ten, that I learned I had another great-grandmother and a whole other set of relatives who lived in Vlora, and that my father had two uncles settled in the United States, one in New York City and the other one in Houston, Texas.

The lifting of restrictions on the right to travel for all Albanian citizens in the early 1990s opened new paths of migration. Given the strict control and surveillance of movement and migration during the communist regime, it was no surprise that the collapse of the regime was set in motion by the silent revolt of thousands of young Albanians storming the European embassies in Tirana in the summer of 1990. This first act of revolution by escape was followed by thousands of others overcrowding the refugee boats to Italy, and by hundreds of thousands regularly crossing the border to Greece by foot. Migration to Italy and Greece continued en masse despite the deportations and other anti-immigrant policies and media campaigns (see, for instance, Kapllani and Mai 2005). The mass escape toward these neighboring countries has been attributed to many factors. Some of the most obvious were economic. Albania came out from the communist regime impoverished, and it experienced high levels of unemployment in the 1990s as state-run enterprises, factories, and cooperatives closed down. In addition, media images of life on the other side of the Iron Curtain played a role in depicting life of leisure and luxury in an imagined Europe (see Barjaba and King 2005; Mai 2001).

Over the years, most of these migrants have taken jobs in construction, agriculture, and services. For the most part, they were unregistered, underpaid, and insecure. Many migrants experienced "occupational deskilling" (Barjaba and King 2005, 17) as they could only find low-skill jobs, despite having completed higher education. In the first years of transition, migrants became a primary source of income for thousands of families who lost their jobs with the closing of state-owned factories and the dismantling of agricultural cooperatives. For those remaining in Albania, having kin abroad provided access to different value regimes—in multiple currencies and various sources of employment. Access to remittances thus constituted a valuable source of value and wealth. Remittances and migrant networks continue to provide economic support to a large number of people in Albania, especially those at the margins of official economic opportunities and resources.

In addition to being "great escapers" (Barjaba 2003), Albanian migrants have proved to be great remitters, sending a large portion of their incomes to relatives back home (Piperno 2005; Vullnetari and King 2011). By 1996, estimates Nicholson (2004), remittances constituted 17 percent of investments in microenterprises (101), a higher percentage than state and international investment. From 1994 to 2001, remittances constituted a significant portion of the national GDP, fluctuating between 9 to 15 percent (IMF 2003, 11), thus showing a steady flow before and after the collapse of the firms. Scholars have noted that migration was an unofficial source of economic development in Albania over the first twenty five years of the free-market economy (Korovilas 1999; Nicholson 2001, 2004).[10] Contribution to development back home was not just in remittances but also through investment in local businesses (microenterprises, house building, etc.).

Migration scholars and development practitioners have acknowledged the role of remittances as a significant source of economic development (Maimbo and Ratha 2005; Ratha 2016). Studies on the Albanian migration note that the very act of migrating is a type of investment, a form of financial security, a source of credit (Hoti 2009; King, Mai, and Schwandner-Sievers 2005; King and Vullnetari 2003; Nicholson 2001). But, often, development analysis of migration and the remittance economy isolate economic drivers and effects from other social and cultural aspirations. Stories of migration and participation in the firms point to other calculations and aspirations at play in decisions to invest in both of these economic spheres.

According to King and Vullnetari (2003, 49), remittances were used for the following reasons (in decreasing order of priorities): basic economic survival, making repairs or extensions on the home, performing social obligations (funerals, weddings, baptisms, etc.), as a means of maintaining respect in the community, education of children, and small business projects. James Korovilas (1999) notes that in the early to mid-1990s, remittances were used as deposits to the firms. The author attributes the large scale of the firms as well as the relatively gentle impact of their collapse to the size and ongoing flow of remittances to Albania at that time (see also Nicholson 1999, 2004).

Remittances are a case in point for how money and social ties intertwine in expected and unexpected ways. June Hee Kwon describes remittances as "a promise of love" that build connections across transnational families while also causing tension in the discussions over the "ambiguous ownership of remittances" and over the distances that couples, parents, children, and siblings have to negotiate (2015, 492–93). Transnational migrant networks help facilitate transfers of wealth in money as well as materials, dreams, and lifestyles (see also Dalakoglou 2010a). People at the margins use migrant networks as ways to get ahead financially and socially in their localities. Remittance transfers constitute a form of social payment, a gift (Kusimba, Yang, and Chawla 2016; Small 2019). They entail the imbrication of market and social exchanges, of money from work with payments to kin. Relations thus play a crucial role in the transmission and conversion of remittances. In turn, the flow of remittances reshapes relationships among transnational families and kin.

Family structure has shaped the patterns and amounts of remittance transfers among Albanian migrants (Vullnetari and King 2011). Notably, these exchanges have been dominated by patriarchal family structures, with men being the primary source of remittances to families back home. These relationships between migrants and their kin, and between social norms and wealth accumulation, played an essential role in transactions with the firms. Remittances from various countries accounted for the multicurrency nature of the operations of the firms. Also, the flow of remittances from transnational kin networks to the firms entailed the negotiation of different social ties.

Remittances and Kinship Relations

The decisionmaking process around investing remittances at the firms varied widely among the kreditorë. The three individuals I discuss were colleagues at a government office in Vlora. They all came to work there from different parts of the city and nearby villages. Their stories exemplify the main patterns of the post-1990s migratory movements—Albania to Greece, rural to urban.

Dalipi was fifteen in 1996 and worked illegally in construction in Greece. He sent remittances regularly to his father living in Gjuerin, a village near Vlora. He described how he and his immediate family had invested in and then lost their remittances to Vefa: "We weren't here [in Albania]. We would come back for one month. That's it. We all worked in migration, the whole family. We would work there like horses, and these ones here gave all the money away. These ones were circulating [*xhironin*] the money."[11] Dalipi's angry comments pointed to the relational tensions generated by participation in the firms. Dalipi distinguished between the migrant family members ("we") and the ones staying behind ("these ones"), scolding the latter for wasting the money earned with so much sacrifice. More specifically, Dalipi directed his wrath toward his father, who had unilaterally decided to deposit Dalipi's remittances to the firms.

As in Dalipi's case, remittances were often considered obligatory "payments" to the heads of the family and thus not subject to the earners' investment plans or wishes. These payments were an expression of the "filial duty" of migrants abroad (King, Castaldo, and Vullnetari 2011). The entanglements of remittance money with the firms' activities thus further reinforced existing gendered hierarchies that organized relations among kin (see also King and Vullnetari 2011). In other words, kinship relationships structured the flow of remittances through the firms.

In Manjola's case, the structure of kin relations had a slightly different trajectory. As the wife of the youngest son, Manjola was obliged by customary standards to remain back in Narta to care for her in-laws.[12] Thus, her positioning was structured by similar norms as those of Dalipi's family. At the same time, Manjola asserted her agency in the decisionmaking process around investing the remittances at the firms. By consensus among her kin abroad, upon her return to Albania, she assumed the authority of administering everyone's money. Her kin trusted her with the decisionmaking power over their remittances and were fully aware of the investment in the firms. Unlike Dalipi's father, however, Manjola acted as a sekser of the investments into the firms. She received the additional 1 percent interest for her work but took great care in keeping track of the individual accounts so that each family received their respective interest.

A third example is Andon, who resided in Albania at the time and who administered his savings and his brother's remittances at the firms. Andon was a civil engineer by training and had worked for the city hall in Vlora in the early 1990s. During this time, he had been able to save some money. Unlike Manjola, Andon had not migrated; but like Manjola, in addition to depositing his savings, he also managed his brother's money at the firms. His brother was a migrant in Greece. The brothers had agreed to invest at the firms together. They deposited the money under one account and planned to build a home that would accommodate both of their families. Andon had invested at Gjallica and Kamberi starting in 1994. He had been able to withdraw some interest over the years. Andon used the interest to invest in the construction of their house, designed with two stories, one for each brother. He continued the construction in a piecemeal fashion until he had lost the deposits with the firms' collapse.

After the collapse, Andon's brother returned from Greece and settled in Vlora. It had taken Andon a decade to complete the ground floor of the house. He used his brother's remittances and his own meager savings to complete the first stage of construction. He offered his brother the chance to move in first, partly because the latter had a bigger family and partly because Andon felt responsible for his brother's loss of remittances to the firms. Andon was still waiting to move into his part of the house at the time of our conversation in 2008. The brothers continued to be on good terms and had remained committed to their plan to live together in one house on two separate floors.

These three examples capture how migration and remittances constituted key "investment repertoires" (Guyer 2004, 97–99) in postsocialist Albania. These financial flows are mediated by kinship networks organized by norms of obligation, reciprocity, and social hierarchy. Remittances also flowed to the firms of the 1990s through these social networks. But the particular configurations of kinship ties and specific investment decisions varied from family to family. In Dalipi's case, for instance, the circulation of remittances through the firms was subject to and further reinforced a patriarchal and centralized family structure. Dalipi's father collected remittances as social payment and had full authority to decide how these would be invested. In this particular case, money was fully subjected to norms and hierarchies of kinship.

Manjola gained the authority to manage the remittances of her kin by being the wife of the youngest son and the only one of the wives to have returned from migration. Her return followed other social norms among families across the south—that of the youngest son being responsible for caring for the parents. This social positionality afforded Manjola some agency over the administration of remittances. In her case, the money was bundled together and invested as a family, and her position as mediator was derivative of kinship norms. However, within the big bundle, each account was treated as a separate account. Kinship ties served as a conduit of the cash to the firms. Meanwhile, Manjola gained a different status by mediating the money from kin—an experience that had come in handy in her job as an accountant for the municipal office.

Finally, Andon's investment also followed in the footsteps of traditional norms of shared property among brothers, yet here the decision-making process was consensual and, to a certain extent, egalitarian. In this case, money and kinship ties intertwined in a mutually reinforcing way. Kinship ties translated into business partnerships while monetary gains and losses restructured kinship hierarchies (such as the priority given to the migrant brother to enter the new house first).

A comparison of these three cases indicates diverse configurations of kinship relations, remittances, and deposits to the firms. These findings resonate with other research on remittances. According to Vullnetari and King (2011), by and large decisions around investing remittance money at the firms were often guided by patriarchal family structure and by filial obligations. But exceptions were quite common. Women are increasingly in charge of remittances and engaged in migrant work.[13] Although the hierarchies of the decision-making process differed across families, the intertwining of social ties with financial decisions remained constant. Investments at the firms were directed by family structure.

This interplay between social ties and money was not one-directional. While kinship relations, with their forms of reciprocity and obligation, channeled the flow of remittances through the firms, the outcome of these investments in turn shaped social relationships. For instance, in Dalipi's case, the loss of remittances to the firms caused conflict and resentment between father and son. Consequently, Dalipi assumed more authority over his finances once back in Albania. He now sidelined his father when making decisions about managing his money. The restructuring of financial authority in Dalipi's family took place without severing relations as such. In Manjola's case, managing the family's remittances gave her more agency and accounting experience, all the while conforming to the cultural norms of caring for the elderly. For Andon, the collapse of the firms, while not necessarily straining relations with his brother, nonetheless was a factor in determining who had priority of entitlement over the property.

These different trajectories point to complex ways in which social ties channeled remittances through the firms and were, in turn, shaped and reshaped by the outcome of the firms' rise and fall. But in addition to social relations, the firms' collapse played a crucial role in people's life trajectories. Here, too, the speculative firms intertwined with the remittance economy insofar as participants sought in the former the fulfillment of some of the same aspirations and plans for future financial and social mobility that they had also sought through the latter. As migration yielded slower income at a high price of labor and low social status, the firms promised to accelerate wealth accumulation as well as social mobility. The collapse of the firms altered the expectations and trajectories of these life plans and aspirations.

"Working the Money" to Change the Future

Manjola's trajectory since the collapse of the firms captures how the plans and aspirations that fueled the mass migration of the early 1990s intertwined with and were reshaped by the rise and fall of the firms:

Sometimes we did not withdraw the interests [at the end of the contract]. The worst was that we were working the money [*e punonim paranë*], we would deposit the interests back into the firms. So that it would multiply [*shtohej*] even more. . . . On January 7, [1997], Gjallica experienced the first tremors; our contract ended on the 24th, we were able to collect the interests from Vefa. I had 14,000,000 lek [about US$140,000], I was only able to get one installment of interest, and that was it, everything else was gone. I was left without a house, without money, the troubles [*trazirat*] started. It was catastrophic . . . I lost 13,000,000 lek [US$130,000], let's say that 5,000,000–6,000,000 lek [US$50,000–60,000] went there [the accrued interest] but at least that 8,000,000 lek [US$80,000] was mine. It was the sweat of my and my husband's labor, both husband and wife we suffered migration [*e hëngrëm imigracionin*] and then came here and threw it all into the firms [*e hodhëm te firmat*].

Manjola's analogy between the remittance money and "the sweat of [migrant] labor" evokes a Marxist understanding of the social relations of production in a global capitalist economy. Manjola had experienced firsthand the reality of low wages for hard labor and she, as many others, tried to turn her positionality around by seeking to make capital. This is what she meant by "working the money" at the firms, thus capturing a classic capitalist logic of wealth accumulation.[14] Manjola's description of this transfer of capital from migrant wages to cash for the firms illustrates how the migration economy intertwined with speculative finance.

Remittances became a lifeline for most migrant families, and many sought to accelerate the accumulation of this form of wealth.[15] In some cases, this desire for accelerated wealth revealed the eagerness to end the hard labor in the underground economy in Greece, Italy, and elsewhere. By providing a mechanism (albeit unsustainable) for such acceleration of wealth, the firms offered a possible way out of migration. In other words, the firms presented kreditorë with an alternative financial temporality than the one provided by migrant labor. These different financial temporalities informed people's decisions and plans for their futures.

Manjola lost all her remittances to Gjallica and Vefa in early 1997. Manjola's lament of "throwing" the sweat of her migrant labor to the firms pointed to the broader aspirations and losses that kreditorë experienced by participating in the firms. In addition to the eighty thousand dollars, Manjola lamented losing the years of migrant labor that she and her husband had endured. In a sense, this loss highlighted the various forms of value (money, time, labor) negotiated through the firms. Her lament is especially bitter, given her life trajectory since the collapse of the firms. Manjola's husband saw no other choice but return to

Greece, where he continued to work at the time of our conversation in 2008. At that time, most residents of Narta were in migration, and the village resembled the tales of kurbet in nineteenth-century Albania: the elderly and women caught in between waiting and mourning their husbands. Manjola did not express the same degree of sadness that permeates kurbet stories, however. She had accepted her fate and had created an active life for herself between her job at the municipality and enjoying the trips to the seashore with her children and friends. Economically, she had survived and was financially comfortable, thanks in large part to the flow of remittances from her husband and kin.

Indeed, the collapse of the firms set off what is known as the third wave of migration in Albania; many of the returned migrants and new migrants headed abroad (Barjaba and King 2005). Migration continues to be an important aspect of life in Albania. Some migrants leave for good and settle in other countries taking their families along. Others work seasonally and return home for part of the year. Often these migrants set up small businesses in Albania. This is the case in the south of Albania, especially the coast, where many migrants have set up bed and breakfasts in the small tourist towns and villages. Migration to obtain higher education is also a way for young Albanians (such as myself) to go abroad. Once settled as students, many seek opportunities to stay abroad. Some return temporarily or permanently.

Remittances have outlasted the firms and they continue to contribute to Albania's economy. Although still taking place mostly outside the official banking system, remittances are calculated alongside other sources of wealth contributing to the GDP. Some have argued that remittances helped buffer the drastic economic consequences of the collapse of the firms (Korovilas 1999). As migration out of Albania is ongoing, remittances continue to be a significant source of investment and development funds for those staying behind. Remittances and migration, thus, constitute an enduring investment repertoire in postsocialist Albania. This investment repertoire continues to be mediated by transnational kinship and social ties.

Conclusion

Though much of the rubble of the infamous year *nëndhteshtata* (year ninety-seven) has been cleared, and the country has experienced significant economic and infrastructural growth since then, the collapse of the firms has left a visible imprint on the national economy and individual life trajectories. For Manjola, Dalipi, and Andon, the collapse of the firms entailed a radical rewriting of their lives. Manjola's husband returned to Greece, leaving her to care for her in-laws and children, with all of her other kin abandoning any plans for returning to Albania. Dalipi returned to Albania; his lack of status in Greece discouraged him from seeking employment there again, and his lack of remittances made it harder to rebuild a life in Albania. He managed to get by but remained bitter about his lost years of migration and the dreams of a good life in Europe. Andon's brother, too, returned, and they both struggled to recuperate from their losses by seeking work and slowly building their joint house.

The social norms and networks facilitated the channeling of cash to the firms, but the collapse of the firms also had a significant impact on restructuring social relations. Most important, these intertwined dynamics between money and social ties underscore the emergence and endurance of investment repertoires that have become important modes of accumulating wealth in postsocialist Albania. Intermediaries such as sekserë and të njohur continue to play a crucial role in business life in Albania. The use of të njohur in business is widespread, especially among small- and medium-sized enterprises and family businesses, which continue to constitute a large portion of employers and sources of income. Meanwhile, the figure of the sekser has become an institution, especially in dealings with businesses and the state. Sekserë act as brokers for business deals. They also intermediate ethically ambivalent transactions between public officials and private citizens or businesses (Musaraj 2018). Further, the remittance economy continues to constitute a key source of economic development and stability, a source of investment capital, and a point of access to other forms and scales of wealth and other employment, education and life opportunities.

A crucial aspect of both types of enduring investment repertoires is social ties. Social ties played an essential role in the firms' recruitment efforts. This Albanian story is not unique; similar use of social networks played a role in the original Ponzi scheme by Charles Ponzi as well as in the Bernie Madoff scam. Likewise, community ties drew the Maya in Guatemala into the pyramid scheme *El Millionario* (Nelson 2012). The stories of the Albanian firms are crucial to understanding how financial speculation can take hold through highly personalized financial transactions rather than the abstraction of capital.

Further, participation in the firms shaped social ties in unexpected ways. While migrant networks and the flow of remittances unintentionally fueled the speculative activities of the firms, the collapse of the firms affected relations among kin. It also affected people's plans and life goals. Used by migrants as a means of shortening their time in migration, the firms sparked another wave of migration abroad when they collapsed. The temporalities of the social and economic transformations that many of the kreditorë aspired toward have been slower than the ones anticipated at the time of the firms' boom. It took Manjola multiple years, for instance, to build her new home that she planned to complete in 1997. The construction of her house materialized the unpredictable and often unreliable temporality of remittance transfers while also entrenching migration as a permanent (rather than temporary) condition.

In addition to relying on remittances, Manjola, Dalipi, and Andon accepted government jobs as a means of securing regular (albeit meager) income and benefits. Having access to multiple sources of income has become a must in Albania, where economic insecurity continues to plague the majority of the population, especially in the rural areas and urban peripheries. It is common, for instance, for families to have at least one member employed in a government job, a brother or sister in migration, and a private business on the side. These forms of income generation exemplify a postsocialist pattern of wealth making and investment that privileges the ability to access multiple regimes of value. The collapse of the firms crushed the dreams of accelerated wealth, leaving behind an entrenched condition of marginality for many investors. Kreditorë, such as Manjola, Dalipi, and Andon continue to rely on diverse sources of income as a means of generating new forms of wealth from their marginal socioeconomic localities.

"ALL WE WANTED WAS A BEAUTIFUL HOME"

Housing and Temporalities of Speculation

> This had become a common narrative among Albanians: "I will sell my house and will invest the money at Xhaferri, I will collect the interests and invest them at Vefa, then I will buy a car, then I will buy a house with a yard and live happily ever after in abundance."
>
> —Armand Shkullaku, *Revista Klan*, 1997

During my research, I heard many first- and secondhand accounts about people selling the privatized communist apartments so they could participate in the firms. These apartments were built during communist times and state-owned until the 1993 privatization law, which passed on ownership to their occupants. This phenomenon was so widespread in Vlora, in particular, that, as one kreditor noted, "one felt stupid *not* selling their apartment."[1] For many who did not have access to remittances, selling the privatized communist apartments was often the only way to access the large stacks of cash needed to invest at the firms. When I asked Isuf where he had come up with the two million lek (approximately US$20,000) that he deposited at Gjallica, he said that he sold his apartment that was located at the center of Vlora. At the time, the apartment was highly desirable for its location. It was built during the communist regime, followed the tight rules of allotted living space (Buchli 2000) and hence was quite small for a family of four. Isuf elaborated on why he and his wife decided to sell their apartment:

> Well, my first incentive came when a neighbor of mine migrated to Greece. And he left me his empty apartment to look after. I noticed at the time that apartments were being sold en masse. Yes, a lot of homes were for sale. And we had this empty home there. Our downstairs neighbor sold his apartment, then another one over there sold his, and then everyone in Vlora seemed to be selling. All those who sold their apartments were renting out other homes. I didn't even need to rent because I could stay in my neighbor's empty apartment [for free]. But as soon as

I made a deal with a buyer, my neighbor in Greece found out and told me that we couldn't continue to stay at his apartment because he too intended to sell. At that point, I had already given my word to the buyer. It seems stupid now but I felt bad because I gave him my word. He was ready to move in. He was coming from the village. And, so, I sold my apartment and rented another.[2]

Isuf sold his privatized apartment in the fall of 1996, a few months before the firms collapsed. He deposited the money at Gjallica, which offered to double his deposit in six months. He hoped to buy a bigger apartment or even a villa with the expected returns from Gjallica. He anticipated that he would be renting only temporarily. Alas, when the firms collapsed, Isuf lost his deposits. It took him a decade to purchase an apartment similar to the one he had "lost to the firms."

Isuf's story exemplifies the negotiation of different temporalities of finance and life through participation at the firms. His plans for how to invest in the firms and, further, how to invest profits from the firms, speak to widely shared desires for new homes. *Shtëpi*, which in Albanian refers both to house and home (see also Bon 2017; Dalakoglou 2010), continues to be a prime object of desire, a key component of the imagined good life. In this chapter, I follow the trajectories of the sale/demolition and the purchase/rebuilding of homes by several former kreditorë as a way to explore the entanglements between investing in the firms and the real estate market. This chapter is based on interviews and home visits with the kreditorë in 2008–9 and follow up conversations in 2013 and 2015. These recollections underscore how housing played a crucial role in the kreditorë's desires and decisions to participate in the firms. They also provide insight into the kreditorë's enduring aspirations to purchase new homes. The trajectories and conditions of their housing were present in discussions about the gains and losses and the progress or lagging behind that kreditorë experienced after the collapse of the firms. Obtaining the desired home was a prime subject of debate, laments, and preoccupation for the kreditorë during the time of my research, and remained so still in the mid-2000s.

By turning attention to housing, I show how financial speculation is not an isolated event but is interconnected with other market and cultural forces. Indeed, intertwined real estate bubbles and financial market crashes are legion throughout the history of capitalism. The 2008 global financial crisis and the subprime mortgage crisis in the United States is a case in point. Economic historians make a similar point when locating bubbles and crashes in periods of credit expansion (Kindelberger and Aliber 2005). Such intertwined dynamics have emerged as a consequence of increased financialization of everyday life, especially the expansion of mortgage lending (Krippner 2012; Langley 2008). As I discuss, the change in the housing regime in Albania and the emergence of a real estate market also intertwined with speculative investments in the firms. This intertwining was of a different nature than the ones fueled by financialization in the United States and elsewhere, primarily because kreditorë turned to the firms as a way to access alternative forms of housing financing because they did not have access to bank loans or were avoiding such loans. By participating in the firms, kreditorë sought to create different temporalities, of both finance and life, to those proliferating alongside the postsocialist financial institutions.

My discussion of temporality is informed by Jane Guyer's (2012) analysis of the temporal transformation from the Keynesian economy of postwar Europe to the post-Fordist neoliberal condition. Guyer describes this shift as an evacuation of the temporality of "the near future," that is, economic institutions and regimes that make it possible for people to plan and predict the short-term aspects of their lives. Instead, writes Guyer, our economic lives (in Euro-America and beyond) are increasingly shaped by a dual temporality of "the long run" (a future as a distant arrival, different and disconnected from the present) and the "punctuated present" (dated events that are sporadic and unpredictable), temporalities generated by monetarist economic policies and a progressive disappearance of the welfare state.

Similar changes to the temporalities of financial policies and practices were the backdrop of participation in the pyramid firms. As Katherine Verdery (1996) notes, the postsocialist transition entailed a profound change in the temporalities of finance and of life. During late communism, many looked up to the West for the promise of a predictable capitalist modernity. Instead, the experience of postcommunism was an intensified version of the dual temporality of the long run and punctuated present, as financial authorities pushed monetarist policies while everyday financial horizons became increasingly more uncertain. It is not surprising then that the temporalities of wealth making and life were at the heart of kreditorë's discussions about their participation at the firms. I discuss these concerns with temporality, focusing on kreditorë's decisions to sell or buy homes in conjunction with their strategies of investing in the firms. Further, I reflect on the assessments by kreditorë relating to their progress or "lagging behind" of the life trajectories that became possible and imaginable at the time of the firms' boom. I suggest that, by participating in the firms, kreditorë sought to recreate a temporality of the near future, which they viewed as the promise of a capitalist future. Buying a new home was seen as a way to materialize this modernist temporality.

The desire for new homes in the early 1990s Albania echoes those of millions of others across postsocialist and postdevelopment contexts, where buying a new home provides the promise of upward mobility, urbanization, and access to a Western consumer lifestyle (Féhervary 2013; Halawa 2015; Zhang 2010). In the early 1990s Albania, homes became a commodity; further, they became another form of capital. Homes also carried more durable value, as compared to cash. They materialized cultural and historical aspirations for the good life—a process that involves not only the search for more assets and commodities but also "the cultivation of new lifestyles, mentalities, dispositions, and aspirations" (Zhang 2010, 15). The aspirations voiced around homes that kreditorë bought or sold during the time of boom of the firms carried different visions of the future, informed in part by ideas of the good life during late communism. Based on location and appearance homes represent competing modernities. While the privatized apartments embodied a failed communist modernity, the desired new homes (apartments or villas) represent what is often described as a "European" modernity (see also Bon 2017; Dalipaj 2016). Tracing the different trajectories of housing—and the assessment of such housing by various kreditorë—I explore people's efforts to negotiate these different modernities by manipulating financial temporalities of investment at the firms and in homes.

Communist Housing and Postsocialist Real Estate

The changes to the housing regime, from one of allocation to a real estate market, constituted one of the most profound shifts that affected people's everyday lives across the postsocialist world. Zhang notes that in post-1990s China "private home ownership and commercialization of urban land are two of the most palpable changes that indicate the end of the socialist mode of city life" (2010, 26). The postsocialist transformations in Albanian were similarly made palpable through changes in the housing regime.

Housing policies and practices under communism in Albania were a peculiar bricolage of the Soviet universal right to a minimalist "living space" (Buchli 2000) and the Chinese hukou system of residence allocation (Solinger 1995; Zhang 2001). Following Stalinist practices, in the early postwar years (1945–60), the communist party-state in Albania invested in building housing blocks in both urban and rural areas (Aliaj 2008; Andoni 2010). Access to a state-owned apartment became a de facto universal right.[3] In the late 1960s, following the fallout with the Soviet Union, the Socialist Republic of Albania allied with Mao Zedong's People's Republic of China. Replicating the Chinese Cultural Revolution, the Albanian government adopted policies that resembled the hukou housing regime (Solinger 1995; Zhang 2002). This entailed a state-controlled right to housing, administered by a regime of allocation that interlocked one's residence with access to a wide range of goods and services. These transformations occurred at the same time that other Eastern European countries relaxed their ban on private property and encouraged a dual economic system as well as a market for private homeownership (see especially Bodnár and Böröcz 1998).

By law, two institutions allocated housing in Albania: work units (*vendi i punës*) and neighborhood councils (*këshilli i lagjes*). Both institutions issued the permits (*autorizim*) that assigned one's right to housing and specified the location of one's residence. In practice, these allocations became subject to one's political biography, one's connections to higher-level officials, and one's relations to local cadres and local administrators. As in other parts of the former socialist world, urban housing thus became a means of privilege or punishment due to its status as an access point to other goods and services. In addition to segregation based on occupation and social group (Szelenyi 1987), housing in Albania was highly politicized. Thus, one's residence was subject to change. Political persecution often began with moving one's family, and often close relatives, from urban areas to remote villages or, in the best-case scenario, from the center of town to its periphery.

These policies were designed to control population movement and urban development. But in practice, the policies generated discontent, especially because the state and local authorities controlled one's right of residence. The lifting of this housing regime in the early 1990s unleashed a mass rural-urban migration (Aliaj 2008). The capital, Tirana, experienced the most dramatic demographic changes, with its population quadrupling in a decade. Other cities, including Vlora, experienced growth as well. For instance, Durim sold his apartment in Shkodra (a town in the northwest) and relocated to Vlora, to be near his extended family. He contrasted his decision to those of others who lived in Vlora at the time:

> Others sold their homes and deposited the money [to the firms]. I sold [my home] out of necessity [*halli*]. If I were residing in Vlora then, I wouldn't have sold my home. I was forced to sell because I did not want to live there [in Shkodra] because I am not Shkodran. And, so, I rolled the dice. Wavering different plans that I discussed with my wife, night after night, because our children then were young. I prayed for the first moment I would find a home to buy. Others would say, "don't rush, wait for your money to multiply so you can buy a two-bedroom apartment." But I decided to put my head under a roof first because it had been almost three years that I lived in angst.[4]

Durim justified his decision to sell his apartment by his need to return to Vlora, his place of birth, from which he had been relocated due to his "bad biography."

Others moved to Vlora, looking for better work opportunities and living conditions. Isuf's buyer, for instance, relocated from the rural areas outside Vlora. Older
urban residents also sought new housing as they lamented the lack of space their
location on the peripheries of the city. In other words, there was a widespread
urge for people to move not just to places outside of Albania but also within,
whether in the same city or from rural to urban areas (see also Vullnetari 2012).
Construction boomed at this time, consisting of new housing developments and
(informal) self-built homes on the peripheries of the city.[5]

Others still sought to accelerate their earnings to be able to buy a home and
start a business. Durim shared the story of a relative who had sold a three-bedroom
apartment in Vlora planning to invest the money in the firms and later be able to
double the money and buy a bigger home and start a new business. His relative
had asked Durim for advice on whether to accept an offer of US$26,000 for a
three-bedroom apartment. Durim recalled that he had persuaded his relative not
to sell the apartment: "'Listen,' I told him, 'if I were in your place, I wouldn't sell
it, I wouldn't give you my blessing [marshalla] for selling, I do not agree with this
decision.'"[6] Although he disagreed with the plan of selling the apartment to invest in the firms, Durim had proceeded to offer financial advice to his relative: if
he had made up his mind on selling, US$26,000 was a good price. Durim told his
relative that if he were to do this, he should act fast since the price of housing had
started to fall due to the rush to sell apartments for cash. He noted that while a
few years back a one-bedroom apartment cost around US$15,000, Durim bought
his in 1996 for US$11,000. Durim's relative had sold the apartment and depos-
ited US$10,000 to Vefa at 9.5 percent interest, deposited another US$10,000 to
Gjallica, and distributed the rest to the other fondacione—Silva and Xhaferri. Alas,
the relative had eventually lost the cash after Gjallica's collapse. The relative had
incurred significant losses as he deposited his money to the firms in late 1996, a
few months before the firms froze their assets and collapsed.

In retrospect, Durim blamed a new interest scheme introduced by Gjallica in
late 1996 that incentivized homeowners to sell their apartments for cash to invest in the firms. According to him, "Gjallica, seeing that people started to withdraw their money, offered a high interest return, 24 percent in hand and 6 percent
going forward." This interest scheme, noted Durim, was an incentive for depositing large sums of cash, and apartment sales were one way to generate such sums.
For many, their communist apartments or houses were the only private assets that
they could turn into liquidity.

These decisions and strategies around the sale of apartments to participate in
the firms speak to broader aspirations to obtain new homes at a time of changing
property forms, housing regimes, and overall demographics. Housing became an
object of high demand as well as one of distinct sociocultural meaning and value.

The firms played a crucial role in mediating new forms of housing financing. As Durim suggests, the firms incentivized kreditorë to sell their homes and invest large sums of cash for high interest returns. This scheme was effective because many desperately wanted to buy a new home but did not have access to bank credit. Bank credit, the only formal means of credit available for home purchases, had just been introduced in Albania. Banks were cautious about lending to consumers, especially since average Albanians came out of communism with no assets to use as collateral, many had lost their jobs as factories closed down, and most had no savings. Some credit lines were available but only for limited populations (e.g., bank employees) and for low amounts.

Throughout our conversation, Durim mentioned in passing that he had been able to take a loan from the bank that he intended to use to buy an apartment in Vlora. As an officer, he was eligible for what he described as a soft loan (*kredi e zbutur*), with a low interest rate of 3 percent. His loan was US$10,000 with a fifteen-year payment plan. Durim had not mentioned this loan earlier in the conversation when he discussed his move to Vlora. But as we continued to talk about his experience as a moneychanger, and then as sekser, he revealed that, indirectly, this loan had brought him to work with the firms.

He had taken out the loan to purchase an apartment in Vlora, but the loan was not big enough for him to afford his desired apartment. He had then used parts of the loan to convert into hard currency and "play" (*luaj*) at the informal exchange. This was the time of drastic devaluations, and Durim lost US$800 within a few days. He panicked and tried to make up the losses by trading with the *menaxherë* (managers) of the firms. Gjallica's menaxherë would come to the informal exchanges to "borrow" large sums of cash at 1 to 2 percent interest to pay off kreditorë the promised interests. This is how Durim had decreased his losses by US$300–400. These transactions with the menaxherë introduced him to the financial alternatives that the firms offered. Once he had recuperated most of his original loan Durim rushed to buy a one-bedroom apartment.

Isuf and Durim followed a similar pattern of participation in the firms as a means of purchasing new homes. This practice was so widespread that every kreditor I talked to, when asked what they intended to do with the expected profits, noted that they planned to buy a new home. The lack of a lending market during the first decade of postsocialist reform pushed many people toward the firms as a source of nonbank credit.[7] Though technically not banks, and not licensed to give out loans, the firms provided an alternative form of housing financing. For many, the firms were even better than banks. They promised double or triple returns—in cash—within short periods (three months to a year), thus providing kreditorë with the ability to purchase a home in cash and not have to pay interest. In other words, a key draw for the firms was their alternative temporality of finance.

Temporality and Speculative Finance

Temporality is a crucial aspect of finance, but it is especially important to the allure of speculative finance. The economist Hyman Minsky distinguishes between different stages of finance—ponzi, speculative, and hedge—based on the projected or expected returns on investments. Financial activities are deemed as "pyramid" or "Ponzi" schemes based on the assessment that they constitute "unsustainable patterns of financial behavior" (Kindleberger and Aliber 2005, 13) by entities that promise exorbitant returns on investments with a very quick turnaround. Temporalities of finance also intertwine with cultural-historical ideas of time and the future.[8] Hirokazu Miyazaki (2003) notes how the temporalities of the market shape an individual's experience of the present and imaginaries of the future. Looking at security traders in the late 1990s Japan, Miyazaki (2003) describes how their experience of temporal incongruity in the practice of arbitrage intersected with a broader sense of being behind that permeated postwar Japan and was renewed after the shift from an economy based on production to one relying increasingly on finance. In Albania, the accelerated temporalities of gain at the firms provided a horizon of expectation (albeit faulty) that entailed an accelerated purchase of desired new homes which, in turn, would accelerate reaching the good life. These financial temporalities promised by the firms constituted an alternative to the realities of the new economic regimes introduced through the shock-therapy reforms.

Jane Guyer's (2007) temporal notions of the near future, the long run, and the punctuated present are useful for thinking about the changing postsocialist temporalities. Guyer (2007) notes a historic phenomenon that set out with the spread of monetarist policies in Anglo-American world since the 1950s, which she describes as an evacuation of the "near future" (the regular, short-term provisioning, ensured by welfare economic policies) and the simultaneous intensification of the temporality of the long run (monetarist policies with long-term macroeconomic goals) and that of the punctuated present (embodied in the uncertain, unpredictable every day, punctuated by specific events).[9] The concept of the "near future" and its evacuation is particularly relevant to the sense of time and aspirations that Albanian kreditorë experienced as they decided to invest at the firms. These experiences and aspirations were rooted in the changing financial and life temporalities in the postsocialist context.

Verdery describes postsocialist transformations as a "collision of two differently constituted temporal orders" (1996, 37), namely communist time and capitalist time. Communist time, she notes, was increasingly experienced as "spastic, arhythmical, and unpredictable" (189) thanks in large part to the failures of the economy of redistribution and of the plan. To the people on the ground capitalist time represented modern, linear, progressive time. This binary of temporalities structured local imagination in postsocialist Albania. People living under the communist regime looked to capitalist markets as a promise of functioning modernity.[10] However, the experience of capitalist transformations in the early 1990s strayed from this modernist utopia. Rather than the linear, progressive, and predictable time imagined as the hallmark of capitalism, people increasingly experienced the postsocialist transformations as a time marked by unpredictability, a time of multiple, but unconnected, events that did not follow any predictable cycle; in other words, of punctuated time.

The temporality of everyday life in early postsocialist Albania in particular was organized by the dual temporality of the long run and of punctuated time. On the one hand, government authorities implemented monetarist policies mandated by the International Monetary Fund and the World Bank as a condition of their structural adjustment loans; these policies focused on the long run. On the other hand, everyday economic life became increasingly experienced as punctuated time: frantic devaluations of the local currency, loss of secure employment, constant hustling, short- and long-term loans from friends and family, short-term contracts with unpredictable payment dates, and the unstructured temporalities of remittances.

For some, transactions at the firms promised to generate a temporality of the near future, that is, financial dates that were predictable and conducive to planning in the foreseeable future. Durim described one pattern of investment at the firms that simulated the financial temporality of planned, predictable, and stable income: "I had a friend that invested around US$3,000 at 8 percent. He would withdraw US$240 per month." This was a fortunate case of a kreditor who had technically lost the principal but over time had been able to make the amount he had invested. Wins and losses aside, the case also represented a scenario whereby the monthly "interests" from the firms served as a form of regular, stable salary. Though many kreditorë reinvested their interest (in the hope of gaining even more in the end), the alternative of withdrawing the interests to cover basic expenses was also common. This practice would seem to generate a temporality of a near future, that is, of regular, predictable payments.

Investing in homes was also an effort to generate different temporalities of life. The location and style of one's home shaped personal and national experiences of time as well as specific imaginaries of the future. By seeking to change their housing condition through the spoils of the firms, kreditorë sought to accelerate the temporality of their socioeconomic and cultural transformation. However, the losses at the firms were often experienced as loss or delay of the purchase of the desired home. This delay, in turn, was often described as "lagging behind" (*mbetur mbrapa*) an imagined trajectory of progress (see also Jansen 2015). It is therefore not a coincidence that conversations with kreditorë about wins and losses from the firms often revolved around the assessment of their housing conditions since the collapse of the firms.

Pyramid Families

One of my most memorable conversations about housing and investment at the firms took place at the home of Manushaqe, a former kreditorë who had "lost" her privatized communist apartment to one of the firms. I met Manushaqe at the Tirana City Hall while searching the archives for records on the subsidized housing given to a select number of so-called pyramid families (*familjet e piramidave*). Manushaqe invited me to visit her at her subsidized apartment in Lapraka, a neighborhood at the periphery of Tirana.

During my visit to her two-bedroom apartment, she arranged for two other women to join us. The women lived in the same building and represented families who had sold their homes in the early 1990s to participate in the firms. After losing their homes and savings to the firms, they had waged protests, sit-ins, and hunger strikes that drew public attention in the early 2000s. The problem of housing lost to the firms was acknowledged in official reports by the Supervisory Group. The socialist government had initially taken the issue seriously and promised to provide compensation. But little has been done. Even the apartments assigned to the forty-four families in Tirana were initially "sold" to the residents with a 0 percent interest loan. By the time of my visit in 2008, the city was requiring 3 percent interest on the loan. The families were split between those who accepted these terms (and continued to pay the monthly payment plus interest) and those who challenged the interest payments. Manushaqe and the other women I talked to vehemently opposed these new terms. At the time of our conversation, the women were considering stopping payments as another sign of protest. During a visit in 2015, I learned that some of the families had indeed stopped making payments altogether.

The buildings inhabited by the families of the pyramids were initially constructed by the firm Vefa (figure 4.1). Construction began in 1996 and the buildings were hailed as the new "contemporary housing" (*banesa bashkëkohore*) that would bring Albanians closer to Europe. The timing of this construction was not random. Nineteen ninety-six saw a boom in construction licenses in Tirana. At the start of construction of the Vefa buildings, Mayor Brokaj commended

FIGURE 4.1. A former kreditorë at one of the Vefa buildings that house pyramid families. Lapraka, Tirana, October 2008.

(Photograph by author.)

Alimuçaj (Vefa's owner) for "solving the housing question," and vowed to assist the construction project by speeding up licensing and providing water and electricity lines (M. B. 1996, 9). The construction was interrupted when Vefa froze its assets. Manushaqe recalled how she had "found out" about these buildings through her inquiries at the Supervisory Group. The head of the Supervisory Group, Farudin Arapi, had suggested that funds from firms as well as a loan by the Greek government allocated for housing the pyramid families to specifically be used to complete the construction of the Vefa apartments for subsidized housing. City authorities then determined which families were eligible for the subsidized housing. Forty-four families were granted subsidized housing in Tirana. The selection process was based on the council of ministers' decisions regarding the "families that lost their homes to the pyramid firms" (VKM NR 585 1997). Eligibility criteria went beyond the mere loss of a home to the firms and included the lack of adequate housing or other forms of wealth and a member of the family with chronic health problems.

The Vefa buildings are located in Lapraka. Once a semirural outskirt, Lapraka is now a densely populated area, with a mixture of post-1990s high-rises and informal self-built homes. Despite its development and sprawl, Lapraka still stands for the messy periphery in the local imagination. The Vefa buildings are nestled between the new high-rises and self-built homes. During our conversation, Manushaqe led me to the balcony that overlooked the informal constructions. The women expressed frustration that they still did not have definitive ownership of their apartments while these once-informal self-built homes were being legalized.

The women who gathered at Manushaqe's home had different socioeconomic backgrounds and positionalities during the communist regime. Manushaqe, for instance, worked as a salesperson in a diesel shop—a valued job given its access to a scarce and rationed commodity. Nafie worked at the textile factory in Kombinat, while Drita was a janitor. Some, like Manushaqe, had sold communist apartments located at the center of the city hoping to buy bigger apartments in the same area; others, like Drita and Nafie, had sold communist apartments located on another periphery of the city hoping to move closer to the center. Despite these differences, the stories of relocation all spoke to the general phenomenon of internal mobility. Some were moving from rural areas or smaller towns to bigger urban centers; others sought to relocate to the city center. Many wanted to leave their communist apartments and search for better residence locations. These movements were shaped by the shifting housing regime, changing demographics, and the subsequent transformation of the home as a form of wealth.

Home Value during Communism and Postsocialism

Homes constituted a highly valued and highly desired possession for most former kreditorë I talked to. This was grounded in the specific history of the transformation of housing from the communist regime of allocation to the postsocialist free market for real estate.

The communist housing regime embodied a philosophy of materiality and infrastructure that was decoupled from private ownership. According to this philosophy, the materials and objects of everyday life, especially housing and infrastructure, were means of generating new persons, new socialities, and new cosmologies (Féherváry 2012; Humphrey 2005; Kiaer 2005; Mëhilli 2012). Housing was considered a key material object that molded individual consciousness. It was the pride of many a communist country to make access to housing a universal right. By providing housing, the communist state claimed to emancipate the working class. At the same time, private ownership of housing was limited, if not banned. Albania took extreme measures against private property. In cities, it nationalized housing owned by wealthy businessmen and landowners, Italian personnel working for the Zogu regime in the 1930s, and politically persecuted individuals. The state housed other families in these properties. New apartment buildings were built to house the working class.

Although private property was increasingly limited in Albania, and most housing was state-owned, housing constituted a fundamental form of sociocultural wealth. It held value as a point of access to other entitlements, goods, and services. It was an aspect of communist citizenship (see also Zavisca 2012; Zhang 2002); it determined or translated one's political and socioeconomic status within a differentiated society. Given the shortage of housing in the late 1980s, come the early 1990s, housing came to constitute an object of the high market as well as sociocultural value.

After the privatization law of 1993 passed, housing became commodified. As such, its value became subject to the market. For kreditorë, however, the home value extended well beyond its commodity form. Although the term "shtëpi" technically refers to a detached house, it also refers to an apartment, a single-family detached house, or a villa (vilë), whether owned or rented. Growing up in Albania during the communist regime, I knew to refer to detached houses as "private homes" (shtëpi private), a vernacular term used even when these homes were appropriated and rented out by the state, often to multiple families. The term "private" was a bit of a misnomer. Because private property was abolished during late communism, "private" referred to the particular structure of the house—detached single-family home—rather than property form or even use. In many cases, shtëpi private, like communal apartments in Soviet Union (Boym 1994), were inhabited by multiple families that were not the original owners. Shtëpi, thus, refers both to a type of privately owned housing and to a place of belonging. In the vernacular speech, shtëpi also stands for family. Young Albanians in the early 1990s referred to parents and the family more generally as "those of the home" (ata të shtëpisë). I use the term "shtëpi" to encompass these various meanings. Shtëpi refers to housing as well as a place of belonging and attachment. This dual meaning of shtëpi played a significant role in the kreditorë's decisions to buy and sell different types of homes alongside their participation in the firms.

From Kombinat to Lapraka: Housing, Citizenship, and Geographies of Difference

Nafie's trajectory, in particular, foregrounded the tensions and negotiations of these different forms of the value of the home. Before the firms' boom, Nafie lived in a one-bedroom apartment in the district of Kombinat. The peripheral district

was built to house workers moving from rural areas to the city to work in the Stalin textile factory. These units replicated other housing projects built across the
former socialist world to support widespread industrialization efforts (see also
Fehérváry 2013; Jansen 2015; Kotkin 1997; Zhang 2010). This type of housing materialized a broader philosophy of infrastructure whereby "carefully designed
living quarters could eliminate the conditions for individualistic and meshchan-
skie (petty-minded bourgeois) ways of life, and on this basis a new human type
would become the norm: Socialist Man and Socialist Woman" (Humphrey 2005,
39). Such state-sponsored housing projects retained a holistic philosophy of dwell-
ing whereby the home was attached to the workplace. Together these infrastructures entailed entitlements in goods and services, from childcare to food rations.

The apartment that Nafie had occupied before getting involved in the pyramid firms was a typical communist apartment, allocated to her as a worker-citizen.
Given this symbolism, and given that she could now own this apartment at a low
cost, I wondered why was Nafie so eager to turn it into liquidity and take the risk
of depositing the cash to the firms. Nafie described her decision to sell the apartment as follows:

> I urged my husband and son to sell our apartment. . . . They did not want
> to go against my wishes . . . because I am entrepreneurial [*jam inisiatore*].
> I do a lot for the home [*bëj shumë për shtëpinë*] for my husband, for my
> children. My husband said, "I am not selling the home [*shtëpinë*]. We
> can buy another one, but we still should keep this one." I said, please,
> for my sake. We had an apartment in Kombinat, my sister was in Ti-
> rana e Re [a Tirana neighborhood], we had never seen villas before, we
> were living in mayhem [*ku thërret qiameti*]. And I was obliged [*u dety-
> rova*] to sell the apartment. . . . We committed the biggest crime, God
> punished us. The home [*shtëpia*] should not be sold; it is like a sacred
> place [*teqe*].[11]

In her expression of self-defense and regret, Nafie evoked the multiple senses of
shtëpi. She described her reputation as a savvy entrepreneur as "doing a lot for
the home," by which she referred to both the apartment and the household. This
implied skills in managing the household budget and the ability to procure for
the family throughout the late communist shortages.[12] Indeed, during late communism, women such as Nafie and Manushaqe were described as *të shkathëta*
(savvy) as they used their networks of friends and family to access the black market to procure scarce consumer goods in times of shortages. Turning the apartment into cash at the time of the firms' boom was also seen as a savvy move. At
the same time, Nafie (and her husband) maintained that the (privately owned)
shtëpi was valued as a sacred object and, thus, was not to be sold.

Nafie's justification for her decision to sell the apartment referred to a complex geography of citizenship that mapped onto the layout of the city. Nafie expressed that the imperative to sell her apartment and to participate in the pyramid firms was the only way out of Kombinat. The contempt that Nafie showed toward her Kombinati apartment represents the discontent around the actual living conditions that many people experienced in these communist apartments. Drita, who had also sold her one-story house at another peripheral neighborhood of Tirana vented:

> SMOKI: Where was your house?
> DRITA: At the train tracks [*shinat e trenit*]. I sold it. A one-bedroom [*dhomë e guzhinë*] . . . We wanted a better home. Like everyone else. We sold it. The whole population went to the pyramids. And for what? For a home [*shtëpi*], for providing better housing for the children. Even us adults started to develop asthma, let alone the children. It was very damp.[13]

The discontent with communist housing was one of the unintended consequences of centralized housing planning and the disintegrating infrastructure in the early years of postsocialist reform (see also Féhérváry 2013; Schwenkel 2015).

For Nafie and other former kreditorë, the privatized communist apartments were far from the clean, well-lit spaces of the ideal home. By the late 1980s, this housing stock was in dire need of renovation and upkeep, but the state could no longer afford it. Meanwhile, consumer shortages always hit the peripheral areas the hardest. With the closing of the factories in the early 1990s, neighborhoods such as Kombinati experienced even greater losses in infrastructure, services, and a sense of community. State factories and kombinats had been the source of provisioning and services as well as the center of local cultural activities and social organizing (Za 2012). With the privatization of the apartment stock in 1993, the market value of the communist apartments drastically differed from the nominal value at which these apartments were appraised. Those who inherited apartments in the peripheries of major cities or smaller towns found themselves with the short end of the stick—owning assets of lesser market value and stuck in neighborhoods that were already receiving lesser-quality services and experiencing rapid deterioration of their infrastructure. It was this context that helps explain what I describe as Nafie's double imperative.

On the one hand, for Nafie, moving out of Kombinati was a way out of her marginal position as a second-rate citizen in the late-communist context. This explains the first imperative: to sell her Kombinati apartment. On the other hand, Nafie also expressed another imperative: that the home cannot or should not be sold. This sentiment echoed new ideas about the value of the private property,

especially housing, as a form of wealth. This valuing of housing as a sacred possession resonates with the socialist philosophy of materiality, which considered
objects of everyday use as crucial to molding one's subjectivity and citizenship
(Humphrey 2005; Kiaer 2005). Thus, Nafie and other women lamented their current poor housing conditions by pointing to individual and family problems.
They enumerated physical and mental illnesses that plagued members of their
families as a symptom of the poor quality of their housing. They blamed state
authorities for not having solved their housing conditions. Although disposing
of socialist materialities, it seemed that these women held on to the socialist philosophy of materiality that grounded forms of personhood and citizenship in the
materiality of the home. The laments also pointed to a differentiated urban geography of the capital city, underscoring the legacy of the unequal social geographies of the communist regime into the present ways of valuing homes. Indeed,
Nafie's contrast between the highly desired Tirana e Re versus the mayhem of
Kombinati speaks to such inequalities within the social geography of Tirana during the communist regime. These differentiations contradicted the official philosophy of universal and equal access to material and social entitlements.

In contrast to Kombinat, Tirana e Re was closer to the center of the city and
home to the much-revered *blloku*—the cordoned-off block of prewar villas expropriated and reclaimed for use as dwellings for the party's elite. Italian architects and engineers built the prewar villas and the low-rise apartment buildings
of Tirana e Re in the late 1930s, when Albania was de facto protectorate of Italy
(Lubonja 2007). The construction of these earlier structures followed an urban
plan that envisioned a modernist European capital, organized around a grid structure that contrasted with the Ottoman circular layout of the older neighborhoods. The villas of blloku housed the Italian elite and pro-Italian local officials
during the prewar and war times, whereas the low-rise apartments housed former army officers and other functionaries of Italian and Albanian governments at
the time. Although most other detached houses in Tirana were demolished after
the war to make room for high-rises, this particular neighborhood was kept in-
tact and appropriated as living quarters of the new communist elites. Blloku
became a fetishized space, closed off to the public. Blloku residents lived under a
different housing regime than the rest of the population. The spacious detached
villas housed single families, thus overriding the specifications of the mandated
"living space." Further, blloku residents were not subject to the rationing system
and had access to the forbidden consumption of goods from the West.

The villas of blloku and the Kombinati apartments represent two opposite ends
of the spectrum of urban housing in communist Albania. The differences between
these residential locations reflected the inequalities of access and entitlements
for different types of socialist subjects. When the communist apartments were

privatized in 1993, such inequalities translated into market value, leaving those with the apartments on the periphery with the depreciated properties. In addition, the variations of access and quality of life between the communist city's center and periphery were exacerbated during the first few years of the postsocialist transformations. The selling of recently privatized apartments for pyramid firm deposits, thus, constitute strategies for creating new forms of wealth across asymmetric scales of value, including communist and market-based notions of property, an emerging real estate market, and changing geographies of urban space. For people like Nafie and other families of the pyramids who had lost their jobs and their social entitlements with the closing down of the state factories, housing remained one of the few possessions that, at least in these kreditorë's imaginations, could ensure access to a particular set of entitlements. In other words, housing was an object that defined one's citizenship in a new socioeconomic reality. It was these multiple forms of value that congealed on the desired new homes and made them highly sought objects of wealth at a time of increased economic instability and volatility.

Postsocialist Aspirations and Competing Modernities

In addition to their value as commodities and as markers of citizenship, the different statuses of the Kombinati and Tirana e Re homes capture competing notions of modernity and aspirations toward the good life that centered on housing.

In the early years of postsocialist transformation in Tirana, Kombinati embodied socialist modernity that for many seemed to have failed and belonged to the past. Blloku, instead, was fetishized as a space of the forbidden West and represented what I describe as a European modernity. This longing for European modernity played a key part in the kreditorë's involvement in the firms.

By European modernity, I refer to a particular "horizon of expectations" (Koselleck 1985) that is ubiquitous in contemporary Albania and that has a long history in the national imagination. The longing for European things and lifestyles was nestled within the communist experience as a "chronotope of a forbidden elsewhere" (Musaraj 2012). This longing was shared across the Eastern European space during late socialism (see, for instance, Berdahl 2010; Borneman 1991). In Albania, such longing targeted more specifically consumer cultures or simply the desire to move to countries such as Italy and later Greece (see Bon 2017; Mai 2001). The fascination with the villas of Blloku is a case in point. The villas were associated with Europe because they were built by Italian architects and because the communist elite that inhabited the villas lived a life of exception, acquiring (Western) European consumer goods forbidden to others and defying the laws of living space enforced everywhere else. The villas embodied the forbidden Europe and thus became an icon of a shared imaginary of alternative modernity.

With their assurance of quick high returns, the firms promised to make this modernity possible in a shorter and finite temporal horizon. In other words, the firms outlined an accelerated path toward Europe—in both the consumer and sociocultural senses. The specter of Europe as a horizon of expectations and aspirations came up in conversations with former kreditorë as they described their motivations for participating in the firms. In the mid-1990s, the specter of Europe was both vaguer and more specific to particular countries, often the countries of migrant destinations: Italy and Greece. Dimitri Dalakoglou (2010a) and Gerda Dalipaj (2016), for instance, have documented migrants' efforts at buying, building, and furnishing their "Greek" houses or apartments back in Albania. Even before the creation of the European Union (EU), Europe constituted a general category of democratic political systems as well as the particular lifestyles and culture of consumption.

By 2008, the EU had become a political reality, and the desire to join informed everyday consumer choices and aspirations in Albania. Europe and Europeanness often appeared as a measure of quality and as an aesthetic for the desired homes. Manjola alerted me to these aesthetic distinctions as she recalled demolishing her old house in anticipation of rebuilding a new home with the firms' gains. Manjola's socioeconomic and citizenship status was somewhat unique. She belonged to an ethnic Greek minority community in the village of Narta that had been recognized as a minority group during the communist regime.

Although Manjola continued to live in Narta at the time of our conversation, her kin had established new lives in Greece. They maintained ties to their hometown by sending remittances, making annual visits, and building new houses. Rebuilding homes, according to Dimitri Dalakoglou (2010a), constitutes a way of extending the self and maintaining the transnational kin relations. These investments are visible in the landscape of rural areas, in particular. Walking around the sleepy town of Narta, one notices the new two- to three-story villas built since the mid-1990s, and many others under construction.

These house-building projects have constituted a prime object of investment of remittances across the board. During the early 1990s, however, many sought to accelerate such efforts by channeling remittances through the firms. Unlike the pyramid families mentioned above, Manjola was not strapped for cash, so she did not sell her home. Like the majority of the kreditorë, Manjola planned to build a new house with the gains from the pyramid firms. She described her decision to demolish her previous house as well as her plans and wishes for a new home as follows:

I demolished our house . . . We had an Elbasançe house [*shtëpi El-basançe*]. Two bedrooms and a hallway . . . My father-in-law had built it in 1960 or 1962. It was an old house but well kept. We thought of building a new one, a European house [*shtëpi Evropiançe*]. And we had some money on our hands. Most important, we had a strong desire to make a new house. That's all the Albanian wanted then, a beautiful European-style home [*një shtëpi të bukur Evropiançe*].[14]

Manjola justified her decision to demolish her old home by drawing distinctions between the types of housing design. The Elbasançe house referred to the house built by her father-in-law during the communist regime. Per the architectural model approved for self-built rural housing by of the Tirana Institute of Design (Instituti i Projektimit, Tiranë), the Elbasançe house consisted of "single-story dwellings with three rooms and a veranda" (Hall 1990, 377). In the original design, these houses were a significant improvement over Ottoman-style homes— built with mud bricks and with outdoor or "Turkish" bathrooms—by incorporating "modern European" design elements such as industrial bricks, indoor bathrooms, and modern plumbing systems. As such, Elbasançe houses represented a socialist modernist infrastructure and aesthetic that evoked tropes of Europeanness (see also Féherváry 2012, 2013). This aesthetic included, for instance, the "French" bathroom versus the Turkish outhouse, straight angles versus rounded lines, separate rooms rather than shared common spaces.

At the time of our conversation, Manjola believed the Elbasançe house embodied a failed modernity that she was eager to leave behind. As was also the case with city dwellers, Manjola's desire for a shtëpi Evropiançe translated into more space, more rooms, multiple floors, balconies, and more privacy (see also Zavisca 2012, 5–6). This contrast in space and scale is visible throughout Narta as many of the residents have built new homes next to their old homes. The new homes that Manjola describes as Evropiançe are typically two- to three-story houses with more rooms and windows and with large balconies. Unlike Manjola, who had rushed to demolish her old house, others kept their old Elbasançe houses and built their new European houses slowly, one floor at a time, adding more walls when new resources and remittances materialized. This piecemeal construction is widespread in rural areas and urban peripheries in Albania, and it accounts for the ubiquitous unfinished houses as well as the sight of iron rods sticking out of the roof terraces (figure 4.2).

Such piecemeal construction reflects the actual temporalities of people's financial lives in contemporary Albania. It is a temporality of the punctuated present (Guyer 2007), marked by the random and sporadic bursts of cash (from immigrant relatives or one-time jobs) and a loss of a predictable near future

FIGURE 4.2. Communist-era Elbasance house (foreground) and postsocialist-era "European" house (background). Narta, Vlora, July 2015.

(Photograph by author.)

(loss of regular employment and related social benefits). For people like Manjola, who aspired toward living in new "European" houses, the firms promised an accelerated source of financing that would circumvent both the temporalities of the long run (namely, of long-term bank loans and interest payments) and those of the punctuated present (the unpredictable, piecemeal, do-it-yourself construction financed through remittances and other sporadic sources of cash). In this sense, these efforts at accelerating the purchase or building of "European" homes through the firms' profits need to be understood as efforts at materializing a temporality of the near future.

Longing for Europe and Lagging Behind

This longing for a European modernity extends well beyond homes and encompasses other aspects of the national imaginary in Albania. Europe and Europeanness are ubiquitous in official and vernacular discourse in Albania. They signal a temporality of progress that conflates specific political projects (such as joining the EU) with broader cultural claims (of being recognized and becoming culturally European). In the 2016 local elections, for instance, the left-wing coalition named itself "The Alliance for a European Albania," while the winning candidate for mayor in Vlora promised to turn the city into "the European city that it merits to be."

On the one hand, this longing for European homes resembles patterns of consumption prevalent in other parts of the developing world, where Western goods became a symbol of another temporality of progress and modernity. On the other hand, in the Albanian context, the longing for Europe as a marker of cultural identity spans the national history and literature of the nineteenth and twentieth centuries. In this discourse, claims toward a European cultural identity are often juxtaposed to other forms of undesired identities, such as the Ottoman (and implicitly Muslim) or communist. Enis Sulstarova (2006) notes how historians, linguists, and ethnologists of communist Albania reached back into pre-Ottoman Albania to advocate for European cultural and historical belonging (often inferred in the opposition between an imposed Ottoman-Muslim identity versus a historical Roman-Christian one). Under the communist regime, since the Cultural Revolution in the 1970s, consumption of European goods became fraught with political meaning, and was cause for critique, demotion, or even political persecution. At the same time, the illicit access and consumption of forbidden European goods was one of the few means of critique and resistance to an increasingly isolated communist regime, especially since the 1970s (see also Mai 2001; Musaraj 2012).

This longing for Europeanness imparts a dual temporality: it reaches toward a future in the European political and economic space while also reclaiming a European cultural identity that predates the Ottoman Empire. This dual temporality overlaps in the materiality of "European" things—commodities, designs, styles, political platforms, and homes. By investing their cash returns from the pyramid firms into the desired "European" homes, former kreditorë sought to appropriate such sociocultural qualities. Buying new European homes with the pyramid firms' gains was simultaneously an effort at transforming their socioeconomic class and at materializing a temporal orientation toward Europe as a political and cultural horizon. Manjola's statement that "all the Albanians wanted was a European home" best captures this logic of material and cultural transformation.

This temporal dimension of "European" homes often emerged in kreditorë laments of "lagging behind" the trajectories of life (and housing) they anticipated at the time of their involvement in the firms. Many former kreditorë I talked to were marginal citizens within the communist regime. Turning the firms' gains into European homes was simultaneously an effort at transforming their socioeconomic class (see also Féhervary 2012) and cultural identity. This next trajectory of change of housing speaks to the enduring relationship with the home as an object that can (and does) transform one's socioeconomic and cultural status.

Fatmira was a former kreditore to several firms and a cashier for one firm. I met her in Vlora in the summer of 2008, but her life trajectory had brought her through multiple homes within the span of a decade. Fatmira grew up during the late communist regime in a village outside of the industrial town of Fier, a second-tier city an hour drive north of Vlora. Her family was originally from a village outside Vlora but had been relocated to rural Fier following the political persecution of one of Fatmira's uncles. Since her childhood, Fatmira has been sentenced to life in the rural villages of Fier because of her "bad biography." She was barred from pursuing higher education and limited to working on a collective farm. When she managed to find a job at the chicken factory in Fier in the late 1980s, she rejoiced. The job enabled her to move closer to the urban center of Fier and afforded her access to urban goods and services; in other words, the job provided upward mobility. In the 1990s, Fatmira embraced the free-market reforms as these allowed her to carve a different path from the one limited by her bad biography. She sold her apartment in Fier for pyramid firms' deposit but withdrew it just before their collapse. Although she did not receive the triple returns she was hoping for, she was eventually able to move to Vlora and start a new life there as the owner of a small upholstery business.

In Vlora, she bought a one-bedroom ground floor apartment in a low-rise brick building. During the communist regime, the apartment block housed families of army officers—a professional and social group that made up a large part of the Vlora population and enjoyed such privileges as better housing. Fatmira had bought the apartment at market rate after losing her job with the firm in Fier in 1997. She was still living there with her husband and son in 2008. This is where we had our first interview. From the mixed use of the main room (which served as a living room during the day and bedroom at night) to the *aneks* (a mini-kitchen) to interior design (the pullout couch, the coffee table with handmade doilies), the apartment reminded me of a typical communist apartment. The apartment's prime location—off the main boulevard of Vlora—made this a preferable home to Fatmira's previous ones. Overall, Fatmira's relocations were entangled with her social transformation—from a political and social outcast to cashier for one of the schemes to currently owning her own business. Still, Fatmira relayed a similar sense of incompleteness, of lagging behind, which I also heard from Nafie and Manjola. According to Fatmira:

> Many things were revealed [with the fall of the communist regime]. Stuck as we were in a vicious circle thinking that Tirana was the wonder of the world . . . And to see how they lived so much better than us. It was an emotional downfall [*rënie shpirtërore*], a collapse of consciousness [*rënie ndërgjegje*]. We have deeply suffered [*përjetuar*] the 1990s. In 1990 I was

thirty years old. To me, at the time, to think that I needed ten years to get settled [*për t'u rregulluar*] seemed like an entire life. And to think that it has been twenty years and we're still not entirely settled.

Fatmira's reminiscing about her suffering of the early 1990s captures the range of emotions that the changes of that period had generated among those at the margins of communist citizenship. One of the things that hurt people most was discovering that the blloku elite had indeed been consuming those same Western goods that were forbidden for the rest of the country. The homes of these elites, made up of single-family houses, embodied the shtëpi private that had been too bourgois to inhabit by the average urban citizen. Further, as images of European lifestyles and consumer culture flooded local TV waves, Fatmira and others had felt the gap between their own lives and those of the West increase that much more. The differences in styles and sizes of homes translated into temporal gaps. Assessments of homes were thus a measure of individual progress or lagging behind the imagined trajectories toward the desired European modernity.

Despite the positive socioeconomic transformations that she had experienced since the collapse of the communist regime, the overarching sentiment in Fatmira's narrative was that of "not yet being settled." The local idiom, "getting settled," refers to a general sense of satisfaction and contentment with one's place in the world. It refers to economic as well as social well-being. Buying a good home constitutes a key element of getting settled. I often encountered this expression with young married couples who felt that buying a new home was a key part of "getting settled" into married life. By "not yet being entirely settled," Fatmira hinted at her dissatisfaction with her current housing situation. The fact that she was still living in a communist (rather than a new, European) apartment in Vlora (rather than in Tirana or, as she noted with bitterness, "in Athens or Rome") contributed to the sense of lagging behind.

Fatmira's lament is indicative of how changes in housing conditions intertwine with the never-ending process of postsocialist transformation in Albania. This sense of ongoing and incomplete transformation is articulated simultaneously as lagging behind and as not-yet becoming European, politically and culturally.

Conclusion

The chaos that followed 1997 is often described as "a derailment from the trajectory toward Europe." Such assessments conflate broader events—the failure of subsequent governments to make progress toward EU inclusion, the lack of economic growth, the continuous migration abroad, the persistent infrastructural and political crisis—with sociocultural claims toward middle-class consumption and lifestyles. The immediate material surroundings, especially homes, become a key site for materializing such aspirations and for witnessing their failure.

This sense of lagging behind from the desired temporal orientation was experienced by kreditorë who lived in housing that did not match their ideal homes and who lacked stable economic lives. Manushaqe and Nafie continued to live in two-room apartments (one bedroom and a living room), inevitably resorting to their pre-1990s strategies of maximizing space by turning a balcony into a miniature kitchen or aneks (figure 4.3), and using the main room as living room, dining room, and bedroom for the kids. The fact that many of the former kreditorë continue to live in similar conditions as they did during communism marks postsocialism as an extension rather than a break from the punctuated time of late communist Albania.

Since the early 2000s, a construction boom has been a significant driver of economic growth in Albania. Construction of high-rises in urban areas, of self-built houses in urban peripheries and rural areas, and of suburban housing complexes, has continued at a steady pace. At the same time, many of the kreditorë I spoke to had taken longer to obtain the homes that they desired. In some cases, they had only been able to purchase homes similar to the ones they had lost to the firms. Bank loans have become a more common way to purchase homes, but distrust in banks and resistance to paying interest long term persists. Piecemeal construction and cash purchases continue to constitute a significant way of obtaining new homes. The building of homes in rural areas and urban peripheries best exemplifies the temporality of the punctuated present. Construction of such houses depends on the sporadic and often unpredictable bursts of cash from immigrant remittances or short-term jobs. Delayed and piecemeal construction is common among developers of high-rises as well. Developments at city peripheries in particular often suffer from the lack of financing or the lack of presales, which is a common way in which such developments are financed. I take up this phenomenon in the following chapter.

Unfinished, suspended, or ongoing construction projects are legion in contemporary Albania—in informal urban and rural areas, the tightly knit high-rises of urban peripheries, and the new suburban-style neighborhoods on the city's outskirts. During subsequent trips, I noted similar construction landscapes, even as new types of home construction, such as gated communities of single-home villas or luxury apartment complexes, have added another aesthetics of middle-class living that mimics global trends.

Such ubiquitous landscapes of ongoing piecemeal construction speak to the enduring temporality of a punctuated present that dominates the postsocialist experience in Albania. In their laments about lagging behind, kreditorë thus

FIGURE 4.3.   Former kreditorë in her *aneks* of the Vefa apartment subsidized to her as one of the pyramid families. Laprakë, Tiranë, October 2008.

(Photograph by author.)

refer to the failure to materialize the desired temporality of the near future that they hoped to achieve by using the firms to buy or build Western/European homes and thus accelerate their move toward a European modernity. Other studies of similar forms of speculation in other financial margins liken the temporalities of speculation to the financial temporalities of global capital and millennial capitalism (Comaroff and Comaroff 2000; Piot, Lachenal, and Mbodj-Pouye 2014; Verdery 1999). Although contemporaneous with these other instances of financial speculation, the Albanian firms did not merely mimic the financial temporalities of the emerging neoliberal economic institutions. Instead, participants sought in these firms the possibility of circumventing the temporality of the long run and that of the punctuated present. They did so by turning sporadic and unpredictable remittances into regular monthly payments or by accelerating their purchase of a new home. By taking a long view of desires, plans, and actual processes of constructing or buying homes since the early 1990s, we can better appreciate kreditorë's participation into the firms as not simply a search for quick wealth but also as an effort to circumvent the new financial and life temporalities introduced by the shock-therapy reforms. Despite the failure by most to achieve this goal, what becomes visible is the enduring aspiration and plans for procuring particular forms of wealth, such as the home, as the materialization of modernist temporalities.

5

THE PYRAMID WAY
Speculation in Construction

During multiple research trips to Albania since 2008, I have been intrigued by a recurring analogy that people draw between the firms and financing practices in the construction industry. Ever since the collapse of the firms, construction had been the only local industry driving up national growth. Nevertheless, behind this apparent boom, many see yet another Ponzi scheme threatening to wreak havoc once again. Tahir, a former *kreditor* (creditor/investor), expressed this fear early on: "*Ndërtimet* [constructions] are like *piramidat* [pyramid firms]. Pray to God that they don't collapse! Nëntdhteshtata [year ninety-seven] was nothing by comparison to what would happen to us if ndërtimet collapsed."[1] In local popular imagination, "piramidat" and "nëntdhteshtata" continue to be a shorthand for the traumatic experience of the violence and anarchy triggered by the collapse of the firms in 1997. By comparing construction to the pyramid firms, Tahiri, as many other kreditorë I talked to during 2008–9, suggested an analogy between practice forms of financing and accumulation deployed by these distinct economic activities. Kreditorë draw on their experience of the defunct firms to critique financial practices in construction. One specific method singled out in these analogies is that of *klering*, a vernacular term locally translated as barter (*shkëmbim në natyrë*) or exchange (*shkëmbim*) (Çela 2009).[2] People working in construction use the term to refer to payments in apartments (rather than capital). These exchanges are frequently made with apartments that are not yet built (*Monitor* 2009, 2010).

The kreditor Andon (introduced in chapter 3), explained the practice of klering as follows:

This is what happens in construction today: I am a developer . . . You are a tile salesman. I don't give you money to pay you for the tiles, but I tell you that you will receive a new apartment. I tell the same thing to the one that provides the iron, to the one that provides the concrete, to the carpenter, to the plumber, and so on. But where does this bring us? The carpenter is a team not a single person. Let's say you gave the apartment to the head of the company, what about the employees? They want to eat so they need work. Thus, the circle keeps getting tighter until it will all explode one day.[3]

Klering thus is a form of payment that has become quite common in the construction industry. As apartments have been used as payment from the developer to the subcontractors, the inability to sell the apartment at the appraised rate sparked a chain of debt and illiquidity among subcontractors and their employees. Andon had some experience with construction and knew the ins and outs of the industry. As mentioned in chapter 3, he was trained as a construction engineer during the communist regime and had built his own house in the late 1990s. In describing the pattern of financing in construction, Andon captured the cycle of debt and illiquidity incurred by the subcontracting firms and suffered most by their workers. Andon compared this "ever-tightening circle" of debt to the patterns of investments at the pyramid firms. In both cases, promised returns were exorbitant as well as uncertain and, in both cases, these payment arrangements had led to a widespread shortage of liquidity.

This chapter looks at the analogies that different constituencies—former kreditorë, public intellectuals and journalists, and actors in the construction industry—draw between the financial activities of the firms and klering in construction. Why, decades after the collapse of the firms, do people in Albania invoke their experience with the firms to critique contemporary financial practices in construction? What do these analogies tell us about forms of accumulation and investment in postsocialist and neoliberal economies?

In approaching these local analogies, I look for what Marilyn Strathern (2005) defines as "partial connections." The notion of partial connections allows for connectivity and relationality without necessarily implying isomorphism. Strathern uses the term to refer to partial connections between cultural forms and meanings, but I use her analytic here to reflect on the relationalities between forms of accumulation and investment proliferating in postsocialist Albania and, more broadly, in neoliberal economic contexts.

I focus on the partial connections between the economic logics of the firms and financing in construction. I ask what this analogy might tell us about postsocialist economic institutions, especially about forms of accumulation

and investment that have proliferated since the 1990s. My approach to "accumulation" and "investment" includes practices that go beyond the narrow definitions
by banking and credit institutions (see also Appadurai 1986; Elyachar 2005;
Guyer 2004; Maurer 2005, 2006; Roitman 2005). I suggest that the analogies between the firms and klering point to particular modalities of accumulation and
investment locally referred to as the "pyramid way" (*mënyra piramidale*). The
pyramid way captures an asymmetry between investments and profit, and an
unsustainable temporality of wealth accumulation. The analogies also point to
enduring regulatory frameworks and repertoires of credit, including the ambivalent legal framework around nonbank financial activities, the use of immigrant
remittances and housing as capital, and the use of social ties to enable financial
speculation.

These partial connections between the activities of the firms and those of the
construction industry in postsocialist Albania help us understand the relationality between speculative forms of accumulation across various contexts at the
center and margins of global capital. To explore these broader implications, I draw
a comparison between the pyramid way and Minsky's (1986) notion of Ponzi finance.[4] The term "Ponzi finance" refers to highly speculative and unsustainable
investment practices in the expanding money-manager capitalism of postwar
United States, whereby "financing costs are greater than income, so that the
amount of outstanding debt increases" (1986, 207). Like Ponzi finance, the pyramid way refers to an unsustainable temporality of profit making, where the investments of the present cannot match the liabilities of the future. Further, like
the proliferation of Ponzi finance in various moments of the post-Fordist economy in the United States and elsewhere, the pyramid way has been fueled by new
forms of capital and credit expansion. In the Albanian case, however, these have
been nonbank forms of capital and credit, such as migrant remittances and real
estate.

The Albanian context is a key site for exploring speculative economies at a time
when a critique of capitalist institutions "from the borderlands of capitalism"
(Guyer 2004, 170) could not be more pertinent. Many of the practices I discuss
here have flourished alongside the implementation of the Washington Consensus policies—deregulation, privatization, and strict monetary policy. Thus the lessons that emerge from these analogies speak to broader contemporary forms of
"spectacular accumulation" (Tsing 2000, 139–42) in margins and centers of global
finance. Although historically shaped by the postsocialist experience, the pyramid way resonates with economic practices that have proliferated alongside neoliberal policies implemented across the global North and South, especially since
the end of the Cold War.

The Pyramid Way

The notion of a pyramid way was suggested to me by Fatos Lubonja, a former political prisoner who, since the 1990s, became involved in politics and is now an active writer, political analyst, and public intellectual. Lubonja's insights about the firms were not simply those of an outside observer. As he has detailed in the autobiographical novel, *Nëntëdhjeteshtata* (2010), Lubonja was also a victim of the firms. Fresh out of prison and in search of a new life, he deposited and lost a significant amount of money in a minor scheme ran by a relative. During a conversation initially intended to reflect on his experience with the firms and their legacy, Lubonja evoked the analogy between the firms and the construction industry:

> [The construction firms] started by telling people "buy an apartment here or there" or "you need a villa outside Tirana" and naturally the money of average Albanians, instead of being invested in rational ways, were driven toward this dead industry because it does not produce anything, because you cannot even rent out these apartments. *This is the pyramid way*.[5]

Lubonja drew this analogy between the firms and construction based on their similar Ponzi logic of investment. Many kreditorë echoed Lubonja's analogy. For instance, Fatmira, the kreditor and cashier who had moved from Fier to Vlora, lamenting her husband's experience of work without pay in construction, invoked a similar analogy to the pyramid way:

> In the construction business, it has become very bad for small businesses like us. For instance, one subcontractor comes and provides *beton* [the concrete]. He doesn't get paid at first but later paid in apartments. The building is complete, residents move in and still the subcontractors do not get paid. Payments are increasingly delayed. [The subcontractors] borrow money. Debt after debt [*borxh pas borxhi*], it's like a pyramid. They are all connected to one another like in a chain.[6]

Fatmira described the practice of klering by referring to her experience with the firms. In klering, the source of liquidity and potential illiquidity are apartments. Actual payments for materials and services depend on when and for how much these apartments are sold. If, as is often the case, apartments are not sold, a crisis of liquidity ensues, and payments to subcontractors and their workers are delayed. Fatmira's husband had not received payment for work completed more than a year. This pattern was endemic in the industry in the 2000s and continued to the late 2010s. Fatmira suggests that this pattern entails an unsustainable logic of wealth accumulation similar to the firms. In both cases, the promised returns (the cash from the firms or sale of apartments) rely on an unsustainable pyramid way of investment.

The analogy between the firms and construction is also frequently evoked by economic journalists and people working in the construction industry (see Çela 2009, 2010; Kola 2013; *Monitor* 2009). Since 2000, a construction boom has unraveled in Albania, concentrated primarily in Tirana and cities along the southern Riviera. In national terms, construction constituted 12.9 percent of the GDP in 2006, 19.9 percent in 2010 (the peak), and fell to 12 percent in 2014 (INSTAT cited in Malaj and Shuli 2015). The initial construction boom in the early 2000s was financed in cash, thanks in large part to presales. Since the late 2000s, as presales began to dwindle, liquidity began to dry out. Construction firms practiced klering as a means of financing their construction. They expected demand in housing to continue to rise with migrant remittances and investments. Developers paid subcontractors in future apartments (rather than capital). But these expectations exceeded actual sales and by 2009, many subcontractors reported an increase in delayed payments—from 180 days up to a year—and an increase in high-interest black market loans (*Monitor* 2009). Many described this crisis of liquidity through the metaphors of the pyramid; economic journalists wrote about "the pyramid of debt" (Hoxha 2016) and the "chains of debt" (*zinxhirët e borxheve*). This analogy between the firms and klering goes beyond mere metaphor. It entails a comparison of modes of accumulation and investment as well as broader social and legal configurations that play into these speculative forms of finance.

The Ambivalent Legal Status of Klering

Let me recap how klering works. A developer hires subcontractors to fulfill a required number of jobs in a building that is in construction. These jobs might include installing electrical wires, plumbing, tiles, and so on. Rather than using cash or bank credit, the developer "pays" the subcontractors in apartments (from that same building or others). The subcontractor accepts the payment arrangement with the assumption that he/she will sell the apartment(s) in the future and thus collect the liquidity it needs to pay its workers. Workers, in turn, accept the delayed or insecure payment arrangements for their labor because they are desperate to work. When subcontractors are not able to sell these apartments, they run out of cash to pay employees.

In theory, klering payments can be more lucrative or come at a loss to the subcontractors—depending on whether the apartments are sold at a higher or lower value than estimated. More often than not, subcontractors experience loss as the apartments given in klering are often located in riskier real estate areas, such as city peripheries. These are areas that lack basic urban infrastructure and typically populated by newcomers from rural areas. New buildings located within the inner ring (*unaza*) of the city usually sell quickly, whereas those at the peripheries are often filled with vacancies. Developers often try to push these apartments as payments for klering contracts. This phenomenon has left its mark on several city sites such as the peripheral neighborhoods of Kodra e Diellit and Kashar (figure 5.1), where many buildings are not yet inhabited or even not yet completed. Walking through these neighborhoods one notices empty buildings, partially inhabited buildings, or buildings under construction. Often, it is not clear if the construction is still going on or has been suspended indefinitely, as subcontractors have abandoned their work to protest the lack of payments. A closer look at some of the construction information boards, for instance, reveals that the buildings were slated for completion years ago. In addition to the incomplete buildings, these areas also suffer from a lack of infrastructure. Roads between buildings are unpaved or poorly paved, sidewalks, public spaces, and playgrounds are absent. This urban landscape is a result of rushed building in areas that used to be farmlands and where the high-rises were built before the roads and other forms of

FIGURE 5.1. New high-rises in ongoing construction at Tirana's eastern periphery. January, 2009.

(Photograph by author.)

infrastructure. Overall, the sense that permeates these peripheries is that of ongoing construction zones. The sense of incompleteness in the urban landscape of
these areas materializes the sense of risk and uncertainty that permeates the construction industry. The risk factor is written into the gray legal framework that
enables klering.

The practice of klering is widespread and legitimate, sometimes described in
legal documents as "jo formale" (informal). As some of the people in the construction industry explained, klering arrangements are often spelled out in written contracts and signed by the parties in the presence of a notary public. Indeed,
a court case in the Circuit Court of Elbasan details the terms of a klering agreement that was not observed by the developer:

> The accuser was owed 46,900 euros for the value of the commodity (de-
> livered steel). This price would be paid for in klering by transferring the
> property title of six apartments, 490 square meters [5,274 square feet],
> located in this apartment building. (*Myzeqari vs. Beu Konstruction sh.p.k.*,
> 2016)

The contract in question described the exact location of the klering apartments
by the block, section, staircase, floor. The promised apartments were to be built
in the district of Kashar, at the time outside of but adjacent to Tirana's city line.
In this particular case, the accused party (the developer Beu Konstruction sh.p.k.)
was found guilty of not fulfilling their obligation of klering. Construction experts,
employed by the court, found that all the promised apartments were located on
the eighth floor. However, building inspection revealed that there was no eighth
floor. In other words, the contract had been a scam. Although this is not how klering usually unfolds, the case reveals the risks and uncertainties associated with
this payment practice as apartments used as capital are not yet built at the time
of the agreement. The legal grayness around klering adds to this uncertainty. In
this particular case, the District Court of Elbasan had accepted the klering contract as valid evidence; however, in other cases, klering contracts were not deemed
as binding or legal.

Another court case between the legal firm CMS Andonnino Ascoli & Cavasola Scamoni and the developer AJM SLOVENIJA Sh.p.k, centered around the
use of klering as payment for legal services rendered (*CMS Andonnino Ascoli &
Cavasola Scamoni vs. AJM SLOVENIJA sh.p.k.*, 2011). The disagreement had
emerged when the developer disputed the request by the legal services company
to pay in euros as opposed to apartments. The case went through three trials—at
the District Court of Tirana, the Court of Appeals, and the High Court. The different courts disagreed on whether the "informal contract" (*kontrata jo formale*)
between the developer and the legal services company conformed to the Alba-

nian Civil Code. The Court of Appeals recognized the "informal contract," but the District Court and the High Court disagreed. The case was finally closed with the High Court siding with the accused, not recognizing the legality of the klering contract.

These and other similar cases point to the ambivalent legal status of klering. This legal grayness constitutes one crucial partial connection between klering and pyramid firms' activities. In both cases, the ambiguity around the legality of such practices enables their proliferation. This lack of clear legal framework around klering further legitimizes it but without clarifying the boundaries of accountability in the exchange.

Real Estate and Remittances as Capital and Credit

Another key point of partial connections between the activities of the firms and the practice of klering is the use of real estate and remittances as forms of capital and credit. These two forms of wealth have contributed to a nonbank credit expansion that has fueled financial speculation.[7] Housing booms and busts have taken place in other centers and margins of global capital, mostly fueled by financialization (the expansion of bank credit to consumers or developers) or by a resource boom (cf. Grant 2014; Woodworth and Ulfstjerne 2016). In Albania, as discussed earlier, by investing at the firms, kreditorë circumvented bank credit, which was inaccessible to most at the time. Similarly, the boom in housing construction in the 2000s was enabled in part by nonbank forms of capital and credit. In this case, too, two significant nonbank sources of financing construction have been real estate and remittances. In other words, these two forms of wealth have continuously enabled financial speculation without liquidity.

In the klering exchange, homes (in this case, future apartments) have replaced capital as a means of payment. As discussed in chapter 4, this was also the case during the time of the firms. Kreditorë used their recently privatized apartments as capital to invest in the firms. In both cases, a boom in real estate (in the first case due to the privatization of the housing market, in the second case due to the growth in construction) fueled the respective speculative financial practices. In both cases, housing constituted not only a form of wealth but also a form of capital (Guyer 2016).

Klering practices resemble other forms of barter that have proliferated across the postsocialist world because of a similar lack of liquidity (Humphrey 1999; Woodruff 1999, 2000). For instance, David Woodruff studied the widespread use of barter in the new Russia. As money dried up, companies accepted barter payments for their services (for instance, gas, electricity). To a certain extent, the Albanian klering is similar to these barter practices. As in the Russian context, the most common reason given for engaging in klering is lack of liquidity or inability to meet bank requirements for loans (only 26 percent of construction is financed through bank loans [Malaj and Shuli 2015]). Given that many apartments used in the exchange are not yet built, the risk of bankruptcy and crisis of liquidity is ever present. The Russian companies that accepted in-kind payments faced the reality of further losses as, often, they were not able to sell these commodities at the price they had paid. Likewise, housing in Albania is an uncertain commodity. Depending on location and construction quality, apartments given in klering can become a liability rather than an asset. Many subcontractors went bankrupt when not able to liquidate these assets.

But in the Albanian context, klering is not only used as a means of exchange; by using homes as capital, klering enables a form of "financialization without liquidity" (Mattioli 2018). This kind of financialization avoids some of the risks associated with bank credit while introducing other risks. In klering, debt and risk are socialized. The inability to sell apartments exerts social pressure on the members of the subcontracting firms and introduces tension between subcontractors and developers.

"Debt," writes Roitman, "represents a moment when particular truths are revealed" (2005, 15). The new forms of credit/debt relationships introduced by klering practices carve out new networks of debt and new relations of hierarchy and dependency. Klering shifts the risks of construction and the real estate market from developers to subcontractors and from subcontracting firms to their employees. An architect familiar with klering, described the practice as another way of delegating sales from the developer to other parties. By paying subcontractors in klering, he noted, the developer is "hiring sales agents for free" (*Merr gratis agjentet e shitjes*).[8]

Subcontracting firms were hit the hardest by the crisis of liquidity in construction in the late-2000s. These consist of small- and medium-sized local businesses that provide the construction firms with the essential materials and infrastructure (concrete, bricks, tiles, plumbing equipment). Given the initial rush in apartment presales in the early 2000s, subcontracting firms fell prey to promises and calculations from the construction companies that the real estate market would continue to expand at the same exponential rates. Based on these calculations, construction firms started investing by paying their subcontractors in nonliquid payments, by engaging in klering. By the late 2000s, however, sales had gone down leaving many subcontractors with empty apartments. In 2009, according to a survey conducted with small subcontracting businesses in the construction industry, "Almost all administrators of the [subcontracting] companies surveyed affirm that they own some apartments in the capital that they have received in exchange for contracts with developers. While they have invested their own money in construction, they have to wait two to three years to obtain the profit from their investment" (Çela 2009).

One administrator explained that he owned seven apartments in Tirana, which he was eager to sell to obtain capital that would pay him for his work as well as his employees (Çela 2009). But given the decline in demand for apartments, he feared going bankrupt if he were not able to sell them. As a nonliquid form of credit/debt, klering introduces some of the same risks—illiquidity and bankruptcy—that are at the heart of more traditional forms of bank credit and debt (James 2014; Stout 2016), but it distributes these risks to different actors and by other norms and temporalities.

Although it leads to illiquidity and bankruptcy, klering is also "productive" (Roitman 2004) in the sense that it generates economies and social relations. Klering, thus, enables developers to complete new developments without having access to the necessary capital and without having to worry about accruing interest. Klering is also productive of work. As Fatmira confessed, her husband, who was not paid for months due to an unfulfilled klering contract, continued to work for the subcontracting firm because he wanted to work, to be active. Work and activity are very much part of these workers' notion of self. The inability to work is viewed by many as a form of social death. Fatmira's husband was willing to take the risk of nonpayment to maintain his social persona as an active, working man. Laborers in such cases do not have the choice of being paid in liquidity. Instead, they are forced into klering arrangements and become dependent on the developers and the real estate market.

Another source of capital and credit in construction has been the continuous flow of remittances, which constituted a significant source of cash for investing at the firms. In the aftermath of the firms, immigrant remittances have continued to be the prime source of income and credit. They constitute an important source of financing the purchase or construction of homes. Such was the case of Andon, who finished the house for his brother and himself with the help of the brother's remittances. The exact contribution of remittances toward construction and real estate sales are hard to estimate, but the promise of remittances as a source of financing of future homes is a factor mentioned by many developers.

Developers frequently reference immigrant investments as evidence of a need for more real estate. "I see a strong interest from immigrants," said Hajredin Fratari, the president of Fratari Construction, "especially from those living in England." He then proceeded with an explanation that is popular among other developers:

Many [immigrants] are considering their return to Albania as something that will happen in the future, something that makes them buy a house here now. Equally, I see their interest in purchasing an immovable property here as an investment. I disagree with what has been said lately: that there is a saturation of the market. On the contrary, there is still a hunger for dwellings, just look at the population of Tirana or the new couples in need of new apartments. But the real destination, I think, will be toward the coast. I expect that fifty to a hundred thousand apartments will be bought from Albanians outside of national borders. (*Monitor* 2010)

In addition to being a resource for housing financing, the flow of remittances is also an object of speculation for developers rushing to build before the immigrant buyers come. This has led to overbuilding. As with the flow of remittances in multiple currencies to the firms, the use of remittances (predominantly in euros) to purchase new homes is mediated by social relations. Migrants buy new apartments or villas in Albania as a way to maintain social ties. They often help their kin to purchase or remodel their existing homes with remittances. Dimiter Dalakoglou (2010) and Gerda Dalipaj (2016) studied the transnational kinship relations that have been negotiated and extended through the building, purchasing, or remodeling of homes in Albania or abroad. As is the case among migrants and diasporas elsewhere (see, for instance, Chu 2010; Kwon 2015), homes become a means of maintaining transnational kinship relations.

Financial Speculation and Social Ties

Social relations play an essential role in mediating klering. This is yet another partial connection between the firms' activities and financing practices in the construction industry. The anthropological literature on credit/debt has historically situated such financial relationships in social relations (Elyachar 2005; Mauss 1954; Peebles 2010; Roitman 2005; Taussig 1987). Indeed, finance and social ties were intertwined in the activities of the firms and those of klering. Both entailed nonbank forms of credit and debt that were mediated by different types of social ties.

Klering is made possible through the active use of relations among kin, acquaintances, and friends as well as clientelistic networks. A similar phenomenon had enabled firms to expand their reach. As discussed in chapter 3, *menaxherë* (managers) and *seksere* (brokers) acted as mediators between the firms and kreditorë to attract chain deposits. These brokers invited family members and acquaintances to invest in the firms. These chains of credit allowed menaxherë to deposit larger amounts of money that the firms' owners rewarded with higher interest rates. In a similar vein, subcontractors use their social networks to sell apartments.

In both cases, illiquidity often resulted from off-the-books loans to family and friends of the companies' heads. As one economist working with a construction company pointed out, some of the outstanding payments for sold apartments that contributed to the shortage in liquidity of a developer (and which led to the developer's eventual bankruptcy) were also ones from family members who were "given" the apartments with the informal promise of payment in the future. Similarly, former insiders of such pyramid firms as Cenaj and Gjallica, often blamed for their scarcity of cash the off-the-books loans to relatives or other acquaintances of the owners. For instance, Fatmira, the cashier for one kompani, claimed that one of the greatest mistakes of these kompani at the time was "hiring their relatives":

> FATMIRA: There were some practices that I did not like at the time.
> SMOKI: Were there relatives that profited from your boss' income?
> FATMIRA: Yes, for instance, they [the relatives] would ask me to withdraw a 500 or a 100,000 [lek]. I always insisted on drawing up a receipt. How could one throw a stash of cash in the bag without a receipt?[9]

For Fatmira, this use of kinship ties in operating the firms was one of the contributing factors for their collapse. In this sense, social relations were not only mediators of transactions at the firms but also a source of liability and financial distress.

Another way that social ties play a role in transactions within the construction industry pertains to the use of connections to government officials. Although developers are all private companies, it is well known among people in the field that contracts for public works are awarded to connected firms. People involved in the construction industry talk about corruption as a widespread phenomenon. Corruption allegedly takes place in the issuing of construction licenses and in tenders for large-scale public works.

When discussing relations between construction companies and government officials, the architect subcontracting for various firms, declared with cynicism:

> Every government has its circle of collaborating and privileged construction firms. For instance, Ilir Meta [a politician and current president] takes the owner of the firm that he will give the contract to and asks him for his opinion on the project—everyone else understands that this guy will get the contract, so they don't even bother applying [for the tender].[10]

These tacit signals of favoritism often lead to lower competition at the public bid for the contract, which allows the select firms to receive the maximum allotted funds by the government.

The use of social ties recalls similar practices in other postsocialist contexts. The networks of private-public developers in China offer a good comparison. There, too, public-private companies receive contracts through connections and bribes (Zhang 2012).[11] In Macedonia, a similar practice of in-kind payments in the construction industry has fueled "forced credit" while also directly benefiting the ruling party, the VMRO-DPMNE (Mattioli 2018). In Albania, accusations of similar clientelistic networks are legion. For instance, critics of Prime Minister Edi Rama, a popular former mayor of Tirana for three consecutive terms, state that it was under his administration that the city turned into "a jungle of construction" as permits were issued en masse, allegedly to firms with ties to the mayor. In reality, construction permits peaked in the late 1990s, right before Rama's tenure as mayor, and remained high during his time in office. The first few decades of postsocialist urban transformation in Tirana witnessed an intensification of the city. New high-rises were erected in between old communist low-rises, stifling any available public space planned for social interaction and play in a city where social time in public spaces is a crucial cultural ritual. The construction, noted an architect, enfolded in a "rushed manner" and "against any concept of the urban condition."[12]

Rama's tenure as mayor has carved out a new role of the mayor as such in national politics and has brought construction to the center of political campaigning and debate.[13] Since his tenure, several allegations surfaced against Rama construction licensing for political purposes. Rama's loss of his fourth bid for mayor took place while the central government was run by Sali Berisha, who returned to power as prime minister in 2005. During the time that they overlapped (2005–11), the two engaged in a bitter war over construction licenses and urban plans of Tirana. Berisha suspended construction plans of public works approved by Rama.

In 2011, Rama lost his bid for mayor to PD's Lulzim Basha. Rama won the national elections in 2013, becoming prime minister. In this capacity, he continued the war against construction with mayor Basha. Rama quickly issued a moratorium on all construction licenses across the country; this affected the construction firms with ties to PD and suspended Basha's plans for redevelopment of key areas in the city. In 2015, when beginning more research on construction, I expected the moratorium to be welcomed by local people who resented overbuilding. On the contrary, I found that many lamented that "everything was dead" because of the moratorium. People referred to the effect of the moratorium on jobs and business opportunities. Further, my informants were suspicious of continuing clientelism in the construction industry. With private construction of high-rises limited under the moratorium, public works' contracts became the only source of income and jobs for those in the construction industry. The few public works contracts available were given to a select set of design and construction firms with ties to government officials.

Public works are a key contributor to unfulfilled payments and chains of debt in Albania. A report on the increasing "pyramid of debt" stated that public tenders have further fueled illiquidity in construction (Hoxha 2016). A consultant familiar with the construction industry explained that "public tenders are concentrated in few companies. The winners have to pay a large bribe to the grantors of the tender. The company that wins the tender assigns the remaining funds to the subcontracting company (*kompani nënkontraktore*). When the same company wins multiple tenders simultaneously, it cannot meet the liquidity necessary for all jobs and so it does not pay subcontractors" (Hoxha 2016, 6). Ties between developers and state officials thus suck up liquidity from the construction industry, leading to more chains of debt. This trajectory of illiquidity doubles up as "most payments in construction are handled through klering" (Hoxha 2016, 6).

Social ties—both in the form of kinship and clientelistic relationships—play a role in enabling construction. They also play a role in fueling financial speculation and risk, as is evident in the return of *fajde* (moneylending) in public debate since the mid-2000s, this time referring to high-interest loans in the black market (*Monitor* 2009). The emergence of a black market in high-interest (up to 18 percent) moneylending is attributed to a combination of factors that have led to illiquidity in the construction industry and beyond. These factors include the high bribes to state officials, the widespread use of klering, the drop in remittances, and the restriction of bank credit to consumers since the late 2000s (mostly due to the credit limit set in the aftermath of the world financial crisis of 2008 by the banks' headquarters in various European capitals). These factors combine informal clientelistic networks, social ties among developers and subcontractors, and official relations between banks and consumers. Together, they contribute to widespread illiquidity that has created the conditions for high-risk financial practices.

These patterns are analogous to the social dynamics that enabled the firms. Anthropological studies of economic relations, understand social ties as a buffer to the uncertainty of the abstract market. The two cases in question challenge this premise by demonstrating how social relations are used to fuel speculation and enable further financialization. The respective financial schemes are exerting more social pressure on various groups of people, recreating relations that are not ones of even barter but of uneven debt.[14]

From Stacks of Cash to Betonizim (Concrete-ization)

Partial connections suggested between the firms and klering go beyond analogies in the patterns of investment. Some draw a direct financial trajectory from the wealth that disappeared at the firms to the new apartment buildings that mushroomed in the years following the collapse of the firms. Pointing to the row of new high-rises lining Vlora's transformed beachfront, Isuf, a former kreditor, who happens to work for a major construction firm in the city, said:

> That's where the money of the pyramid firms [*firma piramidale*] lies. Do you see how the buildings rise every day? Do you see how Vlora is transformed? All these apartment buildings [*pallate*], all these vilas [*vila*].[15]

Isuf left the last sentence incomplete, assuming we both shared a tacit understanding of the material connection between the cash of the firms and the boom in construction of high-rises at the beachfront. Isuf had hinted at this by gesturing toward the new apartment buildings and later by stating bluntly: *that's where the money of the firms lies*. The incompleteness of his statement allows for so much more than a causal explanation of the material correlation between pyramid cash and what is widely referred to as *betonizim* (concrete-ization).

These allegations, though not substantiated in actual investigations, echo a general suspicion among former kreditorë that much of the money accumulated by the firms had been invested in construction. Whether the allegations are legitimate or not, one thing is for sure: the material connections between the economies of the firms and the construction industry were already established during the firms' boom. By 1996, some firms had announced plans for investing in the construction of dream-like apartment buildings. For instance, in December 1996, a month after the IMF urged local authorities to shut down the firms, the leading kompani, Vefa, announced the inauguration of the construction project of a complex of 380 apartments in Tirana's peripheral district of Laprakë. This was the same compound that was later confiscated by the state and allocated to the pyramid families. Vefa's president Vehbi Alimucaj's "new ambition in the sphere of the construction industry" (M. B. 1996, 9) foresaw the construction rush that followed the collapse of the firms. Alimucaj had anticipated that real estate development would be the next jackpot, as indeed it turned out to be the case.

These allegations speak to another kind of partial connection between the two economies: the feeding of different speculative economies into one another. This observation resonates with the claim by Kindelberger and Aliber (2005) that speculative bubbles often intertwine with other bubbles or other instances of speculation. Thus, just as the flows of cash from the remittance economy served as a source of credit expansion for the firms, the spoils of the latter may have played a similar role in the initial financing of construction projects, both visibly and in ways that are hard to track through a paper trail. These intertwined dynamics speak to the broader factors that make possible speculative forms of finance as well as highlighting the broader implications and legacies of such economies beyond their bust.

"The Pyramid Way" as Ponzi Finance

What emerges from these partial connections are particular modalities of accumulation that have endured throughout the three decades of postcolonial transformation in Albania. The form of accumulation locally defined as the pyramid way brings to mind Hyman Minsky's discussion of the highly speculative type of investment in postwar banking in the United States, which he termed "Ponzi finance" (1978, 1986). Following Keynes, Minsky argued that both bankers and borrowers were faced with a constant uncertainty of the profits expected in the future. Depending on how actors in the marketplace negotiate this uncertainty, Minsky distinguished between three "financing regimes": hedge, speculative, and Ponzi finance. He suggested that these were "characterized by different relations between cash payment commitments on debts and expected cash receipts" (1986, 206). Of the three, Ponzi finance is the most insolvent. Minsky described Ponzi finance as types of investments and borrowings whereby the financial costs of investing are higher than the expected income (1986, 207). This relation between investment and expected income leads to more debt over time. The pyramid way is analogous to this notion of Ponzi finance in three ways.

The first resemblance concerns the insolvent modality of accumulation and investment. It is this particular Ponzi modality of investment—plagued by unsustainability and inability to make the promised payments based on the expected income—that constitutes the basis for the analogy between the firms and klering. In estimating future demand in housing based on the real estate boom of the early nineties as well as in the proliferation of chains of debt and delayed payments as a means of financing future housing developments, the construction companies in Albania are equally involved in unsustainable pyramidal forms of investment.

The second resemblance concerns the relation between these speculative practices in the private sector and official or unofficial regulation that enables them. Minsky's choice of the term "Ponzi" to describe a legitimate, though highly insolvent, financial activities are analogous to the use of "the pyramid way" in describing contemporary klering practices in Albania. In both cases, economic methods embedded in legal institutions are compared to allegedly isolated instances of speculative manias. It is suggested that speculative investment practices could flourish within (rather than outside) established financial and other economic institutions. As such, these analogies aim at targeting regulatory regimes as actors responsible for enabling or preventing future economic disasters.

Thus, for Minsky, regulating the financial sector—through government institutions such as the central banks and the Federal Reserve—was a key policy imperative for averting future crises. It is because of his view on financial fragility and his focus on banking, credit, and debt that Minsky's contributions have reemerged among economic circles in the aftermath of the 2008 subprime mortgage crisis. Among others, Perry Mehrling (2010), for instance, looks at the role that some intermediary institutions, defined loosely as "shadow banking" (Epstein 2001), came to play in the exponential increase in speculative forms of finance. These institutions performed banking services while evading banking regulations.

Likewise, the firms and the contemporary construction industry in Albania engage in a similar form of "shadow banking." Some kompani, for instance, acted as an "informal credit market" (Jarvis 1999), as they engaged in loaning and investment that were not regulated by central authorities. Rather than framing this ambiguous status of the firms to ignorance of capitalist institutions, economist Dirk Bezemer (2001) blames the postsocialist institutions modeled after the policies of the Washington Consensus for creating the conditions for these ambiguous forms of credit to flourish. Likewise, by likening klering to the pyramid way, local residents point their critique to official institutions, the specific regulations around financing in the real estate markets, as well as the politics around the distribution of construction licenses—a politics organized around the economy of rents rather than a studied plan of urban expansion.

The third theme in these analogies is the continuities and discontinuities in the flow, transfer, conversion of different forms of wealth from the firms to construction. This theme brings attention to the materiality of finance and financial speculation (Callon, Millo, and Muniesa 2007; Ho 2009; Knorr Cetina and Brueger 2002; Poon 2009; Zaloom 2005). Attention to the materiality of finance reveals the specificity of the types of flows (credit, debt, investment) that make speculation possible. Like other places around the world, Albania has experienced modest financialization, mainly through the expansion of bank credit to consumers and businesses. The pyramid way, however, did not emerge from this financialization; nor was it shaped by the kind of financial innovation typical in the center of high finance such as new technologies of trading (Zaloom 2005) or the specialization of credit rating agencies (Poon 2009). Instead, it was enabled by nonbank forms of wealth and credit that emerged after the collapse of the command economy and the introduction of free market institutions. These included social ties, new types and temporalities of payment, new forms of capital (remittances, real estate). That said, as some of the examples here suggest, the pyramid way has always been intertwined if not fueled by developments in the formal banking and credit sectors.

Conclusion

According to Strathern, the analytical mileage we get from thinking through the partial connections between different practices and concepts is "[the ability] to hold other positions and perspectives in mind" (2005, 55). Thinking through the Albanian pyramid way with the Ponzi finance in mind allows us to reflect on the distinct effects of such logics of accumulation on the ground. The postsocialist space—especially thanks to the privatization of former state property, the deregulation of the economy, the rapid devaluation of local assets vis-à-vis foreign goods—has constituted a prime site for accumulation through speculative forms of investment.

Albania, in particular, is a frontier par excellence, not just as an "emerging market" but also as a country where postsocialist transformations seem to be a never-ending process. Other borderlands of the increasingly differentiated postsocialist geography mirror Albania's incomplete betonizim. As Mathijs Pelkmans (2003) suggests in the context of postsocialist Georgia, similar unfinished constructions also serve as enactments of "an uncomfortable space between reality and discourse" (132). The reality of an "incomplete present" (Miyazaki 2003, 262) materialized in the unfinished apartment buildings versus the discourse of a coming utopia of becoming European. As such, places like Albania and Georgia, with their concretized landscape of the "not yet" (Bloch cited in Miyazaki 2003, 261) speak to broader aspirations and tensions thereof that proliferate in contexts of radical economic and political transformation.

In the course of this chapter, I have also engaged explicitly and implicitly in "partial connections" between different concepts and sites. Among others, I have touched on the relationality of the Albanian "pyramid way" of accumulation with Minsky's Ponzi finance. As we rethink how get-rich-quick firms take hold and what effects they leave on the ground, it is crucial to adopt this relational form of thinking as a way of identifying new modes of wealth creation as well as the new types of social and political differentiations that these new arrangements bring to life.

The analogies between the ponzi logics of accumulation of the firms and the pyramid way of doing business in construction are not to be taken as rhetorical devices. They point to particular unsustainable logics of accumulation and investment that have endured throughout nearly three decades of postsocialist transformations in Albania. These analogies are an invitation to think about Ponzi logics and temporalities of accumulation and investment as a broader financial reality of a neoliberal economic order that affects both margins and centers of global capital. Such logics and temporalities of accumulation are also shaped by cultural and historical economic rationalities that are often driven by what economists describe as "externalities"—in this case, forms of entrepreneurship, kinship ties, patronage relationship, and aspiration toward European modernity.

The accounts by kreditorë gathered in this book echo Minsky's prediction that Ponzi finance emerges from periods of credit expansion, increase in risky loans, and unsustainable promises of future returns on investment. In the case of the firms in Albania, the waves of credit expansion have taken the form of bank and nonbank credit (such as remittances, apartments, social networks). This pyramid way of doing business in Albania calls attention to types of credit expansion and speculative finance from below (rather than through top-down financialization). But these bottom-up forms of financialization and speculation are not to be studied separately from the official structures of credit and capital. These financial practices provide insight into the diverse economies that proliferate within neoliberal regimes, while also being other to neoliberal logics, institutions, and practices.

Epilogue

PONZI LOGICS IN
POSTSOCIALIST ALBANIA

It has always been difficult to explain how one does an ethnographic study of pyramid schemes, both in my fieldsite (Albania) and in my current home and workplace at Ohio University in Athens, Ohio. During my fieldwork in 2008 in Tirana, I had a long conversation with a relative trying to explain "what I was *doing*" as part of my research. Initially, he had recommended that I check out a new gravesite where old bones had just been discovered. Then, he thought I could be researching the kanun, the honor code of the Albanian highlands that have captured the imagination of travel writers and anthropologists alike. Finally, after a long-winded explanation on my part on the scope of the anthropology of financial speculation, he suggested enthusiastically: "What you should really study is these sports betting cafés that have sprung up everywhere."

As he made this suggestion, he pointed at one such café across the street. It was a modest café, compared to the others in Tirana, where social coffee drinking in stylish open-air settings is a cultural institution. Regular cafés are bustling with people, sitting, sipping beverages, and speaking to one another for hours on end, whereas the betting café looked empty and filled with sadness of the lone customer glued to the TV screens announcing game results. I laughed heartily at my relative's suggestion and could not see at first how my talk about the firms had led him to think about the betting cafés.

I dismissed this suggestion at the time. Yet, over the course of multiple research visits between 2010–19, I frequently remembered this conversation as sports betting cafés continued to spread and multiply, becoming that ubiquitous institution that made for a perfect site to study the "imponderabilia of everyday life"

(Malinowski 1922, 20–22). Indeed, with time, I realized that my relative had a good ethnographic sensibility. Something about my talk about the anthropology of financial speculation had evoked in my relative's mind an analogy between investing in the firms and investing in sports betting; the betting cafés, just like the firms, seemed like a sure losing game, yet people continued to invest. The betting cafés had become as ubiquitous in Tirana in the 2000s as the firms's outlets were in the 1990s.[1]

This popularization of betting games is one of many signs of the persistent economic logics of high-risk and speculation that were at the heart of the firms. In writing about the pyramid firms, I have sought to speak to these persistent speculative economies that proliferate alongside neoliberal reforms. Indeed, the stories of participants in the firms do not only constitute a record of the past, but also speak to concerns of the present, in Albania as in other margins of global capital. As kreditorë (creditors/investors to the firms) warned in their critique of financing practices in construction, Ponzi logics of investment and accumulation continue to persist, even as official financial institutions have become more robust. These logics emerge in the *klering* (in-kind) payments in the construction industry, where construction is fueled by promised payments that hinge on uncertain sales of apartments not yet built. They also materialize in the re-emergence of high-interest nonbank moneylending that is reported to be the last resort for individuals and businesses. Similar forms of speculative finance have proliferated in other sites central or peripheral to global capital—from the Wall Street and subprime mortgage market in the United States to the matsutake foraging rush in postindustrial Oregon (Tsing 2015) to building booms across Central, East, and Southeast Asia (Bissenova 2012; Grant 2014; Woodworth and Ulfstjerne 2016). These speculative economies complement official financial institutions; at times, they provide services and forms of wealth inaccessible through formal channels, in other instances, they proliferate alongside the latter.

These economies share a logic of investment and accumulation that introduces the temporality of a punctuated present. They entail forms of investment that promise quick fixes to make up for lack of stable income. Such types of investments have emerged within the broader landscape of an increasingly neoliberal economy.

Since the collapse of the firms, economic reforms in Albania have maintained a distinct neoliberal flavor. This postsocialist neoliberal economic order has focused on liberalization and privatization reforms. The expansion and consolidation of the private banking sector have been one of the ongoing goals since the collapse of the firms. There are now more than a dozen commercial banks, most of which are owned by or branches of foreign (mostly European) banks (IMF

2014; Musaraj and Sullivan 2014). The official financial system has adopted much of the EU regulation. Bank credit to individuals and businesses has expanded significantly over the past decade. It is curious that, even with the expansion of official credit and proliferation of commercial banks, individuals and businesses continue to turn to the unofficial sources of cash. The answer to these seemingly paradoxical practices lies precisely in the nature and scope of these macroeconomic reforms.

Albania's economy is now rated as an upper-middle-income economy (World Bank 2017) with a few large industries and foreign investments—among others, in energy and mining—but with the majority of the working force employed in small- and medium-sized enterprises in services, agriculture, and tourism. These are mostly family-run businesses. Despite the large size of employment and GDP, these sectors have received the least amount of attention from policymakers. Governments of both sides of the political spectrum have typically sought to attract money from foreign aid to invest in large infrastructural projects or resource extraction. Further, following the guidelines by international bodies such as the World Bank, the IMF, and the European Bank for Reconstruction and Development, the Albanian government has consistently targeted informality and tax evasion and aimed at lowering the public debt and increasing government efficiency. It is not surprising then that I continue to encounter discontent and a general sense of nervous uncertainty about the near future. The feeling of economic insecurity and lack of stable employment is very palpable in everyday conversations. In struggling to make sense of this persistent uncertainty, it is instructive to return to the experience with the firms to explore practices, logics, and relations that have persisted in Albania's postsocialist economy.

Take, for instance, the use of remittances in multiple currencies as cash to invest at the firms. Remittances continue to constitute a significant source of income and credit for investment, and they continue to circulate through kin networks, though their contribution to the GDP has fallen from 15 percent in 1996 to 8.84 percent in 2017 (Bank of Albania 2006; Ven Gelder 2017). Remittances are also a source of investment in self-built housing and housing purchases. In other words, in Albania as in other sites across the globe, remittances constitute a vast informal credit market, often sponsoring development from below (Nicholson 2001; Ratha and Mohapatra 2012). Such remittance flows provide a buffer to the punctuated temporalities of neoliberalism. They, too, become a subject of speculation over financial prosperity or cultural imagination (see also Chu 2010; Kwon 2015; Small 2018). As discussed in chapter 5, developers in Albania often speculate over the anticipated flow of remittances in future housing purchases.

Another example of economies of "marginal gains" (Guyer 2004) that proliferated alongside neoliberal reforms in the 1990s and continued to do so in the late-2000s is transacting in a multicurrency regime. As discussed in chapters 2 and 3, a multicurrency system permeated the firms's transactions. Multiple currencies flowed then through transnational migrant networks. A multicurrency regime continued to prevail in Albania in the 2000s, though it transformed into a dual currency regime since the advent of the euro. This regime has become more formalized as more and more businesses accept payments in euros while banks offer accounts in euros. These multicurrency regimes reflect the uneven political and social geographies of hard and soft currencies (Guyer 2012).

Specific sectors of the Albanian economy thrive on the dual currency regime. For instance, small businesses in local tourism (hotels, restaurants, etc.) announce their fares in euros, catering primarily to European tourists (mostly from Poland, Italy, and Macedonia). They accept payment in lek and euros, the latter being the preferred currency because of its higher durability and higher value in global currency markets. As an Albanian-American withdrawing cash in lek from local banks, I note the slight loss in value when paying local businesses euros. I imagine that this transactional pathway brings marginal gains to local businesses as they save in euros.

Another key commodity valued in euros is real estate. The price of housing is usually set in euros, even when the buyer is paying in lek. This practice is well established and formalized, and it primarily benefits banks and developers. Banks provide the loans in euros while developers gain on the sale of the house by valuing it in euros.

This preference for multiple currencies is a continuation of a strategy of diversification of sources of value and wealth. Like the multicurrency regime that proliferated alongside the firms, the current dual-currency regime provides opportunities for arbitrage and the possibility for storing wealth of more durable value (the euro). This tendency resonates with practices in other sites of the world where people find creative ways of turning their marginality into a source of arbitrage and possibility for value conversion (Guyer 2004; Maurer, Musaraj, and Small 2018; Truitt 2013; Villarreal 2010).

This formalization of the dual-currency regime speaks to yet another continuity between the firms and contemporary financial practices, namely the ongoing longing for Europe as an economic, political, and cultural horizon. The formalization of the dual-currency economy parallels the ongoing efforts toward European Union accession. The euro has economic and cultural cachet. The love of the euro is a quest for more enduring value; it is also a yearning for the temporality of Europe (Halawa 2015; Pelkmans 2003). The euro is symbolic of the EU as a geopolitical and cultural space. This longing, which has a long history in the national imagination, has been appropriated and deployed in the official political landscape. Indeed, the promise of bringing the country closer to Europe is

the only political ideology shared by both sides of the political spectrum. The formalization of this longing raises questions that pertain to a failure of political
actors in Albania and elsewhere to provide a viable political agenda to the economic and social problems that many local people face.

From pyramid schemes to speculative financing in construction to betting cafés, Ponzi logics of accumulation and investment have become enduring economic forms in postsocialist Albania. These economic forms articulate well
with broader neoliberal economic institutions that thrive on risk and speculation.
They are fueled by top-down institutions such as official and unofficial global markets, regional financial flows, and Washington Consensus policies; they are also
sustained by bottom-up repertoires such as remittance flows and official and unofficial markets of multiple currencies. The economies are shot through with
ambivalent politics of wealth gain and redistribution. For instance, while the use
of multiple currencies by kreditorë or family-run hotels is a strategy of wealth accumulation at the margins; the deployment of the dual-currency regime by
banks and developers seems to redirect the gains from currency discrepancies
toward the top (rather than the bottom) of the pyramid. As we consider such
economies of marginal gains alongside neoliberal expansion, we should therefore
attend to the politics of wealth distribution that these economic repertoires and
institutions entail.

Notes

INTRODUCTION

1. For exotic Orientalist literature on Albania, see Durham (2010), Byron (2011), West (2007).

2. For a detailed account of this history of openness to the East in the 1950s and 1960s and the increasing isolation since the 1970s, including the making and the breaking of ties with the former Soviet Union and China, see Mëhilli (2017).

3. For an overview of the events of the 1990s, see Pettifer and Vickers (2009) and Abrahams (2015).

4. These policies are also articulated in two key academic articles (Lipton and Sachs 1991a, 1991b).

5. These processes and practices have been at the heart of ethnographies of postsocialist societies since the 1990s. The rich ethnographic record on postsocialist transformations includes, among others, Creed (1998), Lemon (1998), Stark and Bruszt (1998), Verdery (1996, 2003), Burawoy and Verdery (1999), Woodruff (1999), Humphrey (2002), Dunn (2004), Ledeneva (2006), and Berdahl (2009).

6. The sociologist Artan Fuga (2003) makes a compelling case for how, in its economic program, the Socialist Party took a turn to the right in the 1990s.

7. As I describe in more detail in chapter 4, new apartments built by the state were rentals only. People living in villages could own and build their houses, but the notion of property here too was quite different than the one in a free-market for real estate.

8. Since 1946, crediting shifted quickly and dramatically from the private sector to the public sector. The Albanian National Bank (Banka Kombëtare Shqiptare) lended solely to state enterprises. Individual loans were given to workers building or repairing their homes but these loans became increasingly restricted by the 1970s onward (Shoqata Shqiptare e Bankave 2012).

9. As I describe in chapter 1, a practice known as llotari (lottery) also existed informally in communist Albania. But this refers to the informal pooling of savings through collectives that resemble rotating and savings associations, ROSCAs. These transactions do not entail interest on deposits or a multiplication of investments. By contrast, the government-run lotteries that were allowed in other former-communist countries were typical state lotteries that entailed interest and the potential for winning bigger gains than investments.

10. Some commercial banks were set up at this time, but they were reluctant to give credit to individuals, especially given a lack of assets or capital that would serve as collateral.

11. Ponzi schemes refer to a financial scheme whereby the operator makes money by attracting deposits from a growing base of investors. Rather than investing the money into other types of economic activities, the operator(s) circulate money from newer investors to older ones, until the scheme collapses. The term Ponzi scheme is named after the infamous scheme on international reply coupons orchestrated by Charles Ponzi, the Italian immigrant based in Boston in the 1920s. Ponzi promised investors up to a 50 percent return, which he justified to be drawn from what today would be called a game of arbitrage of the international reply coupons, which exchanged for a different value across

different countries. As is known from the aftermath of the collapse of Ponzi's scheme, instead of driving the returns from profits made through the advertised legitimate exchanges, this and other similar firms, usually paid early investors with the money from later investments, in the hope that the number of investors would keep growing at exponential rates (Zuckoff 2006).

12. Another term used interchangeably with kompani was *shoqëri* (company).

13. While there were significant differences between the kompani and fondacione, in this book I refer to both as "pyramid firms" or "firms" because kreditorë often talked about them as such, and because they were treated as such by authorities, even when the distinction between the two was made based on their other investments.

14. A list of debtors to the firm Vefa, published in 1999, includes relatives of the owner (Vehbi Alimuçaj), the other firm Kamberi, Albanian and Italian businesses, and even the PD Tirana branch (*Gazeta Shqiptare* 1999, 21).

15. As the firms were inconsistent with their record keeping and as kreditorë often bundled their deposits, the number of participants in the firms varies.

16. The course of these events is documented in the print media at the time (see, for instance, Hazizaj 1996a, 1996b); in subsequent memoirs by Zogaj (1999), Lubonja (2010), and Baze (2010); and in other recent historical accounts (Abrahams 2015).

17. Such expectations also were an extension of the particular imaginaries of the state; under communism, the state was the main driver of the economy and hence the primary source of legitimacy of economic transactions. Scholars of state socialism and postcommunism make a similar point. See Verdery (1996) on the paternalistic state in socialist Romania, and Alexander (2003) on the lingering expectations from the state in postprivatization reforms in Kazakhstan.

18. Although Sude and Gjallica differed from one another in so far as the former was a pure Ponzi scheme and the latter had some investments in other industries, I refer to them both as "firms" because they both engaged in fajde.

19. Unlike Sude, Gjallica claimed numerous investments (some of them inflated, but others legitimate) in a wide range of economic activities.

20. The events of 1997 are detailed in several accounts, including Nicholson (1999) and Abrahams (2015).

21. Albania received candidacy status for European Union integration only in 2014. The prospects for integration continue to remain uncertain as the EU continues to delay the integration process.

22. After two terms of the PS in government, Sali Berisha went on to serve as prime minister for two consecutive terms (2005–13). He continues to be a member of parliament with an influence on PD. On the opposite side of the political spectrum, the current prime minister and leader of PS, Edvin "Edi" Edi Rama, was one of the early victims of the 1996–1997 government crackdowns on dissenters. In 1996, Rama was beaten in what was seen as a retaliation against dissidents. Rama was active in the student movement of the early 1990s and was initially a PD supporter, but had a falling out with the party (as did many other founders of the opposition) as Berisha turned increasingly authoritarian. Reentering politics after 1997, this time as a PS member, Rama served as minister of culture, then mayor of Tirana for eight years, and replaced Berisha as prime minister in the 2013 elections. Rama's acerbic relation with Berisha can be traced back to his politically motivated beating in 1996.

23. Insofar as its value is divorced from the real terms of valuation as defined by the social relations of production.

24. For critiques of this dichotomy and line of thinking about capitalism and crisis, see also Derrida ([1994] 2012), Maurer (2005b, 2010), Morris (2005), Roitman (2013).

25. Writing during a time of expansion of financial markets, Minsky (1982, 1986) argued, against the mainstream wisdom at the time, that financial markets are inherently unstable and that the enthusiasm of the growth would inevitably push the financial climate from one of reasonable speculative finance to one of Ponzi finance.

26. Bezemer underscores the impact of IMF and World Bank structural adjustment policies, especially "the strict monetarist policies, financial market policies that were very strict for official banks but extremely lenient for informal financial intermediaries" (2001, 4).

27. Claims to psychological universals (such as irrational exuberance, mass mania, euphoria) run counter to some of the key presuppositions and findings of the vast ethnographic record of economic anthropology. Indeed, the history of economic anthropology is anchored in a critique of the economic thinking that takes for granted the human propensity to "truck, barter and trade" (Smith [1776] 1982). Key works in this tradition include Malinowski ([1922] 2008), Mauss ([1950] 2000), Hart (2001), and Guyer (2004). Contemporary economic anthropologists further explore the diversity of economic and social rationalities and pragmatics (Maurer 2006), the various repertoires (Guyer 2004), cosmologies (Sahlins [1988] 1994), and political configurations (Hart 1986) that shape markets, be they capitalist or otherwise.

28. Anthropological studies of such sociocultural transformations abound; among others, see De Grant (1995), Humphrey (2002), Dunn (2004), Ghodsee (2005), Waal (2005), Truitt (2013), and Verdery (1996, 2003).

29. Albania exported oil, copper, and electricity, and was paid in U.S. dollars (Sandstrom and Sjoberg 1991). But the combination of breaking of ties with China and the global decline of prices in the late 1970s, especially of oil, impacted the country's overall revenues.

30. Anthropologists and sociologists trace the different trajectories of privatization reforms in various parts of the postsocialist world. Key contributions include Verdery (1996), Stark and Bruszt (1998), Burawoy and Verdery (1999), Humphrey and Mandel (2002), Verdery and Humphrey (2004), and De Waal (2005).

31. Lampland further explains that this process of commodification during commusim laid the ground for the transition to capitalism in the early 1990s.

32. Ratha and Mohapatra (2012), for instance, argue that the total amount of world remittances three times the size of official foreign aid.

33. The second notion of temporality builds upon anthropological and philosophical reflections on Euro-centric temporalities of progress and modernity (Benjamin 1969).

34. More specifically, Ponzi finance describes financial transactions whereby "the cash flows from operations are not sufficient to fulfill either the repayment or principle of the interest due on outstanding debts by their cash flows from operations" (Minsky 1992, 7).

35. These self-orientalizing discourses permeate cultural representations across the Balkans (Herzfeld 1989; Todorova 2009) where claims to a European cultural identity articulate a contrast between an imposed Ottoman-Muslim identity versus a natural-historical Roman-Christian one. For more on these conflicting identities, see the intense debate between world-renowned writer Ismail Kadare (2006) and literary critic Rexhep Qosja (2006). Enis Sulstarova (2006) provides a critical overview of the cultural and intellectual history of these claims to European cultural and historical belonging in the work of Albanian historians, linguists, and ethnologists that across various political moments of Albania's modern history.

36. I discuss findings from this research that focus on other assessments of corruption, such as the Corruption Perceptions Survey (CPI), in Musaraj (2015, 2018b).

37. This approach takes after a long tradition in the anthropology of money—in particular, the work of Hart (2001), Parry and Bloch (1989), Guyer (2004), Roitman

(2005), and Maurer (2006). I also draw on the political economy and sociology of money in works by de Goede (2005) and Zelizer (1997).

38. For the ethnographic record on socialist housing, see also Bodnár and Böröcz (1998), Buchli (2000), and Humphrey (2005). For fascinating accounts of housing changes in the context of postsocialist transformations, see Pelkmans (2003), Zavisca (2012), Fehérváry (2013), Grant (2014) and Jansen (2015).

1. FAJDE, PYRAMID FIRMS, OR PONZI SCHEMES?

1. Unless otherwise noted, all translations from Albanian are by the author.

2. Interview with author, Vlora, Albania, September 11, 2008.

3. Kompani/shoqëri and fondacione were shorthand for *kompani/shoqëri huamarrëse* (borrowing companies) or *shoqëri me përgjegjësi të kufizuara* (limited liability companies) and *fondacione bamirëse* (charity foundations), respectively.

4. Generally, these religious connotations were no longer attached to fajde in the early 1990s. One exception was a conversation with a member of the Group of Transparency for the Pyramid Schemes, whom I call Alma. Recalling her decision to not invest in the firms at the time of their boom, Alma explained how this was *haram* (a ban/something forbidden) according to the Quran. Besides Alma, I did not encounter references to this Islamic ethic at the time of my research in 2008–9 or in the archival newspaper record, even though a religious revival was underway in Albania across various religious communities.

5. In other countries of the former Eastern Bloc (such as Hungary, former Czechoslovakia, and former Yugoslavia), some form of private property was sanctioned officially or unofficially, and a parallel private sector flourished alongside the state-owned economy. In Albania, this was never the case. There were no equivalents to the Hungarian "business-work partnerships" or the "micro-plots" (around the house) informal farming (Portes and Börösz 1988). At the same time, a black market (*tregu i zi*) for scarce goods proliferated in Albania, working without any sort of regulatory infrastructure, and further reinforcing ideas about free markets as inherently speculative.

6. By contrast to Bockman's fieldsites (Hungary and former Yugoslavia), one cannot speak of a strong tradition of a similar socialist economic thought about market socialism in Albania. However, for a brief period in the early 1990s, Albania also turned to the Yugoslav workers' self-management model of state enterprises (see Pashko 1993). Soon after these few years of self-management, all small and medium enterprises were put up for sale following the 1993 privatization laws.

7. Minsky's main object of concern was the rise of money managers as key players in finance and the expansion of what has come to be known as "the shadow banking system" (see also McCulley 2009).

8. Sude, the fourth fajde interrogated by the Ministry of Finance, did not cite the Civil Code.

9. In everyday conversation *huadhënës* (creditors) were primarily referred to as *kreditor*, an English cognate that once again gestures towards a global register of business and finance.

10. Interview with author, Vlora, Albania, July 2008.

11. Interview with author, Vlora, Albania, July 2008.

12. *Nder* (honor) and the related term *besa* (also translated as honor and oath) are the pillars of essentialist and Orientalist definitions of Albanian culture—both by outsiders and insiders. In anthropological literature, in particular, nder and besa have been prime objects of study, placing Albania among the honor-shame societies of the Mediterranean (for further anthropological work on honor, see Elsie 2010; Tarifa 2008; Young 2001). In his political career, Berisha appealed to this cultural symbol, presenting himself as an honest (*i ndershëm*) politician.

13. *DI* closed down in 1998 for financial reasons, but the editors continue to hold prominent positions in the Albanian media.

14. The newspaper has since lost its circulation and independent status.

15. Interview with author, Vlora, Albania, July 2008.

16. Many studies have provided rich accounts of postsocialist entrepreneurs (see, among others, Eyal et al. 1998; Humphrey and Mandel 2002; Ledeneva 1998; Stark and Bruzt 1998; Stoica 2004; Verdery 1996; Yurchak 2002, 2003).

17. On patriarchal rule under the party-state model of communist countries, see especially Verdery (1996, 61–82).

18. Interview with author, Vlora, Albania, July 2008.

19. To Vlora kreditorë, especially, it made no difference that I was born and raised in Tirana. It was common for people to ask, "Where are you from?" in search of "deeper," prewar cultural and regional family ties.

20. Classic critiques of the honor and shame constructs in the anthropology of the Mediterranean include Herzfeld (1989) and Abu-Lughod (1993). See also recent critiques of similar Orientalist traditions both in Western literature (Blumi 1998) and among Albanian intellectuals (Sulstarova 2006).

21. One exception is the work of Nebi Bardhoshi (2012, 2013), which identifies some areas (such as the use of the property during the communist regime) where kanun was tacitly applied by various communities during the communist regime as well.

22. That said, mutated version of kanun laws have resurged in specific communities in the north after the 1990s (see, for instance, the ethnography of blood feuds post-1990s by Young [2001]).

23. For a revisiting of the land laws under kanun, see Bardhoshi (2008).

24. In particular, the kanun laws were in constant friction with communist efforts at "the emancipation of women." Numerous icons of Albanian literature and cinematography focus on this tension, often through the narrative of a female protagonist who defies the traditional authority of the kanun, the father, and the "fanatic" home community and joins, instead, the communist working class and its modernizing projects.

25. Engels's work, argues Grant (1995, 52–58), was bolstered by the findings of Russian ethnographer Lev Shtenberg and his research among the Nivkhi in Sakhalin.

26. The Albanian term for the local currency is lek (singular) or lekë (plural). To avoid confusion, I use lek for singular and plural. When discussing prices or costs, Albanians alternate between amounts in old lek (*lek të vjetra*) and new lek (*lek të reja*). The former refers to an older denomination of lek, the latter to the current official denomination of monetary value (10 old lek = 1 new lek). Although the change in denomination took place in the 1960s, people continue to count colloquially in old lek. Kreditorë typically spoke in old lek during our conversations. Unless noted in the text, I have converted all these amounts to new lek to keep consistency with the official values and with the exchange rate to the dollar.

27. Gjallica had a female co-owner, Shemsie Kadria, who shared ownership with Fitim Gërxhalliu.

28. Interview with author, Tirana, Albania, March 2008.

29. As such, llotari consisted of a game of predictable chance, retaining an element of luck that was otherwise forbidden in the official economic cosmologies of planned, redistributive, and interest-free financial transactions of the command economy in communist Albania. I discus these aspects of llotari and of their continuities with fajde in Musaraj (2019).

30. On ethnic minorities and trade in other postsocialist contexts, see also Humphrey (2002) and Lemon (1998).

2. "MONEY FLOWED LIKE A RIVER"

1. For a recent review of the two kinds of literatures, see Roitman (2013).

2. This analysis builds on the analytical tool kit of social studies of finance (MacKenzie 2012; Muniesa, Millo, and Callon 2007), which focuses on the efficacy of "market devices," that is "financial models, instruments, and methods" that are co-constitutive of the economy. These market devices "emerg[e] from socio-technical assemblages, which participate in the production of calculative spaces and agencies, thus generating and sustaining processes of qualification and valuation" (Roitman 2013, 76).

3. Though, arguably, some financialization was taking place, thanks in large part to the influence of the IMF and World Bank loans and other forms of financial assistance.

4. My approach to these changes in the money form draws on anthropological theories of value and money. Alongside this literature, I approach money as a commodity and token (Hart 1986), as a relationship (Hart 2000; Maurer 2015), and as a resource mobilized by people on the ground (Guyer 1995).

5. Interview with author, Vlora, Albania, September 2008.

6. For an example of how this economy is absent from economic reports at the time, see Muço (1997).

7. For instance, Martha Lampland (1995) documents the process of commodification of labor in Hungary long before free-market reform. Patrick Hyder Patterson (2011) tracks the disembeddedness and commercialization of consumption through a thriving advertising culture and marketization in Tito's Yugoslavia. Johanna Bockman (2011) traces the various steps of disembeddedness of the market under market socialism in Hungary.

8. This version of history is one-dimensional. Besides the national liberation and the communist revolution, the transformations taking place in postwar Albania amounted to a civil war between various factions (the national front being a main target of the communist purges) and within the ranks of PPSH itself.

9. For instance, during the 2001 economic crisis in Argentina, middle-class consumers went to banks with suitcases to "save their savings" (D'Avella 2014); in Zimbabwe, one of the most dramatic experiences of devaluation in 2009 led to people needing "bale of notes just to buy a few household essentials" (Frisby 2016).

10. Interview with author, Vlora, Albania, August 2008.

11. Manjola's earmarking of the firms' interests as "our money" recalls a similar distinction between our/their money among participants in the Romanian Caritas scheme, and Verdery's observation that "something isn't one's property, an extension of oneself— 'mine'—unless there is some sort of effort or sacrifice somewhere" (1996, 183).

12. According to the data on the list of the Transparency Group, most of the SMEs owned by Vefa had registered in the private property registry (*hipoteka*) during 1995 and 1996.

13. The official term for these privatization vouchers was interchangeably *letër shtetërore me vlerë*, which translates literally as "a state paper with value" and *bono privatizimi* (privatization bond). I use the abbreviated plural used colloquially *letra me vlerë* (the paper/papers with value).

14. In addition to the free-market model, there were two other privatization models applied in other Eastern European countries: (1) the mixed model (applied in Czech Republic), whereby citizens were given coupons with points that were not exchangeable or tradable, but were securities; and (2) the centralized model (applied in Poland), where citizens were given certificates with no face value and were not tradable, exchangeable, transferable, and were deposited in centrally managed national investment funds, while their exchange for shares in joint-stock companies was strictly monitored by central authorities (Mema and Nevruzi 2001, 2).

15. These mediators collected additional interest on the deposits that they brought into the firm. Menaxherë were those who were able to bring in larger amounts (up to 100,000 old lek, roughly US$1,000).

16. Scholars explored the cultural and nationalist significance and attachment to currencies. Most of these accounts tell the story of national identification (Helleiner 2003; Lemon 1998).

17. Practices of earmarking currencies are legion in many cultural contexts explored by economic anthropologists. From Malinowski to Hart and Guyer, anthropologists have explored multiple objects (cattle, cowries, beads, cash, cards) that have been used as money in different historical and cultural contexts. Some of these studies have documented the coevalness of different forms of money at any given point in time. In other words, operating in multiple forms of money is not novel in and of itself.

18. From the Italian *cambiare* (to change). The term is typically used to refer to informal/unofficial moneychangers.

19. Interview with author, Vlora, Albania, August 2008.

3. "WORKING THE MONEY"

1. The adverse effects of money on the social fabric of various communities constitute a significant part of the canon in economic anthropology. For a critical review of this literature, see Parry and Bloch (1989).

2. In addition to sekserë, there was also the category of menaxherë. The difference between menaxherë and sekserë was based on the amount of money mediated and the interest received. Menaxherë brought in more cash than sekserë. But because sekserë were more numerous and featured more prominently in accounts by kreditorë, I use this term to refer to both.

3. The difference between i njohur and të njohur is one of singular/plural as well indicative of a different case in Albanian grammar.

4. This notion is similar to "investment in social relations" (Berry 1989) described in the context of West African societies.

5. Ellen Hertz (1998) makes a similar point regarding the Chinese capitalism of the post-1990s. She notes how, in the Chinese context, capitalist markets are visibly tied to political and social networks. On abstraction in capitalism and speculative finance, see also Carrier and Miller (1998), Comaroff and Comaroff (2000), and Tsing (2000).

6. The question of minority status was sensitive under the communist regime when most minority groups were not recognized as such (see Bon 2017; de Rapper 2005). Narta and a few other villages were an exception. Being recognized as a minority area entailed being free to speak the mother tongue at home and in public. However, schooling in these areas was also in Albanian.

7. Interview with author, Vlora, Albania, August 2008.

8. By contrast to official representations, some locals recall the times of kurbet as a time of abundance and wealth (de Rapper 2005).

9. During communism, bad biography (*biografi e keqe*) referred to having close kin who were considered enemies of the Party of Labor, political prisoners, or persecuted for political reasons. Often times, the families of a political prisoner would also suffer different forms of punishment on the basis of having a bad biography. These punishments included change of residence to a remote area, lack of access to higher education, and lack of access to good jobs.

10. Nicholson (2002, 2004) has researched the establishment of some of the most common microenterprises—the filling station, the shop, the restaurant.

11. Interview with author, Vlora, Albania, August 2008.

12. According to Albanian customary law, the youngest son and his wife has the obligation to take care of the elderly parents.

13. Aida Orgocka (2005) writes about the migration of high-skill migrant women in the United States.

14. Manjola did not make specific references to Marx, but others did. For instance, Muhamet noted defensively, "you might think that I am a Marxist-Leninist, but money cannot grow from trees." The comment was meant to provide a critique of the mode of capital accumulation promised by the firms. It also aimed at defetishizing the mechanism by which the firms explained their money making.

15. It is worth noting that the sums of money that Manjola discussed with great ease were astronomical to the average person living and working in Albania at that time. The national GDP per capita in Albania in 1996 was US$902, and the average salary around US$100 per month.

4. "ALL WE WANTED WAS A BEAUTIFUL HOME"

1. Interview with author, Vlora, August 2008.

2. Interview with author, Vlora, July 2008.

3. Between 1945 and 1991, state authorities in Albania built 457,300 apartments, on an average of 10,000 per year (Gjika and Shutina 2011, 29).

4. Interview with author, Vlora, August 2008.

5. For instance, the period between 1995 and 1997 marked the peak of construction licenses issues nationwide (INSTAT).

6. Interview with author, August 2008.

7. The first commercial bank was licensed in 1992, and by 1999 there were eleven such banks. However, these provided primarily savings and checking accounts and were generally reluctant to give loans to businesses or individuals (UNDP 2000).

8. For recent discussions of the anthropology of time and the future, see Appadurai (2013) and Guyer (2007). On the anthropology of temporality and finance, see Maurer (2002), Miyazaki (2003), and Zaloom (2009).

9. Guyer (2007) likens the temporality of the long run in monetarist policies to that of millennial religious movements that promise salvation in a future that is a rupture (rather than a continuity) from the present. The abundant wealth promised by the firms in Albania were likewise imagined, as a rupture from the socialist past and the uncertain present but, curiously, millenarian religious undertones (present in other sites of speculative finance) were absent in the Albanian context. Accounts of various pyramid and Ponzi schemes proliferating since the 1990s in various margins of global finance also emphasize temporality and the prevalence of millenarian time. Thus, from the fast money schemes in Papua New Guinea (Cox 2018) to the scam of el Millenario in Guatemala (Nelson 2012), from the Ponzi scheme ReDéMare in Togo (Piot, Lachenal, and Mbodj-Pouye 2014) to the Romanian Caritas (Verdery 1996), the rhetoric of financial prosperity converges with the Messianic time of religious salvation. The Caritas in Romania, writes Verdery (1996), was "suffused with Christian imagery," acting as a "millenarian social movement ushering a radiant counterfuture" (189). Similarly, accounts of pyramid schemes suffused with religious (especially Pentecostal Christianity) underscore a specific temporality of hope and faith whereby the imagined or promised future is a rupture rather than a gradual genealogical progression from the present (see especially Piot, Lachenal, and Mbodj-Pouye 2014, 108).

10. Susan Buck-Morss (2000) described the intertwined dreams and temporalities of East and West during the Cold War. This mutual embrace, competitiveness, and aspiration toward the other side of the Iron Curtain was more even in the early part of the Cold War and became more one-sided (with the West gaining more ground) in the late part of the Cold War.

11. Interview with author, Tirana, October 2008.

12. In the late-1980s, communist economies were fraught in shortages in consumer goods. Many of the basic subsistence consumer goods were rationed and often there were shortages in their supply. Economist Janis Kornai (1979) coined the term "economies of shortage" to describe communist economist organized around central planning and a rationing system.

13. Interview with author, Tirana, October 2008.

14. Interview with author, Vlora, August 2008.

5. THE PYRAMID WAY

1. Interview with author, Vlora, Albania, August 2008.

2. Linguistically speaking, this translation is a misnomer. Etymologically, klering derives from "clearing" (as in, the clearing of checks). In the official banking register it is used to describe the clearing of checks. In the vernacular speech, it is also used to describe the specific practice of payment in apartments rather than money.

3. Interview with author, Vlora, Albania, August 2008.

4. Minsky borrows the term "Ponzi" from the infamous scheme by Charles Ponzi, a typical Ponzi scheme where money is circulated from new investors to early investors until liquidity runs out. Minsky argued that a similar phenomenon could occur in free-market capitalist economies where, inspired by a period of economic boom, bankers and investors expand the level of risk taken into future investments and loans, often leading to a pattern of investment that is unsustainable.

5. Interview with author, Tirana, Albania, July 19, 2008.

6. Interview with author, Tirana, Albania, February 2008.

7. On the concept of housing as "capital," see Guyer's (2014) discussion of the form of wealth that housing has come to constitute in highly valued real estate markets.

8. Interview with author, Tirana, Albania, June 2015.

9. Interview with author, Vlora, Albania, September 2008.

10. Interview with author, Tirana, Albania, June 2015.

11. That said, a significant difference between these two cases is that, in the Albanian case, developers are all private companies.

12. Interview with author, Tirana, Albania, July 2015.

13. Rama's impact on the urban development of Tirana is ambivalent. He won the World Mayor award in 2004 for his initiative to bulldoze informal constructions and kiosk and for painting the communist-era low-rises in bright colors. At the same time, Rama allowed what is now seen as an intensification of the city center through the building of new high-rises in the public spaces within the communist apartment blocks.

14. On uneven and coercive credit/debt relations, see also Elyachar 2005; Roitman 2005; Han 2012.

15. Interview with author, Vlora, Albania, September 2008.

EPILOGUE

1. Incidentally, the betting cafes were all closed down in late 2018 by the government on the grounds that they became focal points of money laundering.

References

Abrahams, Fred. 2015. *Modern Albania: From Dictatorship to Democracy in Europe.* New York: New York University Press.

Abu-Lughod, Lila. 1993. *Writing Women's Worlds: Bedouin Stories.* Berkeley: University of California Press.

Akerlof, George A., and Robert J. Shiller. 2010. *Animal Spirits: How Human Psychology Drives the Economy, and Why It Matters for Global Capitalism.* Princeton, NJ: Princeton University Press.

Akin, David, and Joel Robbins. 1999. *Money and Modernity: State and Local Currencies in Melanesia.* Pittsburgh, PA: University of Pittsburgh Press.

Albanian Council of Ministers. 1997. VKM-ja nr. 585, "Për Evidencimin e Familjeve që Kanë Humbur Banesat nga Rënia e Skemave Piramidale" ["Decree for Identifying the Families that Have Lost their Homes due to the Collapse of the Pyramid Schemes"]. VKM 585 (Government Decree 585), December 11.

Alexander, Catherine M. 2004. "Values, Relations and Changing Bodies: Industrial Privatisation in Kazakhstan." In *Property in Question: Value Transformation in the Global Economy*, edited by C. Humphrey and K. Verdery, 251–74. Oxford: Berg Publishers.

Aliaj, Besnik. 2008. *Misteri i Gjashtë: Cili është Kurthi që Mban Peng Zhvillimin dhe Intergrimin e Ekonomise Shqiptare me Botën Moderne?* Tirana: Polis.

Allison, A., and C. Piot. 2011. "New Editors' Greeting." *Cultural Anthropology* 26 (1): 1–5.

Andoni, Doris. 2010. "Individi, Banesa, Qytetit" ["The Individual, The House, The City"]. *Forum A+P* 3: 26–40.

Andrews, Edmund L. 1997. "Behind the Scams: Desperate People, Easily Duped." *New York Times*, January 29.

Appadurai, Arjun. 1986. *The Social Life of Things: Commodities in Cultural Perspective.* Cambridge, NY: Cambridge University Press.

——. 2011. "The Ghost in the Financial Machine." *Public Culture* 23 (3): 517–39.

——. 2013. "The Future as Cultural Fact: Essays on the Global Condition." *Rassegna Italiana di Sociologia* 14 (4): 649–50.

Arapi, Farudin. 1999. "Strategjia e Ndjekur për Likuidimin dhe Shpërbërjen e Skemave Piramidale dhe Rikompensimi i Vlerave Financiare Kreditorëve" ["The Strategy Followed for Liquidating the Pyramid Schemes and the Compensation of the Financial Sums to Creditors"]. Summary of Material. Tirana: Group for the Transparency of the Pyramid Firms.

Ardener, Shirley, and Sandra Burman. 1995. *Money-Go-Rounds: The Importance of Rotating Savings and Credit Associations for Women.* Oxford: Berg.

Ariely, Daniel. 2010. *Predictably Irrational: The Hidden Forces That Shape Our Decisions.* Rev. ed. New York: HarperPerennial.

Arrighi, Giovanni. 1994. *The Long Twentieth Century: Money, Power, and the Origins of Our Times.* New York: Verso.

Åslund, Anders, and Orjan Sjöberg. 1991. *Privatisation and Transition to a Market Economy in Albania.* Stockholm Institute of Soviet and East European Economics.

Babaramo, Ilir. 1996a. "Berisha: Bankat Urgjent Në Treg" ["Berisha: The Banks Urgently for Sale"]. *Koha Jonë*, December 14.

——. 1996b. "Fajdetë: TreJavë Vdekje Klinike: Sudja: Intrigë ndaj Meje Sajuar nga një Firmë Tjetër" ["Fajde: Three Weeks Clinical Death: Sude: an Intrigue Against me Set up by Another Firm"]. *Koha Jonë*, 9.

——. 1996c. "Luniku: Ku Ka Transparence, Ka Rrezik. Intervistë me Guvernatorin e Bankës së Shqipërisë. Kompaniteë e Fajdesë Nuk Kanë Kërkuar Liçencë për Bankë" ["Luniku: Where There is no Transparency, There is Danger. Interview with the Governor of the Bank of Albania. Fajde Companies Have Not Requested Licence to Become a Bank"]. *Koha Jonë*, December 7.

Baçe, Apollon. 1996. "Politika dhe Dollari ose Politika e Dollarit" ["The Dollar and Politics or the Politics of the Dollar"]. *Dita Informacion*, May 21.

Banerjee, Abhijit, and Esther Duflo. 2012. *Poor Economics: A Radical Rethinking of the Way to Fight Global Poverty*. New York: PublicAffairs.

Bank of Albania. 2006. "Remittances: Albanian Experiences. First Meeting of the Luxemburg Group." http://www.imf.org/external/np/sta/bop/2006/luxgrp/pdf/albani.pdf.

Bardhoshi, Nebi. 2007. "E Drejta Kanunore dhe Shteti i Së Drejtës" ["The Kanun Law and the Rule of Law"]. *Polis* (3): 1–19.

——. 2015. *Antropologji e Kanunit* [*Anthropology of Kanun*]. Tiranë: Qendra e Studimeve Albanologjike.

Barjaba, Kosta. 2003. *Shqiptarët, Këta Ikës Të Mëdhenj* [*Albanians, These Great Escapers*]. Tirana: Korbi.

Barjaba, Kosta, and Russell King. 2005. "Introducing and Theorizing Albanian Migration." In *The New Albanian Migration*, edited by Russell King, Nicola Mai, and Stephanie Schwandner-Sievers, 1–28. Brighton: Sussex Academic Press.

Barry, Andrew, and Thomas Osborne. 1996. *Foucault and Political Reason: Liberalism, Neo-Liberalism, and Rationalities of Government*. Chicago: University of Chicago Press.

Bayart, Jean-Francois. 2009. *The State in Africa*. 2nd ed. New York: Polity.

Baze, Mero. 2010. *Viti '97: Prapaskenat Që Rrënuan Shtetin* [*Year '97: The Backstage of the Crisis That Undermined the State*]. Tirana: Botimet Toena.

Bear, Laura, Karen Ho, Anna Tsing, and Sylvia Yanagisako. 2015. "Gens: A Feminist Manifesto for the Study of Capitalism." *Cultural Anthropology*, March 30. https://culanth.org/fieldsights/652-gens-a-feminist-manifesto-for-the-study-of-capitalism.

Benjamin, Walter. 1969. *Illuminations*, edited with an Introduction by Hannah Arendt and translated by Harry Zohn. New York: Schocken.

Berdahl, Daphne. 2009. *On the Social Life of Postsocialism: Memory, Consumption, Germany*, edited by Matti Bunzl. Bloomington: Indiana University Press.

Berdahl, Daphne, Matti Bunzl, and Martha Lampland. 2000. *Altering States: Ethnographies of Transition in Eastern Europe and the Former Soviet Union*. Ann Arbor: University of Michigan Press.

Berry, S. 1989. "Social Institutions and Access to Resources." *Africa* 59 (1): 41–55.

Bezemer, Dirk. 2001. "Post-Socialist Financial Fragility: The Case of Albania." *Cambridge Journal of Economics* 25: 1–23.

——. 2009. "Growth without Development: The Ponzi Economy and its Lessons." In *On Eagle's Wings: The Albanian Economy in Transition*, 17–33. New York: Nova Science.

Bissenova, A. 2012. "Post-Socialist Dreamworlds: Housing Boom and Urban Development in Kazakhstan." PhD diss., Cornell University.

Blumi, Isa. 1997. "The Politics of Culture and Power: The Roots of Hoxha's Postwar State." *East European Quarterly* 31 (3): 379–98.

——. 1998. "The Commodification of Otherness and the Ethnic Unit in the Balkans: How to Think about Albanians." *East European Politics & Societies* 12 (3): 527–69.

Bockman, Johanna. 2011. *Markets in the Name of Socialism: The Left-Wing Origins of Neo-liberalism.* Stanford, CA: Stanford University Press.

Bodnár, Judit, and József Böröcz. 1998. "Housing Advantages for the Better Connected? Institutional Segmentation, Settlement Type and Social Network Effects in Hungary's Late State-Socialist Housing Inequalities." *Social Forces* 76 (4): 1275–304.

Bohannan, Paul. 1959. "The Impact of Money on an African Subsistence Economy." *Journal of Economic History* 19 (4): 491–503.

Bon, N. G. 2017. "Movement Matters: The Case of Southern Albania." *Ethnologie Française* (2): 301–8.

Borenstein, Eliot. 1999. "Public Offerings: MMM and the Marketing of Melodrama." In *Consuming Russia: Popular Culture, Sex and Society since Gorbachev*, 49–75. Durham, NC: Duke University Press.

Borneman, John. 1991. *After the Wall: East Meets West in the New Berlin.* New York: Basic Books.

Bourdieu, Pierre. 1966. "The Sentiment of Honour in Kabyle Society." In *Honour and Shame: The Values of Mediterranean Society*, edited by JG Péristiany, 191–241. Chicago: Chicago University Press.

——. 1977. *Outline of a Theory of Practice.* Translated by Richard Nice. Cambridge, NY: Cambridge University Press.

Boym, Svetlana. 1994. *Common Places: Mythologies of Everyday Life in Russia.* Boston: Harvard University Press.

——. 2002. *The Future of Nostalgia.* New York: Basic Books.

Buchli, Victor. 2000. *An Archaeology of Socialism.* Oxford: Berg.

Buck-Morss, Susan. 2000. *Dreamworld and Catastrophe: The Passing of Mass Utopia in East and West.* Cambridge, MA: MIT Press.

Burawoy, Michael, and Katherine Verdery. 1999. *Uncertain Transitions: Ethnographies of Change in the Postsocialist World.* New York: Rowman & Littlefield.

Burazeri, G., A. Goda, G. Sulo, J. Stefa, and J. D. Kark. 2008. "Financial Loss in Pyramid Savings Schemes, Downward Social Mobility and Acute Coronary Syndrome in Transitional Albania." *Journal of Epidemiology and Community Health* 62 (7): 620–26.

Byron, Lord. 2011. *Childe Harold's Pilgrimage.* Scotts Valley, CA: CreateSpace.

Çabej, Eqerem. 1996. *Studime Etimologjike Në Fushë Të Shqipes* [*Etymological Studies on the Albanian Language*]. Vol. 4. Tirana: Academy of Sciences of Albania.

Çalışkan, Koray, and Michel Callon. 2009. "Economization, Part 1: Shifting Attention from the Economy towards Processes of Economization." *Economy and Society* 38 (3): 369–98.

——. 2010. "Economization, Part 2: A Research Programme for the Study of Markets." *Economy and Society* 39 (1): 1–32. doi:10.1080/03085140903424519.

Callon, Michel. 1998. *The Laws of the Markets.* Hoboken, NJ: Blackwell Publishers/Sociological Review.

——. 2007. "Why Virtualism Paves the Way to Political Impotence: 'A Reply to Daniel Miller's Critique of the Laws of the Market.'" *Economic Sociology* 6 (2): 3–20.

Callon, Michel, Yuval Millo, and Fabian Muniesa, eds. 2007. *Market Devices.* Hoboken, NJ: Wiley-Blackwell.

Camdessus, Michael. 1995. "Opening Dinner of the 1995 Pew Economic Freedom Fellows Program." Speech at Opening Dinner of the 1995 Pew Economic Freedom Fellows Program. George Washington University, Washington, DC, January 9. imf.org/en/News/Articles/2015/09/28/04/53/spmds9503.

Carrier, James G., and Daniel Miller. 1998. *Virtualism.* Oxford: Berg.

Cassidy, John. 2010. *How Markets Fail: The Logic of Economic Calamities*. New York: Picador.

Cela, Laura. 2009. "Ankthi i Ndërtimit" ["The Anxt of Construction"]. *Monitor*. https://www.monitor.al/ankthi-i-ndertimit-3231/.

———. 2010. "Shitjet, Tani Me Para Në Dorë" ["Sales: Now in Cash-in-Hand"]. *Monitor*. https://www.monitor.al/shitjet-tani-me-para-ne-dore-6596/.

Chari, Sharad, and Katherine Verdery. 2009. "Thinking between the Posts: Postcolonialism, Postsocialism and Ethnography after the Cold War." *Comparative Studies in History and Society* 51 (1): 6–34.

Childress, Malcolm. 2009. "The Unfinished Business of Land and Property Reform in Albania." In *On Eagle's Wings: The Albanian Economy in Transition*, 115–27. New York: Nova Science.

Chu, Julie Y. 2010. *Cosmologies of Credit: Transnational Mobility and the Politics of Destination in China*. Durham, NC: Duke University Press Books.

Comaroff, Jean, and John Comaroff. 1999. "Occult Economies and the Violence of Abstraction: Notes from the South African Postcolony." *American Ethnologist* 26 (2): 279–303.

———. 2000. "Millennial Capitalism: First Thoughts on a Second Coming." *Public Culture* 12 (2): 291–343.

———. 2006. *Law and Disorder in the Postcolony*. Chicago: University of Chicago Press.

Cox, John. 2018. *Fast Money Schemes: Hope and Deception in Papua New Guinea*. Bloomington: Indiana University Press.

Cox, John, and Martha MacIntyre. 2014. "Christian Marriage, Money Scams, and Melanesian Social Imaginaries." *Oceania* 84 (2): 138–57.

Creed, Gerald W. 2010. *Domesticating Revolution: From Socialist Reform to Ambivalent Transition in a Bulgarian Village*. University Park: Pennsylvania State University Press.

Çupi, Frrok. 2005. *E Pashë Shtetin Duke Rënë: Dëshmi dhe Esse* [*I Saw the State Fall: Testimony and Essay*]. Tirana: Dritëro.

Dalakoglou, Dimitris. 2010a. "Migrating-Remitting-'Building'-Dwelling: House-Making as 'Proxy' Presence in Postsocialist Albania." *Journal of the Royal Anthropological Institute* 16 (4): 761–77.

———. 2010b. "The Road: An Ethnography of the Albanian–Greek Cross-Border Motorway." *American Ethnologist* 37 (1): 132–49.

———. 2012. "'The Road from Capitalism to Capitalism': Infrastructures of (Post)Socialism in Albania." *Mobilities* 7 (4): 571–86.

Dalipaj, G. 2016. "Migration, Residential Investment, and the Experience of 'Transition': Tracing Transnational practices of Albanian migrants in Athens." *Focaal, 2016* (76): 85–98.

de Goede, Marieke. 2005. *Virtue, Fortune, and Faith: A Genealogy of Finance*. Minneapolis: University of Minnesota Press.

de Waal, C. 2004. "Post-Socialist Property Rights and Wrongs in Albania: An Ethnography of Agrarian Change." *Conservation and Society* 2 (1): 19–50.

———. 2005. *Albania Today: A Portrait of Post-Communist Turbulence*. London: I. B. Tauris.

D'Avella, Nicholas. 2014. "Ecologies of Investment: Crisis Histories and Brick Futures in Argentina." *Cultural Anthropology* 29 (1): 173–99.

Derrida, Jacques. [1994] 2012. *Specters of Marx*. Translated by Peggy Kamuf. New York: Routledge.

Dunn, Elizabeth C. 2004. *Privatizing Poland: Baby Food, Big Business, and the Remaking of Labor*. Ithaca, NY: Cornell University Press.

Durham, M. Edith. 1910. "High Albania and Its Customs in 1908." *Journal of the Royal Anthropological Institute of Great Britain and Ireland* 40: 453–72.

Elsie, Robert. 2010. *Historical Dictionary of Albania*. 2nd ed. Lanham, MD: Scarecrow Press.

Elyachar, Julia. 2003. "Mappings of Power: The State, NGOs, and International Organizations in the Informal Economy of Cairo." *Comparative Studies in Society and History* 45 (3): 571–605.

——. 2005. *Markets of Dispossession: NGOs, Economic Development, and the State in Cairo.* Durham, NC: Duke University Press.

——. 2010. "Phatic Labor, Infrastructure, and the Question of Empowerment in Cairo." *American Ethnologist* 37 (3): 452–64.

Engels, Friedrich, and Eleanor Burke Leacock. 1972. *The Origin of the Family, Private Property, and the State, in the Light of the Researches of Lewis H. Morgan.* New York: International Publishers.

Epstein, G. 2001. "Financialization, Rentier Interests, and Central Bank Policy." Paper prepared for PERI Conference on "Financialization of the World Economy," December 7–8, 2001, University of Massachusetts, Amherst.

Eyal, Gil, Ivan Szelenyi, Eleanor R. Townsley, and Eleanor Townsley. 2001. *Making Capitalism without Capitalists: The New Ruling Elites in Eastern Europe.* New York: Verso.

Fehérváry, Krisztina. 2012. "From Socialist Modern to Super-Natural Organicism: Cosmological Transformations through Home Decor." *Cultural Anthropology* 27 (4): 615–40.

——. 2013. *Politics in Color and Concrete: Socialist Materialities and the Middle Class in Hungary.* Bloomington: Indiana University Press.

Ferguson, Niall. 2009. *The Ascent of Money: A Financial History of the World.* London: Penguin.

Fishta, Iljaz, and Mihal Ziu. 2004. *Historia e Ekonomisë së Shqipërisë* [*The History of the Albanian Economy*]. Tirana: Dita.

Foucault, Michel. 1991. "Governmentality." In *The Foucault Effect: Studies in Governmentality,* edited by Graham Burchell, Colin Gordon, and Peter Miller, 87–104. Chicago: University of Chicago Press.

Fox, Robert. 2012. "International: Gipsy Queen Tells of Pounds 40m Pyramid. Debt Robert Fox Traces Albania's Violence Back to the Get-Rich-Quick Schemes."

Frank, Robert. 1998. "Jungle Accounting: Auditors in Albania Pick through Rubble of Pyramid Schemes—Tracking Missing Money Wins Scant Sympathy from Scammed Citizens—Some Assets but Few Books." *Wall Street Journal European Edition* (August 6): 1, 7.

Frisby, Dominic. 2016. "Zimbabwe's Trillion-dollar Note: From Worthless Paper to Hot Investment." *The Guardian*, May 14. https://www.theguardian.com/money/2016/may/14/zimbabwe-trillion-dollar-note-hyerinflation-investment.

Fuga, Artan. 2003. *Majtas jo djathtas.* Tirana: Ora.

Gal, Susan. 1991. "Bartók's Funeral: Representations of Europe in Hungarian Political Rhetoric." *American Ethnologist* 18 (3): 440–58.

Gjecovi, Stefan. 1972. *Kanuni I Leke Dukagjini.* [*The Kanun of Leke Dukagjini*]. Prishtinë: Rilindja.

Gjika, Anila, and Dritan Shutina. 2011. "Sfidat e Pushtetit Vendor në Zhvillimin Urban Dhe Strehimin Në Shqipëri" ["The Challenges of Local Governance in Urban Development and Housing in Albania"]. In *Politikëbërës apo Politikëndjekës: Alternativa mbi Zhvillimin Urban, Menaxhimin e Territorit dhe Mjedisit* [*Policy-makers and Policy-followers: Alternatives of Urban, Territorial, and Environmet Development*], edited by Dritan Shutina and Rudina Toto, 17–47. Tirana: Co-Plan.

Godole, Jonila. 1996a. "Ankthi i Qytetarëve Fajdexhinj" ["The Anxt of Fajdexhi-Citizens"]. *Koha Jonë*, September 8, p. 9.

——. 1996b. "Bosët Shqiptarë Të Fajdesë: Ndër Qindra Aventurierë Që Japin E Marrin Fajde, Vetëm Disa Jane Te Sukseshem. Ata Që Quhen 'president,' 'kopetent,' 'bos,' 'shef' janë Nga Më Të Rëndësishmit" ["The Albanian Bosses of Fajde: From Hundred of Adventurers That Give and Take Fajde, Only a Few Are Successful. Those Referred to as 'President,' 'the Competent' 'Boss,' 'Chief' Are the Important Ones"]. *Koha Jonë*, December 8, p. 9.

Graeber, David. 1700. *Debt: The First 5,000 Years by Graeber, David (July 12, 2011)*. Brooklyn: Melville House.

——. 2001. *Toward an Anthropological Theory of Value: The False Coin of Our Own Dreams*. New York: Palgrave Macmillan.

Grant, Bruce. 1995. *In the Soviet House of Culture: A Century of Perestroikas*. Princeton, NJ: Princeton University Press.

——. 2010. "Cosmopolitan Baku." *Ethnos* 75 (2): 123–47.

——. 2014. "The Edifice Complex: Architecture and the Political Life of Surplus in the New Baku." *Public Culture* 26 (374): 501–28.

Greenhouse, Carol J., ed. 2012. *Ethnographies of Neoliberalism*. Philadelphia: University of Pennsylvania Press.

Greenspan, Alan. 1996. "The Challenge of Central Banking in a Democratic Society." In "Speech at the Annual Dinner and Francis Boyer Lecture of The American Enterprise Institute for Public Policy Research," Washington, D.C., American Enterprise Institute. http://www.federalreserve.gov/boarddocs/speeches/1996/19961205.htm.

Guyer, Jane I. 1993. "Wealth in People and Self-Realization in Equatorial Africa." *Man*, New Series 28 (2): 243–65.

——, ed. 1995. *Money Matters: Instability, Values, and Social Payments in the Modern History of West African Communities*. Portsmouth, NH: Heinemann.

——. 2004. *Marginal Gains: Monetary Transactions in Atlantic Africa*. Chicago: University of Chicago Press.

——. 2007. "Prophecy and the Near Future: Thoughts on Macroeconomic, Evangelical, and Punctuated Time." *American Ethnologist* 34 (3): 409–21.

——. 2012. "Soft Currencies, Cash Economies, New Monies: Past and Present." *Proceedings of the National Academy of Sciences* 109 (7): 2214–21.

Halawa, Mateusz. 2015. "In New Warsaw: Mortgage Credit and the Unfolding of Space and Time." *Cultural Studies* 29 (5–6): 707–32.

Halawa, M., and M. Olcoń-Kubicka. 2018. "Digital Householding: Calculating and Moralizing Domestic Life through Homemade Spreadsheets." *Journal of Cultural Economy* 11 (6): 514–34.

Han, Clara. 2012. *Life in Debt: Times of Care and Violence in Neoliberal Chile*. Berkeley: University of California Press.

Hann, Chris, ed. 2003. *The Postsocialist Agrarian Question: Property Relations and the Rural Condition*. Zürich: LIT Verlag.

Hann, Chris, and Keith Hart. 2009. *Market and Society: The Great Transformation Today*. Cambridge, NY: Cambridge University Press.

Hart, Keith. 1973. "Informal Income Opportunities and Urban Employment in Ghana." *Journal of Modern African Studies* 11 (1): 61–89.

——. 1986. "Heads or tails? Two sides of the coin." *Man* 21 (4): 637–56.

——. 2001. *Money in an Unequal World: Keith Hart and His Memory Bank*. New York: Textere.

Harvey, David. 1989. *The Conditions of Postmodernity*. Oxford: Blackwell.

——. 2003. *The New Imperialism*. Oxford: Oxford University Press.

——. 2005. *A Brief History of Neoliberalism*. Oxford: Oxford University Press.

——. 2010. *The Enigma of Capital: And the Crises of Capitalism*. Oxford: Oxford University Press.

Hazizaj, Altin. 1996a. "Berisha Takon Fondin Monetar Ndërkombëtar: Fajdetë E Shqiptarëve Janë Të Pastra" ["Berisha Meets the International Monetary Fund: Albanian Fajde Are Honest"]. *Koha Jonë*, November 26, p. 6.

——. 1996b. "Misioni i Fondit Largohet Nga Shqipëria. Nuk Lidhet Marrëveshja. FMN: Fajdetë i Përkasin Qeverisë" ["The IMF Mission Leaves Albania. The Agreement Is Not Reached. IMF: Fajde Belong to the Government"]. *Koha Jonë*, November 27, p. 1.

Helleiner, Eric. 2003. *The Making of National Money: Territorial Currencies in Historical Perspective*. Ithaca, NY: Cornell University Press.

Hertz, Ellen. 1998. *The Trading Crowd: An Ethnography of the Shanghai Stock Market*. Vol. 108. Cambridge, NY: Cambridge University Press.

Herzfeld, Michael. 1989. *Anthropology through the Looking-Glass: Critical Ethnography in the Margins of Europe*. Cambridge, NY: Cambridge University Press.

——. 2005. *Cultural Intimacy: Social Poetics in the Nation-State*. New York: Routledge.

Hibou, Béatrice, ed. 2004. *Privatizing the State*. Translated by Jonathan Derrick. New York: Columbia University Press.

Hirschman, Albert O. 1997. *The Passions and the Interests*. Princeton, NJ: Princeton University Press.

Ho, Karen. 2009. *Liquidated: An Ethnography of Wall Street*. Durham, NC: Duke University Press.

Hobsbawm, Eric J. 1994. *Age of Extremes: The Short Twentieth Century, 1914–1991*. London: Michael Joseph.

Holmes, Douglas R. 2013. *Economy of Words: Communicative Imperatives in Central Banks*. Chicago: University of Chicago Press.

Hoti, Erudita. 2009. "Migration and Poverty Reduction." Student Paper. Department of Economics, University of Lundt. http://lup.lub.lu.se/student-papers/record/1487481.

Hoxha, Blerina. 2016. "Piramida e Borxhit" ["The Pyramid of Debts"]. *Monitor*, April 23. http://www.monitor.al/piramida-e-borxheve/.

Hoxha, Enver. [1981] 2012. *Kur Lindi Partia [When the Party Was Born]*. Tirana, Albania: Instituti i Studimeve Marksiste-Leniniste Albania.

Humphrey, Caroline. 1985. "Barter and Economic Disintegration." *Man* 20 (1): 48–72.

——. 1999. "Traders, 'Disorder,' and Citizenship Regimes in Provincial Russia." In *Uncertain Transition: Ethnographies of Change in the Postsocialist World*, 19–52. New York: Rowman and Littlefield.

——. 2002. *The Unmaking of Soviet Life: Everyday Economics after Socialism*. Ithaca, NY: Cornell University Press.

——. 2005. "Ideology in Infrastructure: Architecture and Soviet Imagination." *Journal of the Royal Anthropological Institute* 11 (1): 39–58.

Humphrey, Caroline, and Stephen Hugh-Jones. 1992. *Barter, Exchange, and Value: An Anthropological Approach*. Cambridge, NY: Cambridge University Press.

Ingrassia, Catherine. 1998. *Authorship, Commerce, and Gender in Early Eighteenth-Century England: A Culture of Paper Credit*. Cambridge, NY: Cambridge University Press.

International Monetary Fund (IMF). 2011. *Albania: Selected Issues and Statistical Appendix*. IMF Country Report No. 03/64. Washington: International Monetary Fund. https://www.imf.org/external/pubs/ft/scr/2003/cr0364.pdf.

——. 2014. "Albania: Financial System Stability Assessment." IMF Country Report no. 14/79. http://www.imf.org/external/pubs/ft/scr/2014/cr1479.pdf.

James, Deborah. 2014. *Money from Nothing: Indebtedness and Aspiration in South Africa.* Stanford, CA: Stanford University Press.

Jansen, Stef. 2015. *Yearnings in the Meantime: "Normal Lives" and the State in a Sarajevo Apartment Complex.* Oxford: Berghahn Books.

Jarvis, Christopher. 1999. "The Rise and Fall of the Pyramid Schemes in Albania." IMF Working Papers, no. 98/99. https://www.imf.org/external/pubs/ft/wp/1999/wp9998.pdf.

———. 2000. "The Rise and Fall of Albania's Pyramid Schemes." *Finance and Development* 37 (1): 46–49.

Kadare, Ismail. 1968. *Dasma: Roman.* Tirana: Naim Frashëri.

———. 2012. *Spring Flowers, Spring Frost: A Novel.* Translated by David Bellos. Reprint. New York: Arcade.

Keane, Webb. 2003. "Semiotics and the Social Analysis of Material Things." *Language and Communication* 23: 409–25.

Kiaer, Christina. 2005. *Imagine No Possessions: The Socialist Objects of Russian Constructivism.* Cambridge, MA: MIT Press.

Kindleberger, Charles P., and Robert Aliber. 2005. *Manias, Panics, and Crashes: A History of Financial Crises.* 5th ed. New York: Wiley.

King, R., A. Castaldo, and J. Vullnetari. 2011. "Gendered Relations and Filial duties along the Greek-Albanian Remittance Corridor." *Economic Geography* 87 (4): 393–419.

King, Russell, Nicola Mai, and Stephanie Schwandner-Sievers, eds. 2005. *The New Albanian Migration.* Sussex: Sussex Academic Press.

King, Russell, and Julia Vullnetari. 2003. "Migration and Development in Albania." Sussex: Development Research Center on Migration. http://www.sussex.ac.uk/Units/SCMR/drc/publications/working_papers/WP-C5.pdf.

———. 2011. *Remittances, Gender and Development: Albania's Society and Economy in Transition.* Vol. 4. London: IB Tauris.

Kodra–Hysa, Armanda. 2013. "Albanian Ethnography at the Margins of History, 1947–1991: Documenting the Nation in Historical Materialist Terms." In *The Anthropological Field on the Margins of Europe, 1945–1991,* edited by Alexandar Boskovic and Chris Hann, 129–51. Zürich: LIT Verlag.

Knorr-Cetina, Karin, and Urs Bruegger. 2002. "Traders' Engagement with Markets A Postsocial Relationship." *Theory, Culture & Society* 19 (5–6): 161–85.

Knorr-Cetina, Karin, and Alex Preda. 2005. *The Sociology Of Financial Markets.* Oxford: Oxford University Press.

Koha Jonë. 1996. "FMN Kerkon Takim Me Fajdet" ["IMF Seeks a Meeting with Fajde"]. November 13.

Kola, Ard. 2008. "Fajdet, Qeveria: Komision Konsulentit Që Sjell Paratë" ["Fajde, the Government: Commission to the Consultant That Brings Back the Money"]. *Shqip,* October 6.

———. 2013. "Fajdetë Zëvendësojnë Bankat, Interes 5% të Japin hua edhe Politikanët" ["Fajde Replace Banks, 5% Interest Return, Even Politicians Give Out Loans"]. *Monitor,* February 2. https://www.monitor.al/fajdete-zevendesojne-bankat-interes-5-te-japin-hua-edhe-politikanet/.

Kornai, Janos. 1979. *Economies of Shortage.* Stockholm: Institute for International Economic Studies.

Korovilas, James P. 1999. "The Albanian Economy in Transition: The Role of Remittances and Pyramid Investment Schemes." *Post-Communist Economies* 11 (3): 399–415.

Koselleck, Reinhart. 1985. *Futures Past: On the Semantics of Historical Time.* New York: Columbia University Press.

Kotkin, S. 1997. *Magnetic Mountain: Stalinism as a Civilization.* Berkeley: University of California Press.

Krippner, Greta. 2005. "The Financialization of the American Economy." *Socio-Economic Review* 3: 173–208.

Kusimba, S., Y. Yang, and N. Chawla. 2016. "Hearthholds of Mobile Money in Western Kenya." *Economic Anthropology* 3 (2): 266–79.

Kwon, June Hee. 2015. "Love and Money in a Korean Chinese Transnational Migration." *Cultural Anthropology* 30 (3):477–500.

Lampland, Martha. 1995. *The Object of Labor: Commodification in Socialist Hungary*. Chicago: University of Chicago Press.

Langley, P. 2008. "Securitizing Suburbia: The Transformation of Anglo-American Mortgage Finance." *Competition & Change* 10: 283–99.

Ledeneva, Alena. 1998. *Russia's Economy of Favors: Blat, Networking and Informal Exchange*. Cambridge, NY: Cambridge University Press.

——. 2006. *How Russia Really Works: The Informal Practices That Shaped Post-Soviet Politics and Business*. Ithaca, NY: Cornell University Press.

Lelaj, Olsi. 2015. *Nën Shenjën e Modernitetit [In the Sign of Modernity]*. Tirana: Pika pa Sipërfaqe.

Lemon, Alaina. 1998. "'Your Eyes Are Green Like Dollars': Counterfeit Cash, National Substance, and Currency Apartheid in 1990s Russia." *Cultural Anthropology* 13 (1): 22–55.

Lépinay, Vincent Antonin. 2011. *Codes of Finance: Engineering Derivatives in a Global Bank*. Princeton, NJ: Princeton University Press.

Lewis, Michael. [1989] 2010. *Liar's Poker*. New York: W. W. Norton & Company, Inc.

——. 2010. *The Big Short: Inside the Doomsday Machine*. New York: W. W. Norton and Company, Inc.

Lipton, D., and J. Sachs. 1990a. "Creating a Market Economy in Eastern Europe: The Case of Poland." *Brookings Papers on Economic Activity* (1): 75–147.

——. 1990b. "Privatization in Eastern Europe: The Case of Poland." *Brookings Papers on Economic Activity* (2): 293–341.

Lubonja, Fatos. 2010. *Nëntëdhjeteshtata*. Tirana: Ora.

MacKay, Charles. 2011. *Extraordinary Popular Delusions and the Madness of Crowds*. Hoboken, NJ: Wiley.

MacKenzie, Donald A. 2006. *An Engine, Not a Camera: How Financial Models Shape Markets*. Cambridge, MA: MIT Press.

Mai, Nicola. 2001. "Italy Is Beautiful: The Role of Italian Television in the Albanian Migratory Flow to Italy." In *Media and Migration: Constructions of Mobility and Difference*, edited by Russell King and Nancy Wood, 95–109. London: Routledge.

Malinowski, Bronislaw. [1922] 2008. *Argonauts Of The Western Pacific*. 1st ed. Chicago: Malinowski Press.

Maimbo, Samuel Munzele, and Dilip Ratha. 2005. *Remittances: Development Impact and Future Prospects*. Washington, DC: The International Bank for Reconstruction and Development / The World Bank.

Mandel, Ruth, and Caroline Humphrey, eds. 2002. *Markets and Moralities: Ethnographies of Postsocialism*. 1st ed. Oxford: Berg.

Marx, Karl. [1867] 1990. *Capital*. Vol 1. London: Penguin.

Mattioli, Fabio. 2018. "Financialization without Liquidity: In-Kind Payments, Forced Credit, and Authoritarianism at the Periphery of Europe." *Journal of the Royal Anthropological Institute* 24: 568–88.

Maurer, Bill. 1999. "Forget Locke? From Proprietor to Risk-Bearer in New Logics of Finance." *Public Culture* 11 (2): 47–67.

——. 2000. "A Fish Story: Rethinking Globalization on Virgin Gorda, British Virgin Islands." *American Ethnologist* 27(3): 670–701.

——. 2002. "Repressed Futures: Financial Derivatives' Theological Unconscious." *Economy and Society* 31 (1): 15–36.

——. 2005a. "Due Diligence and 'Reasonable Man,' Offshore." *Cultural Anthropology* 20 (4): 474–505.

——. 2005b. *Mutual Life, Limited: Islamic Banking, Alternative Currencies, Lateral Reason.* Princeton, NJ: Princeton University Press.

——. 2006. "The Anthropology of Money." *Annual Review of Anthropology* 35 (1): 15–36.

——. 2010. "Credit Crisis Religion." *Religion and Society* 1 (1): 146–55.

——. 2015. "Money Talk: Has Money Really Changed from Shells to Digital Apps? Underneath, Money is Always a Token of our Social Relationships." *Aeon*, December 14. https://aeon.co/essays/how-money-evolved-from-shells-and-coins-to-apps-and -bitcoin.

Maurer, Bill, Smoki Musaraj, and Ivan V. Small, eds. 2018. *Money at the Margins: Global Perspectives on Technology, Financial Inclusion, and Design.* Vol. 6. Oxford: Berghahn Books.

Maurer, Bill, Taylor C. Nelms, and Stephen C. Rea. 2013. "'Bridges to Cash': Channeling Agency in Mobile Money." *Journal of the Royal Anthropological Institute* 19 (1): 52–74.

Mauss, Marcel. [1950] 2000. *The Gift: The Form and Reason for Exchange in Archaic Societies.* Translated by W. D. Halls. New York: W. W. Norton.

M. B. 1996. "Vefa: Nga Pasuria Në Strehim. Inaugurohet Ndërtimi i 380 Apartamenteve në Laprakë" ["Vefa: From Wealth to Shelter. 380 New Apartments Are Inaugurated in Laprakë"]. *Koha Jonë*, December 19, p, 9.

Mëhilli, Elidor. 2012. "The Socialist Design: Urban Dilemas in Postwar Europe and Soviet Union." *Kritika: Explorations in Russian and Eurasian History* 13 (3): 635–65.

——. 2017. *From Stalin to Mao: Albania and the Socialist World.* Ithaca, NY: Cornell University Press.

Mema, Fatmir, and Nevruz Koçi. 2001. "Mass Privatization Process and Post Privatization in Albania." Paper for the SEED Conference, June 1–3, 2011, Tirana, Albania. https://web.archive.org/web/20140514085318/http://www.seedcenter.gr/projects /MNE/1stconfer/1stconf_papers/Mema.pdf.

Mehrling, Perry. 2010. *The New Lombard Street: How the Fed Became the Dealer of Last Resort.* Princeton, NJ: Princeton University Press.

Minsky, Hyman P. 1982. *Can "It" Happen Again?: Essays on Instability and Finance.* Armonk, NY: M. E. Sharpe.

——. 1986. *Stabilizing the Unstable Economy.* New Haven, CT: Yale University Press.

——. 1992. "The Financial Instability Hypothesis." Working Paper No. 74. Annandale-on-Hudson: The Levy Economics Institute. http://www.levy.org/pubs/wp74.pdf.

Mirowski, Philip. 2013. *Never Let a Serious Crisis Go to Waste: How Neoliberalism Survived the Financial Meltdown.* London: Verso Books.

Mitchell, Timothy. 2002. *Rule of Experts: Egypt, Techno-politics, Modernity.* Berkeley: University of California Press.

Miyazaki, Hirokazu. 2003. "The Temporalities of the Market." *American Anthropologist* 105 (2): 255–65.

——. 2006. "Economy of Dreams: Hope in Global Capitalism and Its Critique." *Cultural Anthropology* 21 (2): 147–72.

Monitor. 2009. "Piramida e Tregut të Zi" ["The Pyramid of the Black Market"]. *Monitor.* https://www.monitor.al/rpiramidar-e-tregut-te-zi-4901/.

——. 2010. "Opinione Ndërtuesish" ["Opinions from Developers"]. *Monitor.* https:// www.monitor.al/opinione-ndertuesish-6356/.

Morgan, Lewis Henry. 1877. *Ancient Society.* New Brunswick, NJ: Transaction Publishers.

Morris, Rosalind. 2005. "Fetishism: Overview." In *New Dictionary of the History of Ideas*, edited by Maryane Cline Horowitz, 882–90. Vol 2. Detroit: Charles Scribner's Sons.

Muço, Marta, 1997. *Economic Transition in Albania: Political Constraints and Mentality Barriers*. PhD diss., University of Tirana.

Muço, Marta, and Drini Salko. 1996. "Some Issues on the Development of Informal Financial Sector in Albania." Unpublished manuscript. Tirana: Albanian Center for Economic Research.

Muehlebach, Andrea. 2012. *The Moral Neoliberal: Welfare and Citizenship in Italy*. Chicago: University of Chicago Press.

Muniesa, Fabian, Yuval Millo, and Michel Callon. 2007. "An Introduction to Market Devices." *Sociological Review* 55 (October): 1–12.

Munn, Nancy D. 1986. *The Fame of Gawa: A Symbolic Study of Value Transformation in a Massim (Papua New Guinea) Society*. Durham, NC: Duke University Press.

Musaraj, Smoki. 2009. "Passport Troubles: Social Tactics and Places of Informal Transactions in Postsocialist Albania." *Anthropology of East Europe Review* 27 (2): 157–75.

——. 2011. "Tales from Albarado: The Materiality of Pyramid Schemes in Postsocialist Albania." *Cultural Anthropology* 26 (1): 84–110.

——. 2012. "Alternative Publics, Alternative Temporalities: Unofficial Collective Practices in Communist Albania." In *Albania: Family, Society and Culture in the 20th Century*, edited by Andrea Hemming, Gentiana Kera, and Enriketa Papa, 175–86. Zürich: LIT Verlag.

——. 2017. "Pyramid Firms and Value Transformation in Postsocialist Albania." *Ethnologie Française* (2): 321–30.

——. 2018a. "Corruption, Right On! Hidden Cameras, Cynical Satire, and Banal Intimacies of Anti-corruption." *Current Anthropology* 59 (S18): S105–16.

——. 2018b. "Corruption Indicators in the Local Legal/Political Landscape: Reflections from Albania." In *The Palgrave Handbook of Indicators in Global Governance*, edited by Deborah Valentina Malito, Gaby Umbach, and Nehal Bhuta, 351–70. Gewerberstrasse: Palgrave Macmillan.

Narotzky, Susana, and Niko Besnier. 2014. "Crisis, Value, and Hope: Rethinking the Economy." *Current Anthropology* 55 (S9): S4–16.

Nelson, Diane M. 2012. "Banal, Familiar, and Enrapturing: Financial Enchantment after Guatemala's Genocide." *WSQ: Women's Studies Quarterly* 40 (3–4): 205–25.

New York Times. 2012. "Eastern Europe's Wild Capitalism."

Nicholson, Beryl. 1999. "The Beginning of the End of a Rebellion: Southern Albania, May-June 1997." *East European Politics and Societies* 13 (3): 543–65.

——. 2001. "From Migrant to Micro-Entrepreneur: Do-It-Yourself Development in Albania." *South-East Europe Review* 4 (3): 39–41.

——. 2004. "Migrants as Agents of Development: Albanian Return Migrants and Microenterprise." *New Patterns of Labour Migration in Central and Eastern Europe*, edited by D. Pop., 94–110. Cluj Napoca: Public Policy Centre.

Ong, Aihwa. 2006. *Neoliberalism as Exception: Mutations in Citizenship and Sovereignty*. Durham, NC: Duke University Press.

Ong, A. 2011. "Hyperbuilding: Spectacle, Speculation, and the Hyperspace of Sovereignty." In *Worlding Cities: Asian Experiments and the Art of Being Global*, edited Ananya Roy and Aihwa Ong, 205–26. Hoboken, NJ: John Wiley & Sons.

Osburg, John. 2013. *Anxious Wealth: Money and Morality among China's New Rich*. Stanford, CA: Stanford University Press.

Parry, J., and M. Bloch. 1989. *Money and the Morality of Exchange*. Cambridge, NY: Cambridge University Press.

Pashko, Gramoz. 1993. "Obstacles to Economic Reform in Albania." *Europe-Asia Studies* 45 (5): 907–21.

Patterson, Patrick Hyder. 2011. *Bought and Sold*. Ithaca, NY: Cornell University Press.

Peebles, Gustav. 2010. "The Anthropology of Credit and Debt." *Annual Review of Anthropology* 39 (1): 225–40.

———. 2011. *The Euro and its Rivals: Currency and the Construction of a Transnational City*. Indiana: Indiana University Press.

———. 2012. "Filth and Lucre: The Dirty Money Complex as a Taxation Regime." *Anthropological Quarterly* 85 (4): 1229–55.

Pelkmans, M. 2003. "The Social Life of Empty Buildings: Imagining the Transition in Post-Soviet Ajaria." *Focaal—European Journal of Anthropology* 41: 121–36.

Peristiany, Jean G. 1965. *Honor and Shame: The Values of Mediterranean Society*. London: Weidenfeld and Nicolson.

Petryna, Adriana. 2002. *Life Exposed: Biological Citizens After Chernobyl*. Princeton, NJ: Princeton University Press.

Pettifer, James, and Miranda Vickers. 2009. *The Albanian Question: Reshaping the Balkans*. London: I. B. Tauris.

Piot, Charles, Guillaume Lachenal, and Aïssatou Mbodj-Pouye. 2014. "Fin des temps et nouveaux départs." *Politique africaine* 135 (3): 97–113.

Piperno, F. 2005. "Albanian migrants' remittances: a development opportunity?" In King, R., N. Mai, and S. Schwander-Sievers, eds., *The New Albanian Migration*. Brighton: University of Sussex Press, 118–38.

Polanyi, Karl. 1965. *The Great Transformation: The Political and Economic Origins of Our Time*. Boston: Beacon Press.

———. 1971. *Primitive, Archaic, and Modern Economies*. Boston: Beacon Press.

Poon, Martha. 2009. "From New Deal Institutions to Capital Markets: Commercial Consumer Risk Scores and the Making of Subprime Mortgage Finance." *Accounting, Organizations and Society* 34 (5): 654–74.

Poovey, Mary. 2008. *Genres of the Credit Economy: Mediating Value in Eighteenth- and Nineteenth-Century Britain*. Chicago: University of Chicago Press.

Portes, Alejandro, and József Böröcz. 1988. "The Informal Sector under Capitalism and State Socialism: A Preliminary Comparison." *Social Justice* 15 (33–34): 17–28.

Power, Michael. 2007. *Organized Uncertainty: Designing a World of Risk Management*. Oxford: Oxford University Press.

Pula, Besnik. 2011. "State, Law, and Revolution: Agrarian Power and the National State in Albania, 1850–1945." PhD diss., University of Michigan.

Raffles, Hugh. 2002. *In Amazonia: A Natural History*. Princeton, NJ: Princeton University Press.

Ramírez, María Clemencia. 2014. "Legitimacy, Complicity and Conspiracy: The Emergence of a New Economic Form on the Margins of the Colombian State." *Antipoda. Revista de Antropología Y Arqueología* 18 (January): 29–59.

Ratha, Dilip. 2016. *Migration and Remittances Factbook 2016*. Washington, DC: The World Bank.

Ratha, Dilip, and S. Mohapatra. 2012. "Remittances and Development." *The Wiley & Blackwell Encyclopedia of Globalization*. Hoboken, NJ: Wiley-Blackwell. https://online library.wiley.com/doi/10.1002/9780470670590.wbeog494.

Reinhart, Carmen M., and Kenneth Rogoff. 2011. *This Time Is Different: Eight Centuries of Financial Folly*. Reprint. Princeton, NJ: Princeton University Press.

Ries, Nancy. 1997. *Russian Talk: Culture and Conversation During Perestroika*. Ithaca, NY: Cornell University Press.

Roitman, Janet. 2004. "Productivity in the Margins: An Anthropology of Economic Regulation in the Chad Basin." In *Anthropology in the Margins of the State*, edited by Veena Das and Deborah Poole, 191–242. Santa Fe, NM: School of American Research Press.
———. 2005. *Fiscal Disobedience: An Anthropology of Economic Regulation in Central Africa*. Princeton, NJ: Princeton University Press.
———. 2013. *Anti-Crisis*. Durham, NC: Duke University Press.
Rosen, Matthew. 2019. "Between Conflicting Systems: An Ordinary Tragedy in Now-Capitalist Albania." *Anthropological Journal of European Cultures* 28 (2): 1–22.
Roubini, Nouriel, and Stephen Mihm. 2010. *Crisis Economics: A Crash Course in the Future of Finance*. London: Penguin.
Roy, Ananya, and Aihwa Ong. 2011. *Worlding Cities: Asian Experiments and the Art of Being Global*. Hoboken, NJ: John Wiley & Sons.
Rutherford, Stuart. 2001. *The Poor and Their Money*. Oxford: Oxford University Press.
Sahlins, Marshall D. 1963. "Poor Man, Rich Man, Big-Man, Chief: Political Types in Melanesia and Polynesia." *Comparative Studies in Society and History* 5 (3): 285–303.
———. [1988] 1994. "Cosmologies of Capitalism: The Trans-Pacific Sector of 'The World System.'" In *Culture/Power/History: A Reader Contemporary Social Theory*, edited by Nicholas B. Dirks, Geoff Eley, and Sherry B. Ortner. Princeton, NJ: Princeton University Press.
Sahlins, Marshall David. 1974. *Stone Age Economics*. New Brunswick, NJ: Transaction Publishers.
Sandstrom, Per, and Orjan Sjoberg. 1991. "Albanian Economic Performance: Stagnation in the 1980s." *Soviet Studies* 43 (5): 931–47.
Schuster, Caroline E. 2015. *Social Collateral: Women and Microfinance in Paraguay's Smuggling Economy*. Berkley: University of California Press.
Schwenkel, Christina. 2015. "Spectacular Infrastructure and its Breakdown in Socialist Vietnam." *American Ethnologist* 42 (3): 520–34.
Sejdarasi, Bardhi. 1996. "Vlora: Kryeqyteti i Fajdesë: Dollareë Franga Sviceriane, Lireta, Dhrahmi, dhe së Fundi Lekë Shqiptare Janë Preja e Domosdoshme e Gjiganteve të Vlorës, Vega, Gjallica, Kamberi, Cenaj & Co, Silva" ["Vlora the Capital of Fajde: Dollars, Swiss Francs, Liretas, Dhrahmas, and Finally the Albanian Lek, are the Inevitable Prey of the Giants of Vlora: Vefa, Gjallica, Kamberi, Cenaj and Co and Silva"]. *Koha Jonë*, September 8.
Shiller, Robert J. 2000. *Irrational Exuberance*. Princeton, NJ: Princeton University Press.
Shipton, Parker MacDonald. 2010. *Credit between Cultures: Farmers, Financiers, and Misunderstanding in Africa*. New Haven, CT: Yale University Press.
Shkullaku, Armand. 1997. "Piramidat e Aventurës Shqiptare" ["The Pyramids of the Albanian Adventure"]. *Revista Klan*, 1, 6.
Siegel, James T. 1998. *A New Criminal Type in Jakarta: Counter-Revolution Today*. Durham, NC: Duke University Press.
Simmel, Georg. 1967. "The Stranger." In *The Sociology of Georg Simmel*, edited by Kurt Wolff, 402–8. 12th ed. New York: The Free Press.
Smith, Adam. [1776] 1982. *The Wealth of Nations: Books 1–3*. New York: Penguin Classics.
Stark, David, and Laszlo Bruszt. 1998. *Postsocialist Pathways: Transforming Politics and Property in East Central Europe*. Cambridge, NY: Cambridge University Press.
Stoica, Cătălin Augustin. 2004. "From Good Communists to Even Better Capitalists? Entrepreneurial Pathways in Post-Socialist Romania." *East European Politics and Societies* 18 (2): 236–77.
Stout, Noelle. 2016. "# Indebted: Disciplining the Moral Valence of Mortgage Debt Online." *Cultural Anthropology* 31 (1): 82–106.

Strange, Susan. 1997. *Casino Capitalism*. Manchester, UK: Manchester University Press.

Strathern, Marilyn. 1988. *The Gender of the Gift: Problems with Women and Problems with Society in Melanesia*. Berkley: University of California Press.

———. 2005. *Partial Connections*. Lanham, MD: Rowman and Littlefield Publishers, Inc.

Sulstarova, Enis. 2006. *Arratisje nga Lindja: Orientalizmi Shqiptar nga Naimi te Kadareja* [*Exiling from the East: Albanian Orientalism from Naimi to Kadareja*]. Tirana: Globic Press.

Szelényi, Iván. 1983. *Urban Inequalities under State Socialism*. Oxford: Oxford University Press.

Tarifa, Fatos. 2008. "Of Time, Honor, and Memory: Oral Law in Albania." *Oral Tradition* 23 (1): 3–14.

Taussig, Michael. 1983. *Devil and Commodity Fetishism in South America*. Chapel Hill: University of North Carolina Press.

Thaler, Richard H. 2015. *Misbehaving: The Making of Behavioral Economics*. New York: W. W. Norton.

Tirta, Mark. 1999. "Migrime të Shqiptarëve, të Brendshme dhe Jashtë Atdheut: Vitet '40 të Shek.XIX–Vitet '40 të Shek.XX" ["Internal and International Migration of Albanians: 1840s–1940s"]. *Etnografia Shqiptare* 18.

Todorova, Maria, and Zsuzsa Gille. 2010. *Post-Communist Nostalgia*. Oxford: Berghahn Books.

Truitt, Allison J. 2013. *Dreaming of Money in Ho Chi Minh City*. Seattle: University of Washington Press.

Tsing, Anna Lowenhaupt. 2000. "Inside the Economy of Appearances." *Public Culture* 12 (2): 115–44.

———. 2015. *The Mushroom at the End of the World: On the Possibility of Life in Capitalist Ruins*. Princeton, NJ: Princeton University Press.

Ulfstjerne, M. A. 2017. "The Tower and the Tower: Excess and Vacancy in China's Ghost City." In *Emptiness and Fullness: Ethnographies of Lack and Desire in Contemporary China*, edited by Susanne Bregnbæk and Mikkel Bunkenborg. Oxford: Berghahn Books.

Verdery, Katherine. 1991. "Theorising Socialism: A Prologue to the 'Transition.'" *American Ethnologist* 18 (3): 419–39.

———. 1996. *What Was Socialism and What Comes Next?* Princeton, NJ: Princeton University Press.

———. 2003. *The Vanishing Hectare: Property and Value in Postsocialist Transylvania*. Ithaca, NY: Cornell University Press.

Verdery, Katherine, and Caroline Humphrey, eds. 2004. *Property in Question: Value Transformation in the Global Economy*. Oxford: Berg Publishers.

Vevaina, Leilah S. 2014. *Trust Matters: Parsis and Property in Mumbai*. Doctoral diss. New York: The New School.

Villarreal, Magdalena. 2010. "Value, Gender, and Capital: Frameworks of Calculation in Micro-Financial Practices." In *Rural Transformations and Development-China in Context: The Everyday Lives of Policies and People*, edited by Norman Long, Ye Jingzhong, and Wang Yihuan, 110–30. Cheltenham: Edward Elgar Publishing Ltd.

———. 2014. "Regimes of Value in Mexican Household Financial Practices." *Current Anthropology* 55 (S9): S30–39.

Villarreal, Magdalena, Isabelle Guérin, and K. S. Santosh Kumar. 2018. "Carola and Saraswathi: Juggling Wealth in India." In *Money at the Margins: Global Perspectives on Technology, Financial Inclusion, and Design*, edited by Bill Maurer, Smoki Musaraj, and Ivan Small. New York: Berghahn Books.

VKM.585 (Prime Minister's Office Decree nr. 585). 1997. "Për Evidencimin e Familjeve që Kanë Humbur Banesat nga Rënia e Skemave Piramidale." ["For Identifying the

Families that Have Lost their Homes to the Fall of the Pyramid Schemes"]. December 11. Tirana: Prime Minister's Office.

Vullnetari, Julie. 2012. *Albania on the Move: Links Between Internal and International Migration*. Amsterdam: Amsterdam University Press.

Vullnetari, Julie, and Russell King. 2011. *Remittances, Gender and Development: Albania's Society and Economy in Transition*. London: I. B. Tauris.

Weber, Max. 2009. *The Protestant Ethic and the Spirit of Capitalism*. Vol. 4. Oxford: Oxford University Press.

Wedel, Janine. 1986. *The Private Poland*. 1st ed. New York: Facts on File.

West, Rebecca. 2007. *Black Lamb and Grey Falcon*. New York: Penguin Classics.

Woodruff, David. 1999. "Barter of the Bankrupt: The Politics of Democratization in Russia's Federal State." In *Uncertain Transitions: Ethnographies of Change in the Postsocialist World*, 83–124. New York: Rowman and Littlefield.

——. 2000. *Money Unmade: Barter and the Fate of Russian Capitalism*. Ithaca, NY: Cornell University Press.

Woodworth, M. D., and M. Ulfstjerne. 2016. "Taking Part: The Social Experience of Informal Finance in Ordos, Inner Mongolia." *Journal of Asian Studies* 75 (3): 649–72.

World Bank. 2017. "Albania, Data." https://data.worldbank.org/country/albania.

Wray, L. Randall. 2009. "The Rise and Fall of Money Manager Capitalism: A Minskian Approach." *Cambridge Journal of Economics* 33 (4): 807–28.

Yang, Mayfair Mey-Hui. 1994. *Gifts, Favors, Banquets: The Art of Social Relationships in China*. Ithaca, NY: Cornell University Press.

Young, Antonia. 2001. *Women Who Become Men: Albanian Sworn Virgins*. New York: Berg.

Yurchak, Alexei. 2002. "Entrepreneurial Governmentality in Post-Socialist Russia: A Cultural Investigation of Business Practices." In *The New Entrepreneurs of Europe and Asia*, 278–324. Armonk, NY: M. E. Sharpe.

——. 2003. "Russian Neoliberal: The Entrepreneurial Ethic and the Spirit of 'True Careerism.'" *Russian Review* 62 (1): 72–90.

——. 2005. *Everything Was Forever, until It Was No More: The Last Soviet Generation*. Princeton, NJ: Princeton University Press.

Za, Luigi. 2012. *Kombinat: Storia e Vita Quotidiana di un Quartiere Simbolo di Tirana* [*Kombinat: History and Everyday Life in a Model Neighborhood in Tirana*]. Lecce: Salento Books.

Zaloom, Caitlin. 2006. *Out of the Pits: Traders and Technology from Chicago to London*. Chicago: University of Chicago Press.

——. 2009. "How to Read the Future: The Yield Curve, Affect, and Financial Prediction." *Public Culture* 21 (2): 245–68.

Zavisca, Jane R. 2012. *Housing the New Russia*. Ithaca, NY: Cornell University Press.

Zelizer, Viviana A. Rotman. 1996. "Payments and social ties." In *Sociological Forum* 11 (3): 481–95.

——. 1997. *The Social Meaning of Money*. Princeton, NJ: Princeton University Press.

Zhang, Li, and L. Zhang. 2001. "Migration and Privatization of Space and Power in Late Socialist China." *American Ethnologist* 28 (1): 179–205.

——. 2002. "Spatiality and urban citizenship in late socialist China." *Public Culture* 14 (2): 311–34.

——. 2010. *In Search of Paradise: Middle Class Living in a Chinese Metropolis*. Ithaca, NY: Cornell University Press.

Zili, Roland. 1996. "Sudja: Ju Garantoj Ne Janar; Perfaqesues Te Kreditoreve Arrijne Te Takohen Me Suden" ["Sude: I Guarantee [Returns] in January; Representatives of Creditors Manage to Meet with Sude"]. *Koha Jone*, December 24.

Zogaj, Preç. 1998. *Uncivil War* [*Luftë Jocivile*]. Tirana: Dita.

Zojzi, Rrok. 1972. "Aspekte të Kalimit nga Familja Patriarkale në Familjen e Re Socialiste" ["Aspects of Transitioning from the Patriarchal Family to the New Socialist Family"]. *Etnografia Shqiptare* 6: 28–36.

Zuckoff, Mitchell. 2006. *Ponzi's Scheme: The True Story of a Financial Legend.* New York: Random House.

Index

Lightning Source UK Ltd.
Milton Keynes UK
UKHW011241040720
366021UK00005B/236